# Integrating Knowledge T
# Interdisciplinary Researc

In this important new text, Holland seeks to explain, by means of social scientific and philosophical inquiry, the difficulties that researchers often experience when attempting to integrate knowledge from different academic disciplines, either individually or as part of a team of subject specialists. It is argued that the difficulty of integrating knowledge from different academic disciplines is the result of, firstly, an inadequate justification of the nature of scientific integration and differentiation and, secondly, the dominance of disciplinary specialization in scientific inquiry.

By focusing on both the theoretical justification for, and the practical feasibility of, integrating knowledge through interdisciplinary research, this book asks what properties of reality make the integration of knowledge from different academic disciplines possible and to what extent it is feasible to integrate knowledge through interdisciplinary research within a traditional, disciplinary context. Accordingly the text is both philosophical and social scientific in content: philosophical in the sense that it presents a theory of causal determination, which will help researchers to understand how reality is both differentiated and interconnected; social scientific in the sense that it presents the results of three case studies of collaborative interdisciplinary research projects.

The book is heavily informed by the philosophy of critical realism. The philosophical argument about the possibility of integration and specialization in science draws explicitly on some of the key concepts of critical realism – particularly those comprising the theory of 'integrative pluralism' – while critical realist assumptions underpin the social scientific argument about the causal influence of the social system of knowledge production. By exploring researchers' conceptions of knowledge and of reality on the one hand and their decisions about what sort of knowledge to produce on the other, Holland shows how the difficulty of scientific integration is both a problem of knowledge and a problem of knowledge production.

This book is essential reading for students and academics interested in the emerging topic of knowledge integration and interdisciplinarity.

**Dominic Holland** holds a PhD from the Department of Politics at the University of Sheffield, where he has taught philosophy of social science, political analysis and social research methods.

## Critical Realism: Interventions

Other titles in this series:

**(Mis)recognition, Social Inequality and Social Justice**
Nancy Fraser and Pierre Bourdieu
*Edited by Terry Lovell*

**After International Relations**
Critical realism and the (re)construction of world politics
*Heikki Patomäki*

**Being and Worth**
*Andrew Collier*

**Beyond East and West**
*Roy Bhaskar*

**Capitalism and Citizenship**
The impossible partnership
*Kathryn Dean*

**Critical Realism and Marxism**
*Edited by Andrew Brown, Steve Fleetwood and John Michael Roberts*

**Dictionary of Critical Realism**
*Edited by Mervyn Hartwig*

**A Social Theory of the Nation-State**
The political forms of modernity beyond methodological nationalism
*Daniel Chernillo*

**Rethinking Marxism**
From Kant and Hegel to Marx and Engels
*Jolyon Agar*

**Transcendence**
Critical realism and God
*Margaret S. Archer, Andrew Collier and Douglas V. Porpora*

**Contradictions of Archaeological Theory**
Engaging critical realism and archaeological theory
*Sandra Wallace*

**Integrating Knowledge Through Interdisciplinary Research**
Problems of theory and practice
*Dominic Holland*

# Integrating Knowledge Through Interdisciplinary Research

## Problems of theory and practice

**Dominic Holland**

LONDON AND NEW YORK

First published 2014
by Routledge
2 Park Square, Milton Park, Abingdon, Oxfordshire OX14 4RN

and by Routledge
711 Third Avenue, New York, NY 10017

First issued in paperback 2014

*Routledge is an imprint of the Taylor and Francis Group, an informa business*



*British Library Cataloguing in Publication Data*
A catalogue record for this book is available from the British Library

*Library of Congress Cataloging-in-Publication Data*
Holland, Dominic.
Integrating knowledge through interdisciplinary research: problems of theory and practice / Dominic Holland.
pages cm. – (Realism and Marxism)
Includes bibliographical references and index.
1. Social sciences–Research. 2. Interdisciplinary research. I. Title.
H62.H578 2013
001.4–dc23
2013008581

ISBN 978-0-415-65762-4 (hbk)
ISBN 978-1-138-91941-9 (pbk)
ISBN 978-0-203-76224-0 (ebk)

Typeset in Times New Roman
by FiSH Books Ltd, Enfield

# Contents

# Figures

# Preface

What justifies the production of integrative, interdisciplinary research? To what extent is it possible to produce integrative, interdisciplinary research in the UK today? These seem to me to be pertinent questions to ask, given the increasing interest in – indeed, public commitment to – producing such research among UK higher education policymakers, research managers and research funders. It is notable that some UK universities have set up institutes and centres explicitly designed to facilitate the production of integrative, interdisciplinary research, while others have recently reorganized academic departments into cognate schools of study in the hope of promoting interdisciplinary interaction. Both policies, I argue in this book, reflect an explicit recognition – although far from complete understanding – of the interconnected nature of reality and of the need to develop forms of knowledge that express this characteristic. Of course, efforts to achieve scientific integration through interdisciplinary research (and teaching) are not new; for example, interdisciplinarity was a founding ideal of the many new UK universities that appeared in the 1960s and 1970s. Yet, if it is an explicit, albeit underdeveloped, understanding of the complexity of reality that is motivating attempts to encourage scientific integration through interdisciplinary research, whether it is organized individually or collaboratively, it is the lack of understanding of what is causing the continuing dominance of scientific specialization in the UK academy that explains why these attempts have often failed – or, at least, why the interdisciplinary research that is produced as a result of them is often not genuinely integrative in nature. Indeed, it is important to understand that, although research may be identified as interdisciplinary, multidisciplinary, cross-disciplinary and transdisciplinary, the use of such terms does not mean that the research will be genuinely integrative in nature. Therefore, I ask readers to keep in mind the distinction between integrative and non-integrative forms of knowledge, and (mono)disciplinary and interdisciplinary research. I say more about this distinction in Chapter 1.

In Chapters 3, 4 and 5 of the book, I attempt to explain why scientific specialization is still the dominant form of scientific inquiry in the UK academy. The key message of the book is that the dominance of this form of inquiry is a property of the academic system of knowledge production. The focus on the UK, and on the disciplines of politics and economics, is appropriate, given my own experience of

UK higher education as an undergraduate student in a department of economics and as a postgraduate student in a department of politics. My prior knowledge of these two fields of social science was a convenient 'way in' and thus a starting point for a thorough examination of the UK academy as a system of knowledge production whose constitutive elements are social and intellectual. I could have chosen different disciplines as my starting point – for example, biology and sociology – and I expect that, if I had done so, I would have discovered that the structures of biology and sociology differ from the structures of politics and economics in the UK. I would, though, have reached the same conclusions about the way the UK academic system of knowledge production works – that is, the effects it tends to have on individual researchers. In other countries, the academic system of knowledge production – if one exists – may have different effects. However, understanding how this system works in the UK – its complexity and tendencies – was the goal of the social scientific part of my inquiry into the problem of integrating knowledge through interdisciplinary research.

Of course, consideration of the extent to which scientific integration is possible presupposes that this sort of inquiry is justified. Hence, the goal of the philosophical part of my inquiry was to set out a clear and coherent justification for scientific integration (and its counterpart, scientific differentiation) – a justification grounded in the nature of reality. Indeed, there is an urgent need to do this given that most justifications for integrating knowledge from different disciplines remain underdeveloped and incoherent. It is this incoherence, I argue, that helps to explain why researchers who attempt to integrate knowledge from different disciplines often run into difficulties. Again, this problem is not new: the classical political economists of the eighteenth and nineteenth centuries ran into similar difficulties – as I argue in the third section of Chapter 2.

I develop my own justification for integrating knowledge through interdisciplinary research using the categories of original and dialectical critical realism, the philosophy of science associated most closely with the work of Roy Bhaskar. Indeed, critical realism is the underpinning philosophy for the whole book because the social scientific inquiry into the conditions of knowledge production that is the focus of Chapters 3, 4 and 5 was explicitly informed by the principles of critical realism. Readers who are new to critical realism will find the first section of Chapter 2, where I summarize its key principles, of particular interest; seasoned critical realists may wish to skip this section and move on to the second section of Chapter 2, where I develop my justification for scientific differentiation and integration using the critical realist theory of integrative pluralism.

If the first feature of the book is the explanation, by means of social scientific argument, of the practical difficulties of integrating knowledge from different disciplines and the second feature is the justification, by means of philosophical argument, for doing so, the third feature of the book is the integration of sociological and philosophical theory; for the social scientific theory of knowledge production that I develop and defend in Chapters 3, 4 and 5 incorporates the categories of philosophical inquiry – an incorporation that enables me to show clearly how the social and intellectual conditions of scientific inquiry are related. In other words, this is a book about integrating knowledge through interdisciplinary research that is itself an example of integrative, interdisciplinary research. What it is not is a consideration of interdisciplinary research methods; that is, it does not consider explicitly how to achieve integration at a scientific level – as Allen Repko (2008) has done. Yet, the continuing existence of inconsistencies in interdisciplinary research outputs that are intended to be integrative in nature suggests that it is now time that we approached the issue of interdisciplinary integration at an ontological level. I hope, therefore, that, on reading this book, scientists who are interested in producing integrative research through interdisciplinary ways of working will have a clearer understanding of how this sort of research is possible and will be more able to avoid the sorts of mistakes that previous researchers have made. I hope, too, that, on reading this book, higher education policymakers, research funders and research managers who are interested in developing policies to encourage the production of integrative, interdisciplinary research will have a clearer understanding of what is blocking the production of such research. In Chapter 6, I consider the policy implications of my argument explicitly and what exactly it is that policymakers need to change if they want to encourage the production of integrative, interdisciplinary research.

Many people have helped me to produce this book. It started out as a PhD thesis; hence, special thanks must go to my PhD supervisor, Martin Smith, for his support and advice throughout the project and to all those researchers who agreed to be interviewed. Thanks are also due to Mike Kenny and Jonathon Perraton, who provided valuable insights into the nature of the fields of politics and economics respectively; to Rick Szostak, who kindly sent me some of his work on interdisciplinarity; to John Hobson and Andrew Sayer, who examined the PhD thesis and encouraged me to develop it into a book; and to Sarah Cooke, who provided secretarial assistance. I am grateful to the two anonymous reviewers who provided constructive comments on a subsequent version of the argument and to Alan Jarvis and Damian Mitchell at Routledge. I must also thank Roy Bhaskar for agreeing to consider the book for publication in the series *Critical Realism: Interventions*. Finally, thanks must go to Clive and Tony Lawson at Cambridge, with whom I have had insightful conversations about interdisciplinarity – especially Tony, whose comment during a plenary session at the conference Economics for the Future at the University of Cambridge in September 2003 was the trigger for my inquiry into the problem of integrating knowledge through interdisciplinary research.

Dominic Holland
Sheffield, February 2013

# Acknowledgements

The author and publishers wish to thank the following for permission to use copyright material: University of Toronto Press for extracts from *Essays on Economics and Society* by John Stuart Mill, published as Volume IV of *The Collected Works of John Stuart Mill* (© University of Toronto Press and Routledge & Kegan Paul, 1967); Pickering and Chatto Publishers for extracts from *Principles of Political Economy Considered with a View to their Practical Application* by Thomas Robert Malthus, published as Volume Five of *The Works of Thomas Robert Malthus* (© Pickering and Chatto Publishers, 1986); Oxford University Press for extracts from *An Inquiry into the Nature and Causes of the Wealth of Nations* by Adam Smith, published as Volume II of *The Glasgow Edition of the Works and Correspondence of Adam Smith* (© Oxford University Press, 1976); Royal Economic Society via Liberty Fund Publishing for extracts from *On the Principles of Political Economy and Taxation* by David Ricardo, published as Volume I of *The Works and Correspondence of David Ricardo* (© Cambridge University Press and The Royal Economic Society, 1951).

# 1 Introduction

## The problem of integrating knowledge

When academics think about integrating knowledge from different disciplines they usually think of interdisciplinary research. Scientists and higher-education policy-makers have become increasingly interested in this form of research. For example, in May 2006, the British Academy organized a workshop on interdisciplinarity, 'Working Together Across Disciplines: Challenges for the Natural and Social Sciences',[1] while, in May 2005, interdisciplinarity was the explicit focus of the third in a series of six ESRC-funded seminars on 'interactive agenda setting in the social sciences'.[2] Moreover, the University of Sheffield has recently established the Informatics Collaboratory of the Social Sciences (ICOSS), which is explicitly designed to facilitate 'high quality interdisciplinary research',[3] while the University of Durham has just established an interdisciplinary Institute of Advanced Study.[4] Finally, the UK Research Councils have also been stepping up their efforts to encourage the production of interdisciplinary research through the Rural Economy and Land Use (RELU) programme, which involves collaboration between natural and social scientists from over 30 disciplines at research institutions across the UK.[5]

In this book, I focus on a particular type of interdisciplinary research, which Barry *et al.* define as the '*integrative* or *synthesis* model of interdisciplinarity' (2008: 28). I am focusing on this type of interdisciplinary research because, in my observation, this is the type that is most often discussed in the academic literature on interdisciplinarity; in other words, it is the dominant (but not exclusive) meaning of interdisciplinary research. (Indeed, as I discuss later in this chapter, the concepts of *integration* and *synthesis* are invoked in justifications of interdisciplinary research.) I am also focusing on this type of interdisciplinary research for the simple reason that, if reality is differentiated and interconnected in the way that I argue it is in Chapter 2, *not* to attempt to understand how it is differentiated and interconnected at a *scientific* (as opposed to a philosophical) level, will be a serious derogation from the enterprise of science and will leave policymakers ill-equipped to address the increasingly complicated problems that have emerged within contemporary society – not least the pressing problem of climate change (Bhaskar *et al.*, 2010). As I show later in this chapter, it is the increasing awareness among scientists and policymakers that traditional, disciplinary-based scientific inquiry is seriously deficient that is driving the growth of interest in collaboration across the social and natural sciences.

Moreover, in focusing on integrative interdisciplinary research, this book marks a departure from existing books on interdisciplinarity in the fields of sociology and philosophy of science, which are typically concerned with the different ways in which interdisciplinarity is understood and which deal thereby with the concept of scientific integration (and differentiation) only incidentally. For example, Klein reflects on the nature of the discourse of interdisciplinarity and the 'internal and external forces' influencing it (1990: 14) and, in a later work, explores the meaning of different forms of interdisciplinarity across the academic spectrum (1996), while Moran examines debates about the 'meaning, purpose and practical applications' of interdisciplinarity from the particular perspective of literary studies (2002: 2). The collection of articles edited by Weingart and Stehr (2000) examines the discourses of both disciplinarity and interdisciplinarity, although, as the title suggests, the focus of this collection is the practice of interdisciplinarity and the different forms of organizing it. The practice, or construction, of interdisciplinarity (in both teaching and research) is also the focus of Lattuca's research monograph, *Creating Interdisciplinarity* (2001), which explores how academics in the United States understand and engage in interdisciplinary work, their perceptions of the impact of the academic context on such work and the different outcomes of their engagement in it. Yet, the concept of scientific integration is incidental to Lattuca's inquiry in the sense that it appears as the concept of 'synthetic interdisciplinarity', one of four types of interdisciplinary research and teaching that she derives from her empirical investigation (2001: Chapter 4).

By focusing on understanding the different ways in which individual researchers construct forms of interdisciplinarity, existing books on this subject reflect – in varying degrees – the influence of social constructionism. However, as I argue later in this book, social constructionism and postmodernism cannot sustain a coherent justification for scientific integration and differentiation and so cannot help to explain the problem that motivates this investigation, which is why attempts to produce integrative interdisciplinary research either fail or become incoherent. Producing a form of knowledge 'that is more than the simple sum of the parts' (SURPC, 1997: xi) is indeed the goal that most advocates of interdisciplinary research demand; yet, it is a goal that researchers have often struggled to meet, even when working in research centres and institutes explicitly intended to facilitate the production of integrative, interdisciplinary research. In subsequent chapters, I attempt to explain why this is the case. I examine researchers' conceptions of knowledge and of reality on the one hand and their decisions about what sort of knowledge to produce on the other, and I argue that contradictions within researchers' thinking place limits on their ability to synthesize knowledge from different disciplines and that the social system of knowledge production, and the intellectual structures of science constellationally contained within it, places limits on the opportunities for researchers to integrate knowledge from different disciplines in varying degrees. In short, I argue that the problem of integrating knowledge through interdisciplinary research is both a problem of *knowledge* and a problem of knowledge *production*.

Accordingly, in the first section of this chapter, I discuss the different meanings of interdisciplinary research that I have identified from a reading of the contemporary academic literature and justify my focus on the integrative form of interdisciplinary research. This leads into the second section, which considers the adequacy of some typical justifications for integrative, interdisciplinary research. In the third section, I attempt to determine whether or not researchers are managing to *produce* integrative interdisciplinary research and present a critical survey of some recent empirical investigations into the conduct and funding of interdisciplinary research. In the fourth section, I consider the nature of *disciplinary* research, which has to be the starting point for interdisciplinary research, and examine critically different conceptions of an academic discipline. In the fifth and final section, I draw together the arguments of the previous sections in defining the key questions of the book and show how the arguments of subsequent chapters relate to these.

## The nature of interdisciplinary research

It is important to acknowledge that interdisciplinary research has different meanings within the academy. The heterogeneity of interdisciplinarity is evident in the most recent research, which distinguishes between three different 'modes' of interdisciplinarity: the '*integrative* or *synthesis*' mode, in which the aim is to integrate knowledge from two or more disciplines so as to generate an increase in understanding of the causes of a complicated problem (such as climate change) that would not be possible were the problem to be addressed from multiple yet disconnected disciplinary perspectives; the '*subordination–service*' mode, in which one or more disciplines are subordinated to the needs of a master discipline – an arrangement that is typical of the interactions between art, science and technology; and finally the '*agonistic–antagonistic*' mode, in which the aim is to challenge traditional disciplinary thinking and thereby 'transcend the given epistemological and ontological assumptions of traditional disciplines' – as in the field of ethnography in the information technology industry (Barry *et al.*, 2008: 28–9). In identifying three different 'modes' of interdisciplinarity (and also three different 'logics' that motivate it), Barry *et al.* are adopting a broad-based definition of interdisciplinarity that stands in contrast to the traditional assumption that the essential characteristic of interdisciplinary research is the integration of knowledge from two or more distinct disciplines (ibid: 27–8).

Similarly, Lattuca explores how academics in the United States understand and engage in interdisciplinary work. She identifies four ideal types of interdisciplinary research: 'informed disciplinarity', in which the concepts and/or methods of one discipline contribute to answering a question posed in another discipline; 'synthetic interdisciplinarity', in which the research question is relevant to two or more different disciplines and thereby acts as a 'bridge' between them; 'transdisciplinarity', in which the aim is to apply a concept or method across different disciplinary domains so as to unify those domains – as in sociobiology or the application of rational choice theory across the social sciences; and finally 'conceptual interdisciplinarity', in which the researcher answers a question that has no 'compelling disciplinary basis' and thereby constructs a critique of traditional, disciplinary approaches to a particular problem or issue (Lattuca, 2001: 113–18).

Lattuca derives her typology of interdisciplinarity from an exploration of the different types of research question that her subjects asked in their research. By adopting this approach, she claims to have rejected the traditional way of defining interdisciplinarity according to the degree of integration of different disciplinary perspectives. For example, Rossini and Porter distinguish between 'type I integration' – or multidisciplinarity – in which the various disciplinary analyses are linked externally as in a 'patchwork quilt' and 'type II integration' – or interdisciplinarity – in which the analyses are linked both externally and internally as in a 'tapestry' (Rossini and Porter, 1979: 72).[6] Lattuca's motivation for rejecting integration as the basis of her typology is that in her view focusing on the issue of integration leads to the problem of how to measure the level of integration within a research project so as to determine the extent to which it is interdisciplinary as opposed to multidisciplinary. In her view, we can avoid this problem by examining how researchers understand the meaning of their work. As she explains:

> A foolproof method for assessing the level of integration of an interdisciplinary teaching or research project has eluded researchers. Some have tried to measure integration by examining the processes by which interdisciplinary research is accomplished, for example, by noting how often researchers on an interdisciplinary project meet to coordinate their work. Others have attempted to judge the final product of an interdisciplinary project typically relying on the judgments of participants or the researchers themselves. If interdisciplinary projects, however, are born, not made, that is, if they begin as I have argued, with interdisciplinary questions, then such attempts are misguided because we must look to the point of origin to understand interdisciplinarity.
>
> (Lattuca, 2001: 113)

In the third section of this chapter, I argue that attempts to determine how successful an interdisciplinary research project is by measuring the level of scientific integration within it are indeed problematic. I argue that integration is not something that may be quantified. However, that does not mean that we should abandon the issue of integration altogether, because this concept is clearly fundamental to the concerns of many interdisciplinary researchers. Indeed, in my observation, interdisciplinary research as integrating or synthesizing knowledge from different disciplines is the dominant understanding of interdisciplinarity in the academic literature. As I show in the second section below and in the second chapter of this book, integration is a recurring feature of justifications for interdisciplinary research because the integration of knowledge from different fields of inquiry meets an important scientific need, which is to understand the way the world *is*. I argue that the relevant question to ask about interdisciplinary research projects is not how much integration there is but *what* is being integrated and *how*.

Little attention has been given to the question of what an integrated research product is in the literature on interdisciplinarity and many reports on interdisciplinarity leave the nature of integration unexamined. Consider Tait *et al.*'s fairly typical distinction between multidisciplinary and interdisciplinary research:

> *Multidisciplinary research* approaches an issue from the perspectives of a range of disciplines, but each discipline works in a self-contained manner with little cross-fertilisation among disciplines, or synergy in the outcomes.
>
> *Interdisciplinary research* similarly approaches an issue from a range of disciplinary perspectives but in this case the contributions of the various disciplines are integrated to provide a holistic or systemic outcome.
>
> (Tait *et al.*, 2003a: 12)

For Tait *et al.*, interdisciplinary is distinguished from multidisciplinary research according to the nature of the research product; yet, they say nothing about what a 'holistic or systemic outcome' is, even when they go on to make further distinctions between 'mode 1' and 'mode 2' interdisciplinarity.[7]

Similarly, Bell *et al.* conclude, from their investigation of interdisciplinarity in two European Union Fifth Framework projects that 'interdisciplinarity is dynamic, being the integration of "ways of thinking" as part of the development of a "way of working" and thus cannot be produced by following a predetermined recipe' (Bell *et al.*, 2005: 34). Bell *et al.* say little about what these 'ways of thinking' and 'way of working' are. Yet, it may be difficult to integrate 'ways of thinking', if these are contradictory; for disciplines are not 'homogeneous entities with clearly defined borders' but are 'heterogeneous' – that is, characterized by competing scientific paradigms (Molteberg *et al.*, 2000: 321). For example, in the social sciences we find different schools of thought in politics (Marsh and Stoker, 2002a, 2010; Marsh and Savigny, 2004), economics (Harley and Lee, 1997, 1998), law (Toma, 1997) and sociology (Turner, 1990; Crane and Small, 1992) that reflect philosophical differences both within and between disciplines. Now, if researchers are unaware of such differences, they may find it difficult to synthesize competing forms of knowledge. In this respect, Bell *et al.*'s proposal that researchers should 'make a conscious effort...to describe to others both the methodological and epistemological foundations of their research and how these are used to interpret their findings' (Bell *et al.*, 2005: 12) is a step in the right direction. But, it still leaves open the question of how researchers, once they have revealed their philosophical assumptions, can 'make their disciplinary contribution mutually intelligible' (ibid.). In other words, how are they to integrate their 'disciplinary research strands' (ibid.), if what one researcher accepts as valid knowledge is not the same as what another researcher accepts as valid knowledge?

Even those scholars who do address the issue of integration directly often fail to shed clear light on what exactly is being integrated. Consider, for example, Allen Repko's definition of integration:

> The integration of knowledge, then, means identifying and blending knowledge from relevant disciplines to produce an interdisciplinary understanding of a particular problem or intellectual question that is limited in time and to a particular context that would not be possible by relying solely on a single disciplinary approach. For example, a single disciplinary perspective cannot possibly explain the complex phenomenon of terrorism, much less craft a comprehensive solution to it. Understanding terrorism in an interdisciplinary sense calls for drawing on insights from history, political science, cultural anthropology, sociology, law, economics, religious studies, and psychology and integrating these to produce a more comprehensive understanding of it.
>
> (Repko, 2008: 19)

In later chapters of his textbook, Repko explains in greater detail what integration entails. He argues that the first key step is to identify the conflicts in disciplinary based insights deemed to be of relevance to the problem under investigation. As he puts it:

> The immediate challenge for the student is to identify conflicts in disciplinary insights and then locate the sources of these conflicts. This is necessary because these conflicts stand in the way of creating or discovering common ground and, thus, of achieving integration. One cannot integrate two things that are exactly alike or that have identical properties. Integration can be achieved only between things that are different, whether those differences are seemingly small or impossibly large. In other words, integration arises out of conflict, controversy, and difference.
>
> (ibid: 248)

Repko explains further that creating 'common ground', which is necessary in the social sciences and humanities but not in the natural sciences, 'where it can be discovered' (ibid: 272), involves *modifying* concepts, theories and assumptions using five different techniques: 'theory expansion', 'redefinition', 'extension', 'organization' and 'transformation' (ibid: 281–92). After creating 'common ground', the third key step in the process of integration is 'using the common ground theory, concept or assumption to integrate disciplinary insights' and thereby 'to produce an interdisciplinary understanding of the problem' (ibid: 295).

Yet, the 'common ground' approach to integrating knowledge is problematic because it loses sight of the significance of scientific *difference*. Repko appears to be unsure about how to deal with scientific difference, at one point stating that 'Integration is the part of the interdisciplinary research process that seeks to *reconcile* disciplinary insights' (ibid: 6; emphasis added) and at another point stating that 'The process involved in achieving integration involves identifying, evaluating, and *rectifying* differences between disciplinary insights' (ibid: 122; emphasis added). Now, reconciling disciplinary insights suggests the possibility of integrating them while at the same time acknowledging and respecting the differences between them; rectifying disciplinary insights, by contrast, suggests the possibility of integrating them by removing the differences between them. This contradiction – between reconciliation and rectification – is apparent across the scientific examples on which Repko comments when illustrating the five integrating techniques in his textbook. For example, his illustration of 'theory expansion' through the case study of suicide terrorism reflects the idea of reconciling disciplinary insights because in this case the author of the study on suicide terrorism is attempting to bring together, reconcile and so integrate different causal factors. (It is puzzling, therefore, that Repko should see 'theory expansion' as a form of rectification.) By contrast, the case studies that Repko cites as illustrations of 'redefinition' and 'extension' reflect the idea of rectification. Yet, in these examples, it would seem that the common ground is created by a kind of distortionary unification. Thus, he cites Boulding's (1981) work on the economy of love and fear as an example of 'theory extension'. However, Repko does not consider whether or not Boulding's manipulation of the meaning of altruism is simply a distortion of this concept as it is understood in psychology and sociology and appears unaware of the serious criticisms of the application of rational choice theory across the social sciences (Archer and Tritter, 2000). Moreover, Repko cites with approval a study by Nagy on the causes of the degradation of tropical ecosystems in Costa Rica as an example of 'redefinition'. Yet, the danger of redefinition, as in this example, is that it will lead to a loss of explanatory power as the researcher overlooks the significance of contradictory causal forces. As I argue in Chapter 2, causal mechanisms are of different types and act in conjunction, either reinforcing or counteracting each other's effects, and with differential force; attempting to rectify these differences will lead to a distorted understanding of their conjunctural effect.

The fundamental problem with the theory of 'common ground', then, at least as Repko understands it, is that it appears unable to combine disciplinary insights in a way that preserves their differences. Repko is clearly confused about this issue, stating that 'The objective of creating common ground is not to eliminate tension altogether between the insights of different disciplines, *but to reduce the level of tension*' (Repko, 2008: 301; emphasis added). From a philosophical perspective, tension, if it is the result of philosophical inconsistency, will be manifest as scientific incoherence and a failure of integration (as I argue in Chapter 2). This sort of tension *must be resolved* through a change of philosophical position if integration is to get going again. By contrast, tension at a *scientific* level may be crucial to understanding the causal complexity of a particular problem so that attempting to reduce it through some sort of rectifying procedure will merely obscure the significance of contradictory causal powers and liabilities and make it more difficult to understand the processes leading to natural and social change.

The cause of Repko's confusion is his failure to articulate a coherent *ontology* of integration. Because he approaches the issue of integration at the level of methodology and epistemology, he fails to understand what features of reality can be integrated and how their differences can be preserved in an interdisciplinary understanding. In Chapter 2 of this book, I set out and defend an ontology of integration and differentiation using the concepts and theories of the philosophy of critical realism. Armed with an ontology of structures, causal mechanisms, powers, liabilities and tendencies, I provide a coherent justification for integrating knowledge from different disciplines. I argue that it is because the objects of scientific inquiry are all causal objects – their commonality – that they can be integrated (through their relations with each other), and that it is because their powers and liabilities have different effects that they can be differentiated and so studied separately.

Finally, it is important to recognize that the process of integrating knowledge through interdisciplinary research need not be organized on a collective basis – that is, where a team of researchers from different scientific backgrounds works together on a common problem. Yet, the assumption in much of the academic literature is that interdisciplinary research is a collective enterprise. Typical in this respect is a definition of interdisciplinary research as

> joint, coordinated and continuously integrated research done by experts with distinctly different disciplinary backgrounds producing joint "staff authored" reports. It differs from multidisciplinary research where experts from different disciplines work individually on different aspects of a specific problem and produce separate reports which may be published individually or as a collection.
>
> (cited in Hickman, 1980: 49)

However, it is clear that, at least in the social sciences, a great deal of interdisciplinary research is carried out on an individual basis. The interdisciplinary field of political economy, for example, has a long history that stretches back to the Scottish Enlightenment and that has developed primarily through the work of individual theorists from a wide range of schools of thought (Redman, 1997; Milonakis and Fine, 2009). Moreover, as I show in Chapter 2, political economy is often held up as an example of interdisciplinary research precisely because it is (implicitly) understood as an integrative field of social inquiry.

In this book, I examine interdisciplinary research both as an individual pursuit and as a collective enterprise. In Chapter 2, for example, I focus on the work of individual classical political economists. By contrast, in Chapters 4 and 5, I discuss evidence from three case studies of collaborative, interdisciplinary research projects, two of which fall into the domain of political economy. By considering both forms of interdisciplinary research, I demonstrate that philosophical contradictions may exist *within* the thinking of individual researchers as well as *between* researchers from distinct scientific backgrounds and that it is these contradictions that prevent researchers from producing coherent, integrative research.

## Justifications for interdisciplinary research

As public demands for interdisciplinary research have grown in recent years, so has the promotion of interdisciplinary research through national and international funding programmes. At an international level, the European Commission Fifth Framework Programme has addressed the issues of sustainable development and technological innovation through 'an integrated approach to research and its exploitation', involving 'close collaboration and interaction, on the one hand, between researchers and practitioners... and on the other, between disciplines both within and between the social and natural sciences' (Bruce *et al.*, 2004: 458). At a national level, the RELU Programme, funded and managed jointly by the UK Research Councils, has emerged in response to growing public concerns about 'sustainable development and the knowledge economy, and associated demands for greater accountability of science' (Lowe and Phillipson, 2006: 160). Significantly, all research proposals submitted to the Programme have to be explicitly interdisciplinary, combining both a natural and social science perspective, although the particular approach taken to integration is left for applicants to determine.[8]

Now, given the increasing external demands for integrative interdisciplinary research, the question we must ask is what justifies this sort of knowledge. We might approach this question by considering what Enlightenment social theorists, who were writing in a predisciplinary age, thought about knowledge production. Adam Smith, for example, argued that specialization in the production of knowledge was a necessary condition for the growth of knowledge as a whole, just as specialization in the production of material goods and services was a necessary condition for the accumulation of wealth. Smith writes:

> In the progress of society, philosophy or speculation becomes, like every other employment, the principal or sole trade and occupation of a particular class of citizens. Like every other employment too, it is subdivided into a great number of different branches, each of which affords occupation to a particular tribe or class of philosophers; and this subdivision of employment in philosophy, as well as in every other business, improves dexterity, and saves time. Each individual becomes more expert in his own peculiar branch, more work is done upon the whole, and the quantity of science is considerably increased by it.
>
> (Smith, [1776] 1976: 21–2)

Whereas Smith was more concerned with the quantity of knowledge, contemporary scientists and philosophers are more concerned with the quality and thus the nature of knowledge and are critical of what they see as the reductionism that characterizes the majority of Western science. For example, Sayer criticizes the increasing tendency towards 'disciplinary parochialism' in academia, the consequence of which is that disciplines become 'incapable of seeing beyond the questions posed by their own discipline' (2000a: 83); Beam argues that 'fragmentation' – the consequence of specialization – 'promotes inadequate access to knowledge and wasteful duplication of effort through inefficient classification and inadequate understanding' (1982: 160); while Blackburn argues that disciplinary '*separatism*' has led to the '*failure*' of social science for the simple reason that '*the object of social science* – society – *may only be comprehended on the basis of the various disciplines working together*' (2004: 168). In short, as Karlqvist puts it,

> There is a price to be paid for fragmentation and specialization... The parts can no longer be put together easily... As science moves closer to applications, decision- and policymaking, problems occur that cannot be confined to narrow disciplines or kept within the borders of specific departments.
>
> (Karlqvist, 1999: 379)

Certain research problems cannot be adequately addressed through disciplinary specialization, it is argued, because reality is *complex*. For example, the report, *Facilitating Interdisciplinary Research*, states that:

> In recent decades, the growth of scientific and technical knowledge has prompted scientists, engineers, social scientists, and humanists to join in addressing *complex* problems that must be attacked simultaneously with deep knowledge from different perspectives. Students show increasing enthusiasm about problems of global importance that have practical consequences, such as disease prevention, economic development, social inequality, and global climate change – all of which can best be addressed through IDR [interdisciplinary problem-focused research].
>
> (Committee on Facilitating Interdisciplinary Research, 2004: 17; emphasis added)

Similarly, in a special issue on interdisciplinary research in the journal *Ecosystems*, contributors argued that the complexity of reality justifies intellectual collaboration across disciplines. Wear, for example, claims that:

> Many of the world's critical problems involve human interactions with nature and their long-term implications for environmental quality and the sustainability of resource/ecological systems. These problems are *complex* – defined by the collective behaviours of people as well as by the structure and function of ecosystems – suggesting that both the social and natural sciences should focus efforts on dimensions of these problems. The separate efforts of social and natural sciences are unlikely to fully illuminate the fabric of or fashion solutions to environmental problems.
>
> (Wear, 1999: 299; emphasis added)

Certain commentators go further in attempting to define complexity. Hickman, for example, identifies it with the *interdependence* of the different parts of reality:

> life in a modern industrial society such as ours is characterized by a growing *interdependence* of many parts. Political, legal, industrial, economic and physical factors are interacting to an extent that has not been experienced before. It is self-evident that the problems which such complex interactions create will be difficult to deal with.
>
> (Hickman, 1980: 51; emphasis added)

Kinzig also recognizes the complexity of reality but acknowledges more explicitly the idea that through a particular interaction of parts something new emerges:

> Solving today's environmental problems requires an understanding of the complex ways in which nature and society interact to make a *whole that is different from the sum of its parts*. An integration of knowledge from many different traditional disciplines will be required to see this whole.
>
> (Kinzig, 2001: 709; emphasis added)

In short, most scholars seem to agree that what justifies the production of integrative, interdisciplinary research is the complexity of reality[9] and that, through this mode of research, scientists will arrive at an understanding of reality that is greater than the understanding they would achieve were they to try to understand it from any single disciplinary perspective. Repko's definition of interdisciplinary studies brings together the key ideas of complexity, integration and progress in understanding:

> Interdisciplinary studies is a process of answering a question, solving a problem, or addressing a topic that is too broad or complex to be dealt with adequately by a single discipline and draws on disciplinary perspectives and integrates their insights to produce a more comprehensive understanding or cognitive advancement.
>
> (Repko, 2008: 12)

However, advocates of integrative, interdisciplinary research have gone only so far with the concept of complexity. We can begin to understand why this is by looking at the way in which interdisciplinary researchers have responded to arguments made against interdisciplinarity. A common (mis)conception of interdisciplinary research is that it is somehow more superficial or less rigorous than disciplinary research and so less valuable. For example, Mar *et al.*, (1981) in their examination of central university research administrators' attitudes to large-scale interdisciplinary research in the United States found that university officials doubted the quality of interdisciplinary outputs:

> Doubts existed in officials' minds with reference to the review of the quality of interdisciplinary research. This difficulty jeopardizes the preparation of graduate students for significant future contributions requiring special expertise... Several university officials indicated that interdisciplinary

> research and affiliation may make the students subject to the suspicion of shallowness and less than solid competence in the fields involved.
>
> (Mar *et al.*, 1981: 31)

The view that interdisciplinarity promotes intellectual shallowness is also the fourth of Benson's 'Five Arguments Against Interdisciplinary Studies' (1982). But, more significant for our purposes is Benson's first argument, which is that advocates of interdisciplinarity seem to be seriously confused about what they are doing, especially when it comes to integrating knowledge. As Benson puts it:

> Quite simply, the practitioners of interdisciplinary studies lack a coherent, defensible sense of their purposes. Interdisciplinary studies purports to be concerned with examining and developing significant lines of connection between two or more disciplines. It is not at all clear, however, just what it means to connect the disciplines nor what the value of such activity might be. Most of the discussion of interdisciplinary or integrative studies assumes clarity in these matters and moves on to other concerns.
>
> (Benson, 1982: 103)

Newell (1983) has responded to this critique and I discuss part of his response here because it illustrates some of the problems into which interdisciplinary researchers run when attempting to provide justifications for interdisciplinary research that expand on the meaning of complexity. Newell is quite clear about the purpose of interdisciplinary studies:

> Interdisciplinary study should be understood to start with the confrontation of the interdisciplinarian with the world... Out of that phenomenological confrontation comes a question, one which is too broad to be answered by any single discipline. The strategy of the interdisciplinarian is to bring the relevant disciplines... to bear upon the question, one at a time, letting each illuminate that aspect of the question which is amenable to treatment by the characteristic concepts, theories, and methods of the respective disciplines. Out of the resulting disciplinary insights, the interdisciplinarian fashions a response to the question that would ideally be a complete answer but which at least leads to a greater appreciation of the nature and complexity of the question.
>
> (Newell, 1983: 109–10)

However, what Newell is much less clear about is the issue of what connecting the disciplines means and what value there is in this connection. Newell continually fudges this issue, stating simply that what is connected in interdisciplinary studies is 'disciplinary insights' rather than whole disciplines and that out of the comparison and evaluation of disciplinary insights will come 'a richness of insight not available to the adherent of any one disciplinary orthodoxy' (ibid: 110). This response leaves the meaning of 'disciplinary insights' and 'richness' unclear.[10] Indeed, similar criticisms could be made of the justifications for interdisciplinary research discussed earlier, which work with very basic conceptions of complexity and interdependence and which raise important questions about what exactly is the nature of the different parts of society that proponents of interdisciplinarity are so quick to emphasize, and how these parts are related to each other such that they form an irreducible, holistic outcome. Given the lack of clear answers to such questions in the literature on interdisciplinarity, it is unsurprising that Newell is forced to admit later on in his response to Benson that 'The process of integration or synthesis is poorly understood and little studied by professional interdisciplinarians. It is no wonder that we achieve synthesis so seldom in our courses' (ibid: 117).

In short, what advocates of interdisciplinary studies lack is a compelling rationale or justification for scientific integration, which is manifest in their failure to elaborate on the meaning of complexity. Yet, we can elaborate on the meaning of this concept using ontological inquiry, as I show in Chapter 2. It is through ontological inquiry that we can start to establish a coherent grounding for scientific integration and differentiation, for these two epistemological concepts are complementary and follow from the structured, stratified and differentiated nature of reality. Indeed, the implication of my argument in Chapter 2 is that integrative, interdisciplinary inquiry can be just as rigorous as specialized, disciplinary-based inquiry and that scientific progress demands both types of inquiry.

## Interdisciplinary research in practice

In the post-war era, higher education institutions throughout the West have established research institutes and centres explicitly designed to encourage the production of interdisciplinary research (Ikenberry and Friedman, 1972). But, to what extent have the objectives associated with the interdisciplinary research carried out in these centres been met? In other words, to what extent is the institutional encouragement for interdisciplinarity actually leading to scientific integration? This is an important question to ask, given the public rationale for these centres and the resources directed towards them, for, although a research centre may claim to be interdisciplinary, it may not actually be producing the sort of knowledge for which it was funded. Klein suggests that this is often the case when she writes that:

> both NASA [US National Aeronautics and Space Administration] and NSF [National Science Foundation] as well as other funding agencies and many interdisciplinary researchers themselves expressed disappointment in the lack of genuine integration. Born of pressures for solving problems outside the narrow scope of the academic world, IDR [interdisciplinary problem-focused research] projects were themselves plagued by disciplinary chauvinism and the psychological, social, and epistemological problems of communicating across disciplines.
>
> (Klein, 1985: 119)

However, there is little in the way of *systematic* evidence to support the view that scientific integration has been difficult to achieve because few analyses of the *outputs* of interdisciplinary research projects have been undertaken. Rather than examining the quality of interdisciplinary research outputs, seminars and workshops have tended to explore individuals' experiences and, hence, perceptions of interdisciplinary research. For example, the British Academy organized a one-day workshop in May 2006, 'Working Together Across Disciplines: Challenges for the Natural and Social Sciences', which 'explored the many challenges that interdisciplinary research faces in a university environment'.[11] Similarly, the third in a series of six ESRC-funded seminars on 'interactive agenda setting in the social sciences', held in May 2005, looked at 'how interdisciplinary agenda and priorities develop'.[12] Also, the ESRC Transdisciplinary Seminar Series, 'Knowledge and Power: Exploring the Science/Society Interface in the Urban Environment Context', held in 2003, had as only one of a range of objectives, 'To explore the difficulties and requirements of interdisciplinarity'.[13] Typically, discussion among the participants at such seminars has focused on the perceived institutional and methodological barriers to scientific integration. For example, Petts *et al.* (2004) report that, during the ESRC Transdisciplinary Seminar Series 'Participants in every seminar... felt the deep structuring of disciplines keenly. They spoke of "disciplinary tribalism" and of the personal (particularly academic career) costs of engaging in interdisciplinarity'.[14] They also report that participants identified the 'funding and organisational practices' of the UK Research Councils, the Research Assessment Exercise (RAE) 2008, and publishing 'policy-related research' as significant obstacles to intellectual collaboration.[15] The discussion at the Royal Society's one-day conference, 'Interdisciplinarity – Transport and the Environment', reached similar conclusions. The report from that conference identified 'three major obstacles to interdisciplinary research: institutional, conceptual/methodological and funding-related'.[16]

More systematically, Bell *et al.* (2005) investigated the experiences of those who participated in two interdisciplinary European Commission Fifth Framework projects. However, Bell *et al.* had as their objective to develop 'a greater understanding of the processes, potential and problems facing research projects that involve more than one discipline' (Bell *et al.*, 2005: 5); hence, they did not look at exactly how the integration of different forms of knowledge might be achieved. They state that 'projects involving a range of disciplines will not necessarily produce interdisciplinary research unless specific steps are taken to ensure the communication and integration of disciplinary perspectives' (ibid: 6). Yet, they do not say exactly what these 'steps' are, and they state that 'for interdisciplinarity to be achieved within a project, where it is most likely that the group is made up specifically of qualitative and quantitative researchers... we must acknowledge the "different worlds" within which qualitative and quantitative researchers work' (ibid: 7). But how can these 'different worlds' be reconciled? How can, say, a positivist and an interpretivist social scientist work together and integrate their results when those results presuppose incompatible methodological, epistemological and ontological positions?

Tait *et al.* also investigated the issue of interdisciplinarity in relation to European Commission Fourth and Fifth Framework projects by means of postal questionnaires, telephone interviews, case studies, participant workshops and meetings. Again, the research objectives focused mainly on exploring the experiences of those managing, evaluating and carrying out interdisciplinary research, their perceptions of what was successful and problematic in interdisciplinary research and their perceptions of what caused these successes and problems (Tait *et al.*, 2003a: 7). Tait *et al.* identify the usual practical difficulties of management and communication, which are associated with cultural differences and geography, and the usual personal qualities necessary for collaborative research, such as keeping an open mind, being flexible in one's approach and being willing to learn from others (ibid: 17–31). They also discuss the typical institutional obstacles associated with the funding and evaluation of interdisciplinary research (ibid: 33–7). But, just as do Bell *et al.*, Tait *et al.* say little about the possibility of scientific integration. They offer 'models' of interdisciplinary research (ibid: 12–13) and consider practical ways in which participants have achieved integration. For example, they find that project co-coordinators have a key role to play in facilitating integration through 'understanding the research methods and assumptions of the different disciplines', 'bringing partners together when this seemed useful', 'interpreting and negotiating between researchers', and 'listening for signals that one partner was suggesting a different way of doing things and not constraining the approach to any particular discipline's accepted methods' (ibid: 25). What is interesting, though, is what they state in their conclusion:

> Even for our sample of FP5 [Fifth Framework] projects funded by the EC [European Commission] over the relevant time period there were disappointingly few projects that one would regard as interdisciplinary rather than multidisciplinary, particularly in cutting across the boundary between social sciences and natural science/engineering.
>
> (Tait *et al.*, 2003a: 54)

Tait *et al.* say no more about this. Yet, their comments raise obvious questions. To what extent was scientific integration an explicit objective of these projects and, if it was an explicit objective, how did project participants understand integration and to what extent did they achieve it in practice? Tait *et al.* do not provide answers to such questions, even in their six case studies of Framework projects (2003b: 73–191). In subsequent chapters of this book, I argue that, to answer such questions, we need to examine project participants' conceptions of science and of reality and, more importantly, the philosophical coherence of their research outputs, if we are to think about success in integrating knowledge through interdisciplinary research.

Interdisciplinary research groups have also been the subject of investigation in management science. Typically, these studies attempt to measure various aspects of interdisciplinary research in order to develop empirical generalizations. For example, Birnbaum (1978, 1979) has measured interdisciplinary research project 'performance' using an aggregate of different 'indicators': the group's average perception of its overall effectiveness, a weighted summation of three 'dimensions' of group behaviour – 'reliability, cooperation, and development' – and the group's perception of the extent to which it achieved differentially important organizational goals 'either concerned with output or support' (1979: 233). But, these output goals, it seems, do not relate to the extent to which interdisciplinary research outputs are *philosophically coherent*. Birnbaum does address the issue of integration directly but either as a dependent variable reflecting different ways of encouraging collaboration (through seminars and joint papers, for example) (1978: 87–8) or as an independent variable reflecting the differential strength of interpersonal group relations (1981: 491–93). In other words, nowhere in Birnbaum's work is the issue of scientific synthesis addressed qualitatively.

Recent work on interdisciplinarity in information science adopts the same sort of approach. Qin *et al.* (1997), for example, examined the relationship between the 'degree' of interdisciplinarity, which they measured by counting the number of disciplines in a research paper (as represented by the number of cited journal articles) and the 'level' (number of authors, number of organizational affiliations, number of disciplines represented by organizational affiliation) and 'type' (intradepartmental, interdepartmental, inter-institutional, international) of collaboration (ibid: 895). But, once again, their study pays no attention to the *nature* of the knowledge that interdisciplinary research outputs represent. It may well be the case that a particular journal article cites a large number of disciplines and that this is associated with a large number of authors having different disciplinary perspectives. But this tells us nothing about how the article treats these different and potentially conflicting perspectives. How, for example, were these different perspectives integrated? Indeed, to what extent was integration an explicit objective of the research? And, to what extent was the integration attempted philosophically coherent? Once again, quantitative analyses of interdisciplinary research leave us unable to answer such questions.

Interdisciplinary research has also provided a focus for investigation in the areas of research policy and administration. For example, Rossini and Porter (1979, 1981), Rossini *et al.* (1981) and Chubin *et al.* (1979) carried out an empirical study of 24 technology assessments (which typically involve collaboration among a wide range of social and natural sciences). Unlike Birnbaum's work, Rossini and Porter's work is directly concerned with the integration of assessment outputs, which they regard 'as a primary indicator of performance' (Rossini and Porter, 1981: 11) and which they measure along a five-point scale for a range of aspects – 'editorial integration, conceptual/terminological integration, systematic integration, and overall substantive integration' (ibid.). However, they offer little in the way of a thorough discussion of this typology. How, for example, are the different types of integration related to each other and how is the issue of philosophical coherence dealt with?

Rossini and Porter do discuss the wider social context of disciplinary specialization within which interdisciplinary research operates and which they argue 'poses further dilemmas in terms of professional achievement, institutional structure, training, and utilization of findings' (ibid: 18). However, their discussion of these issues, and the possible policy responses to them, is rather superficial and begs further questions. How exactly does the social context generate 'dilemmas' for interdisciplinary researchers? How do these researchers deal with the dilemmas facing them? Which social structures and causal mechanisms are at work and how are they related to each other and to the intellectual context of knowledge production? Indeed, Rossini *et al.* seem to be unclear as to what exactly are social structures and causal mechanisms. For example, they identify six 'structural and process' factors as important causal influences on project integration – 'leadership characteristics', 'team characteristics', 'bounding', 'iteration', 'communication patterns' and 'epistemological factors' (Rossini *et al.*, 1981: 510–17). Thus, they argue that 'projects with a democratic leadership show a greater degree of interdisciplinary integration than those characterized by other styles' (ibid: 510) and they explicitly conceptualize this finding as a 'causal relationship' between 'leadership style' and 'integration' for which they calculate a 'path coefficient' (ibid: 511–12). Yet, arguably, what they are identifying are the empirical *effects* – as manifest in observable 'characteristics' – of underlying, *unobservable*, processes and structures. Hence, in this case, it is possible that it is the causal mechanism of participation, stemming from the particular set of relationships between team members (the underlying structure) that is generating both a 'democratic' leadership style and a high degree of integration. Indeed, this particular structure may also allow for satisfactory 'bounding' of the project and for a sufficient number of 'iterations' – two factors that Rossini *et al.* found were also well correlated with integration.

It is unclear whether or not Rossini *et al.* recognize that there is an ontological distinction to be made between the six different effects they identify and the underlying structures and processes generating them. I say more about this particular philosophical critique in subsequent chapters. For now, it is enough for me to say that, by treating 'structural and process factors' as independent variables that can be measured directly, Rossini *et al.* suggest that these are observable rather than unobservable entities. Furthermore, treating these factors as measurable variables makes it difficult to understand how they are related to each other. For example, it is possible that there are more powerful mechanisms, whose effects may override, in certain conditions, the effects of the participation mechanism referred to above. It may be that the intellectual norms and assumptions which team members draw on are conflicting (a cognitive problem) and that team members are too insecure to resolve these conflicts (a psychological problem). Rossini *et al.* are clearly aware of such 'epistemological differences' (1981: 514–17); yet, their preference for measurement again leads them into considering only the epistemological 'distance' between disciplines (ibid: 517), rather than the different ways of understanding the world and of gaining knowledge of it that these epistemological differences reflect and how they might be reconciled. Rossini *et al.* do construct a 'simple index of intellectual distance among core team members' (ibid: 517) in which they differentiate between 'economics' and 'social sciences'. Yet, this index still suggests that the 'social sciences' are homogeneous disciplines. As I discuss in subsequent chapters, the social sciences are far from being homogeneous in their ontological, epistemological and methodological assumptions. Therefore, trying to represent the complexity of such qualitative differences through measurement may be highly misleading.

The most recent investigation of interdisciplinarity is Rhoten's social network analysis of six interdisciplinary research centres in the United States. Significantly, she found that the research networks in these centres (which dealt with both the natural and social sciences) appeared to be 'more multidisciplinary than interdisciplinary' so that there was 'more of an inclusion, rather than an integration, of different disciplines'. She also found that, in certain cases, there were 'clear divisions between represented disciplines and distinct clusters of monodisciplinary relations' and that overall there tended to be more 'information sharing' than 'knowledge creating' collaborations (Rhoten, 2003: 5–6). To a certain extent, then, Rhoten's findings support Tait *et al.*'s findings about the lack of genuine integration discussed above. However, because Rhoten's focus was on understanding how interdisciplinary research centres 'originate and operate' (ibid: 2) and not on evaluating 'the research outcomes produced by these centers' (ibid: 3), it is unclear exactly how centre members understood scientific integration and to what extent they intended to achieve it and did achieve it. Rhoten writes that 'on average, 60% of researchers believe that the research he/she does inside the center qualifies as multidisciplinary or disciplinary' (ibid: 4); yet, it may have been the case that what researchers thought was an interdisciplinary outcome at a scientific level was not a genuine integration of disciplinary perspectives.

Finally, we should also consider the extent to which newly emergent interdisciplinary fields such as the 'new economic sociology' (Swedberg, 1990), the 'new political economy' (Gamble, 1995) and the 'new economic geography' (Martin, 1999) represent a genuine integration of knowledge from different disciplinary domains. In addition, there have emerged fields of inquiry based on supradisciplinary themes and perspectives such as area studies (Ichimura, 1975; Pye, 1975) and cultural studies (Ray and Sayer, 1999) amongst others. There has been very little analysis of the philosophical coherence of these hybrid fields of inquiry, which is an additional motivation for the philosophical analysis of scientific research presented in this study. However, Grace (1996) analyzed a variety of women's studies courses at colleges and universities in the United States and identified seven different types of course, many of which incorporated multiple disciplinary perspectives in the study of women. She found that some of these courses, despite claiming to be interdisciplinary, did not amount to an integration of disciplinary perspectives and so were only multidisciplinary or cross-disciplinary in nature.[17]

Overall, then, existing investigations into the practice of interdisciplinary research suggest that researchers, where they are committed to integrating knowledge from different disciplines, are often struggling to follow through on this commitment. The evidence is far from clear on this because, as we have seen, most researchers have set about trying either to measure scientific integration or to explore the experiences and perceptions of interdisciplinary researchers; few have taken a qualitative approach and have examined the philosophical consistency of research outputs claimed to be examples of scientific integration. In Chapters 2 and 4, I show how this can be done through qualitative case studies of research projects that are either implicitly recognized or explicitly proclaimed as exemplifying integrative interdisciplinary research.

## The nature of disciplinarity

In the previous section, I noted that, in recent seminars and workshops on interdisciplinarity and scientific collaboration, participants discussed perceived *institutional* constraints on producing integrative interdisciplinary research and, in particular, the *structuring* of disciplines. These discussions raise the question of what exactly is a discipline. We should also ask this question because, as advocates of integrative interdisciplinary research have acknowledged, 'interdisciplinarity has a high degree of dependence upon and interaction with the disciplines' (Repko, 2008: 53) so that the relationship between disciplinarity and interdisciplinarity is '*symbiotic*' (Szostak, 2007: 10).

Most conceptions of an academic discipline equate it with the objects, theories and occasionally methods, of scientific inquiry; that is, disciplines are usually thought of as bodies of knowledge – as essentially intellectual things. Consider the following definitions of disciplinarity. The first comes from the seminal Organisation for Economic Cooperation and Development (OECD) study on interdisciplinarity published in the 1970s. One of the contributors to this study defines 'disciplinarity' as:

> the specialized scientific exploration of a given homogeneous subject matter producing new knowledge and making obsolete old knowledge. Disciplinary activity results incessantly in formulations and reformulations of the present body of knowledge about that subject matter.
>
> (Heckhausen, 1972: 83)

Another contributor to the same study defines 'discipline' as 'a set comprising three types of elements'. These 'elements' are:

> 1. observable and/or formalized objects, both manipulated by means of methods and procedures.
> 2. phenomena that are the materialization of the interaction between these objects.
> 3. laws – whose terms and/or formulation depend on a set of axioms – which account for the phenomena and make it possible to predict how they operate.
>
> (Boisot, 1972: 90)

Finally, here are two recent definitions of 'discipline', both from scholars advocating interdisciplinary research:

> At its simplest, we might regard a discipline as a self conscious field of sustained, systematic inquiry with its own distinguishable broad subject matter, questions, and methods – and, moreover, with a relatively specialized vocabulary supplying the terms by which the field, its subject matter, and its methods are described, and by which its questions are framed.
>
> (Evans and Macnaughton, 2004: 1)

> A discipline is a particular branch of learning or body of knowledge whose defining elements – i.e. phenomena, assumptions, epistemology, concepts, theories, and methods – distinguish it from other knowledge formations. History is an example of a discipline because it meets all of the above criteria. Its knowledge domain consists of an enormous body of *facts*… It studies an equally enormous number of *concepts or ideas*… It generates *theories* about why things turned out the way they did…And it uses a *method* that involves critical analysis of primary sources…and secondary sources…to present a picture of past events or persons within a particular time and place.
>
> (Repko, 2008: 4)

There seem to be two key problems with defining an academic discipline as just a body of knowledge. The first problem is that, in reducing the meaning of discipline to the *products* of disciplinary inquiry, we are left with an impoverished conception of the intellectual context of science. In subsequent chapters, I argue that the intellectual context of science cannot be reduced to a collection of facts; for scientific inquiry presupposes ideas that are more abstract and so fundamental than the concepts and theories that the scientist works with directly – ideas about the nature of reality and of science. In other words, what characterizes the intellectual context of science is intellectual *depth*.

Now, certain commentators implicitly understand that the intellectual context of science has depth when they refer to the notion of a 'worldview' or 'thought model':

> Disciplines themselves have been described as stable systemic communities within which researchers concentrate their experience into a particular worldview. This puts limits on the kinds of questions they can ask about their material, the methods and concepts they use, the answers they believe and their criteria for truth and validity.
>
> (Tait *et al.*, 2003a: 12)

> world view points to the conceptual construction which is used by a group to interpret reality. In my view, it is that conceptual framework, the associated images and metaphors, plus the understandings of relationships among them which pre-eminently influence how the members of one discipline think in contrast to the members of another discipline. It is not subject matter or the naming of a single central concept that identifies the essence of a discipline, but the predominant thought model or models.
>
> (Miller, 1982: 6)

> Disciplines are also distinguished from one another by the questions they ask about the world, by their perspective or world view, by the set of assumptions they employ, and by the methods which they use to build up a body of knowledge (facts, concepts, theories) around a certain subject matter.
>
> (Newell and Green, 1982: 25)

However, although these commentators do acknowledge the possibility of an intellectual context underlying disciplinary inquiry, they fail to explore the content of this context. What exactly is the nature of the 'worldview', 'conceptual framework' or 'thought model' involved in scientific inquiry? What sorts of assumptions does the use of particular scientific concepts and methods presuppose? And, to what extent are the different components of this intellectual context either explicit or implicit to scientific inquiry?

The second problem with reducing the meaning of an academic discipline to the products of disciplinary inquiry is that it ignores the *social* basis of knowledge production; for scientific inquiry is no different from any other social activity in having as one of its conditions of existence sets of rules, norms, duties, obligations, etc. Again, certain commentators have in fact recognized that there is something more to the meaning of discipline than just a collection of facts. Goodlad, for example, argues that: 'Whatever else academic disciplines may be, they are political arrangements in which a necessary tension is maintained between ideas and the social institutions through which they are expressed and explored' (1979: 14–15).

Similarly, Newell and Green state that:

> disciplines are not natural species amenable to systematic characterization through a taxonomy, but rather social organizations whose origins and continued existence are as much attributable to educational politics as to the needs of scholarly inquiry. A discipline is perhaps best characterized as a socio-political organization which concentrates on a historically linked set of problems.
>
> (Newell and Green, 1982: 24)

But, recognizing that academic inquiry is socially conditioned raises further questions. How, for example, are ideas 'expressed and explored' through 'social institutions'? How do 'political arrangements' or 'educational politics' enter into this? How, in short, are academic disciplines institutionalized?

We cannot answer these questions and so begin to explain the problems facing interdisciplinary researchers unless we develop an adequate understanding of disciplinary research. In Chapter 3 of this book, I present a theory of knowledge production that encompasses both the social and intellectual aspects of science alluded to above and that allows us to understand the conditions for producing both disciplinary and interdisciplinary research. There, I argue that the context of science has both social and intellectual depth, the implication of which is that conceptions of disciplinarity that reduce the context of knowledge production to what scientists 'do' are seriously misleading.

That two of the contributors to the OECD study on interdisciplinarity should deny the possibility of social and intellectual depth suggests that they are drawing on positivist philosophical ideas. The positivist influence is particularly evident in Heckhausen's statement that 'the subject matter of a discipline consists of circumscribed subsets of observables of a material field' (1972: 84) and Boisot's statement that the 'object' of a discipline is 'a definable personalized element which is recognizable experimentally (observable)' (1972: 90). Now, as I argue in Chapter 2, this epistemological assumption that observation (or more generally sensory experience) constitutes the limit to what we can know about the world presupposes a particular social theory of knowledge production, which is that scientists are simply passive recorders of sensory impressions of naturally occurring atomistic events and states of affairs, the constant conjunctions of which constitute immutable scientific facts. However, if we accept that reality has depth – and in the next chapter I explain why it is intelligible to think this – we can allow that the subject matter of an academic discipline will involve concepts referring to objects that may be either observable or unobservable. We can then arrive at a very different theory of knowledge production, according to which scientists draw upon a pre-existing context of rules and resources to transform a pre-existing set of ideas – all of which will usually be taken for granted by the scientists concerned and will not be immediately apparent to them. In short, what is known as the philosophy of critical realism presupposes that scientific inquiry is a type of human practice involving the active transformation of pre-existing, historically specific, fallible knowledge of the world.

## Conclusion

The preceding discussion of the nature, justification and conduct of integrative interdisciplinary research and the nature of disciplinary research, raises some important issues and questions. We saw in the first section of this chapter that many researchers advocate interdisciplinary research because they are interested in integrating knowledge from different disciplines. In the second section, we saw that they are interested in integration because they recognize, typically implicitly, that reality is complex and that the problems that reality throws up cannot be understood adequately on the basis of isolated disciplinary analyses. However, I argued that justifications for integrating knowledge that invoke the complexity of reality are inadequate to the extent that they fail to elaborate on the nature of complexity and thereby leave interdisciplinary researchers without a clear understanding of what they are integrating.

In light of the absence of a clear and coherent grounding for scientific integration and differentiation, it is not surprising that interdisciplinary researchers should be struggling to integrate knowledge from different disciplines – whether this be a collective or individual pursuit – as the evidence from studies of the conduct of interdisciplinary research indicates. However, I want to suggest that the existence of inadequate justifications for integrating knowledge from different disciplines only partly explains the difficulties interdisciplinary researchers have faced; we also need to take into account the inadequacy of typical conceptions of disciplinarity and the general lack of understanding of the nature of the social (and intellectual) context of knowledge production, which I revealed in the fourth section of this chapter.

What I am suggesting, in short, is that the problem of integrating knowledge through interdisciplinary research is both a problem of *knowledge* and a problem of knowledge *production*, and that to understand this problem we need to find answers to two key questions:

- What justifies the production of integrative interdisciplinary research?
- To what extent is it possible to produce integrative interdisciplinary research?

In this book, I address the first question by means of a philosophical inquiry into the nature of reality, which forms the basis of Chapter 2; and I address the second question by means of a social scientific inquiry into the conditions of knowledge production, which forms the basis of Chapters 3, 4 and 5. Note that the second question presupposes the first because, as I have already indicated, the production of integrative, interdisciplinary research presupposes an understanding of the reasons for scientific integration. It follows that, even if interdisciplinary researchers do have a coherent justification for scientific integration, they may be restricted in their opportunities to produce such research by the influence of the social system of knowledge production.

Given that philosophy enters into the arguments of Chapters 3, 4 and 5, as well as Chapter 2 of this book, perhaps I should say something about the nature of the philosophy on which I am drawing and how it relates to the social scientific argument of the book. The particular philosophy of science guiding my inquiry is critical realism, a body of thought that has emerged during the last 30 years in criticism, and in transcendent synthesis, of the two philosophies that have dominated scientists' thinking in the twentieth century: positivism and interpretivism (Archer *et al.*, 1998). I provide an explanation of the core concepts of critical realism in the first section of Chapter 2. It is, however, appropriate at this point to give a brief overview of the three key building blocks of critical realism: ontological realism, epistemological relativism and judgemental rationality. The methodological approach that I set out in the appendix, the theory of knowledge production that I develop in Chapter 3 and the empirical assessment that I carry out in Chapters 4 and 5 all presuppose these ideas. For example, I am assuming that there is such a thing as a social context of knowledge production that is 'real' – that is, which exists independently of whether it is investigated or not – and which is unobservable but can still be known through the effects it has on the decisions researchers make (ontological realism). Moreover, I am assuming that what I can know about this underlying context is socially and historically situated so that in no way does the theory of knowledge production that I present in Chapter 3 constitute final or absolute knowledge (epistemological relativism). Finally, I am assuming that my theory may be evaluated according to the criterion of relative explanatory power; that is, I am assuming that it can be compared with existing theories of knowledge production and that a rational judgement can be made about how well it explains the problem of integrating knowledge through interdisciplinary research (judgemental rationality).

How, though, does critical realism relate to my social scientific argument? Perhaps I may answer this question by contrasting my approach with that of Steinmetz and Chae, who use critical realism as the 'philosophical basis for (re)constructing Gouldner's proposed project of a reflexive "sociology of sociology"' (Steinmetz and Chae, 2002: 117). Steinmetz and Chae quite clearly want to bring together the philosophy of science, the sociology of science and the sociology of knowledge but they seem to be confused about the differences between philosophy on the one hand and social science on the other. They argue that a 'critical realist sociology of knowledge can be distinguished from two other major perspectives that arose sequentially in the theory of knowledge during the twentieth century: positivism and conventionalism' (ibid: 117). However, what they go on to define are not three different sociologies of knowledge but three different philosophies of science – positivism, critical realism, and conventionalism – so that it becomes unclear what they mean by a 'critical realist sociology of knowledge'. This could mean a sociology of knowledge that presupposes a critical realist philosophy. But, when they come to discuss their proposed combination of critical realism and the sociology of knowledge, it is clear that this is not what they mean:

> The critical realist sociology of knowledge is concerned with tracing the social determination of (scientific) ideas ('unmasking'). But it is also interested in the *philosophical* adequacy of a theory or explanation, that is, with its empirical support. Assessing a theory in philosophical and empirical terms involves Mannheim's refuting dimension. In short, as a philosophy of science, and as a research activity critical realism refutes; as a sociology of knowledge, it unmasks.
>
> (Steinmetz and Chae, 2002: 121)

However, the problem with this proposed combination of critical realism and the sociology of knowledge is that critical realism cannot do the work of social science; it cannot do the work of 'unmasking' the social determinants of scientific ideas because that is a task for sociologists of science. Critical realism is a philosophy first and foremost; it is not a science (although that is not to deny that scientific inquiry may presuppose critical realist assumptions). As a philosophy, it operates at a more general level of reality than does sociology; that is, it develops categories of thought and performs its 'refuting' role in relation to science by drawing on the results of scientific inquiry. It leaves the task of 'unmasking' the social determination of ideas to sociologists because sociology of knowledge operates at a less general level than philosophy and is concerned with identifying specific sociocultural processes thought to be determinants of scientific ideas. Therefore, if the 'unmasking' and 'refuting' roles carried out by sociology and philosophy respectively are distinct and cannot be conflated, the term 'critical realist sociology of knowledge' should be used to refer only to a form of social scientific inquiry underpinned by critical realist assumptions.

How, then, may philosophy and sociology of knowledge come together? If we think of a particular philosophy as a body of thought in its own right, we can introduce philosophical ideas into the content of a sociological argument as an intellectual cause of the production of knowledge.[18] In other words, what we are combining are the *results* of philosophical practice – that is, a particular philosophy – with the *practice* of sociology; more specifically, we are treating philosophical ideas as a specific element within a complex scientific argument. This way of relating philosophical ideas and scientific practice is made clear in Chapter 3, where I develop a (sociological) theory of knowledge production, and in Chapter 5, where I incorporate the argument of Chapter 4 (about the intellectual context of knowledge production) into a broader argument about the social context of knowledge production.

But, if the scientific part of my argument in this book incorporates philosophical ideas as causal objects in their own right, the philosophical side of my investigation works in a different way and thus remains distinct from the scientific part. For example, in Chapter 4, I use a particular philosophical technique called ontographology to draw out (the often contradictory) philosophical presuppositions of scientific theories and scientists' professed understandings of science and thereby reveal the nature of the intellectual causes of scientific activity. I use the same technique in the third section of Chapter 2, where I identify scientific and philosophical inconsistencies in the works of classical political economists. However, in the second section of Chapter 2 and, to a lesser extent in Chapter 3, I am more concerned with the development of critical realist ontology – that is, ontological elaboration – than I am with drawing out the philosophical presuppositions of scientific research.

Hence, what makes this book distinctive in its approach to the problem of integrating knowledge is that in integrating a sociological and philosophical argument it is itself an example of integrative, interdisciplinary research. The approach has to be interdisciplinary and integrative because, as I argue later on, the nature of the object of inquiry – the social system of knowledge production – demands it.

I must point out, though, two important limitations to the scope of my argument. Firstly, I consider interdisciplinary research only in academic settings. Thus, the three case studies of interdisciplinary research projects discussed in Chapters 4 and 5 all relate to UK universities. Now, given that academic employment units have held a monopoly over the production of knowledge, this focus on academia does not seem unreasonable. Yet, as Whitley points out, the academic monopoly of knowledge production is weakening as private and state research laboratories have proliferated and have provided alternative sources of employment for full-time research scientists (1984: 19). If, then, researchers working in non-academic research organizations are subject to different sorts of social and intellectual pressures from those working in an academic context, the feasibility of conducting interdisciplinary research projects in such organizations may also be different. Further research would be required, therefore, to reveal the structural differences between academic and non-academic research settings.

Secondly, although I examine the socio-intellectual conditions of knowledge production, I do not consider explicitly the psychological conditions.[19] This does not mean, though, that the psychology of interdisciplinary collaboration is unimportant; Robertson (1981), for example, has looked at the relationship between psychological attributes and success in interdisciplinary research. There are, in any case, good reasons to suppose that the psychology of individual researchers will have an important bearing on the relative success of their attempts to work in collaboration. When researchers have to engage in interdisciplinary collaboration and have to confront fundamentally different theoretical and philosophical perspectives, they may well experience cognitive strain or dissonance; that is, the experience of questioning largely taken-for-granted cognitive frameworks may be psychologically unsettling for certain researchers. In such circumstances, one may find open-minded persons trying to resolve cognitive differences and closed-minded persons becoming defensive in what they will see as an intellectually threatening situation. I say no more about the socio-psychological dynamics of teamwork simply because there is insufficient space to explore this issue in this book. But, clearly, acknowledging the possibility of interpersonal dynamics in collaborative research opens up further lines of investigation.

# 2 Critical realism and integrative interdisciplinary research

In this chapter, I argue that critical realist philosophy of science provides a coherent basis for justifying integrative, interdisciplinary research. What is distinctive about the critical realist school of philosophy is that it is rooted in questions of ontology – that is, with questions about the nature of reality. For most of the twentieth century, mainstream philosophy of science – in its positivist and interpretivist guises – had been concerned largely with questions of epistemology – that is, with questions about the nature and limits of knowledge. However, the accumulation of intellectual anomalies and antinomies arising from the development of orthodox positivist philosophy, principally those relating to the monistic account of scientific development and the deductivist theory of scientific structure, paved the way for a fundamental reorientation of the philosophy of science, from questions about how knowledge is possible to questions about what must be the case for particular forms of knowledge to be possible. The re-vindication of ontology has made possible the resolution through sublation of a range of dualisms and dichotomies emanating from the basic split between positivism and interpretivism.

The transcendent synthesis that became known as *critical realism* posits a range of assumptions, some of the most important of which are:[1] in the realm of ontology, *transcendental realism*, standing in contrast to the empirical realism and actualism presupposed by both positivism and interpretivism and allied to a qualified, *critical naturalism*, which overcomes the basic split between a naturalistic positivism and an anti-naturalistic interpretivism; in the realm of epistemology, *judgemental rationalism*, presupposing epistemic relativism and entailing epistemic fallibilism, in place of the judgemental relativism (or irrationalism) of the interpretivist tradition and tendencies towards fundamentalism, reductionism, monism and endism characteristic of positivism and interpretivism alike; and, in the realm of methodology, *methodological unity-in-diversity*, replacing the scientism, monism and naturalism associated with the positivist tradition, and the historicism, relativism and anti-naturalism associated with the interpretivist tradition.

My objective in the first section of this chapter is to explain the key concepts of critical realism and to show how they overcome the intellectual problems associated with the positivist and interpretivist traditions. I approach this task from the perspective of the debate about the possibility of mixing research methods in social science. Because this debate emerged out of a desire to overcome the dichotomy between the so-called quantitative and qualitative research paradigms, which, I argue, reflects the basic split between positivism and interpretivism, it thereby offers an opportunity to demonstrate how the concepts of critical realism can be used to resolve this dichotomy. Critical engagement with this debate also allows me to introduce the concept of theory–practice inconsistency, which I discuss further in Chapter 4 when I compare the philosophical presuppositions of scientists' research outputs with their professed understanding of the nature of science.

Having explained some of the key concepts of critical realism, I show in the second section how these concepts can be used to justify the practice of integrative, interdisciplinary research. I start by examining critically alternative philosophical justifications of interdisciplinarity and then show how the critical realist theory of integrative pluralism offers a more promising route to explaining scientific differentiation and integration in general. However, I argue that the theory of integrative pluralism must be revised if it is to take account of the particular differences between the differentiation and interconnection of the social and the natural sciences. I present one such revision in this section of the chapter.

In the third section of the chapter, I develop the argument of the second section by showing how social scientists' failure to sustain a coherent philosophical justification of integration and specialization undermines their ability to achieve social scientific integration and their ability to understand the potential for interdisciplinary integration in social science. I do this by identifying philosophical contradictions implicit in the scientific works of leading classical political economists and in their reflections on the scope and method of political economy. In the fourth and final section of the chapter, I offer some concluding comments.

## Introducing critical realism: the philosophy of social research

Most discussions of methodology in social science methods textbooks typically focus on the distinction between quantitative and qualitative approaches to social inquiry. Traditionally, these two approaches have been construed as a dichotomy but there has been considerable debate recently about the extent to which they are actually complementary. While some authors continue to argue that qualitative and quantitative research cannot be combined, except in a very limited sense (Guba and Lincoln, 1982; Smith and Heshusius, 1986; Buchanan, 1992; Sale *et al.*, 2002), others have argued for their accommodation (Rist, 1977; Reichardt and Cook, 1979; Howe, 1988; Firestone, 1990).[2]

Now, those authors who maintain that quantitative and qualitative research cannot be combined tend to see choice of research methods as deriving from particular epistemological positions, usually positivism and interpretivism (for which the terms 'quantitative' and 'qualitative' are often used as synonyms respectively). Thus, Smith and Heshusius distinguish between 'method as logic of justification' and 'method as technique' (1986: 8) and argue that, since the former informs the latter, quantitative and qualitative methods of inquiry can supplement but not complement each other because the two paradigms from which each research tradition derives presuppose incompatible theories of knowledge. Indeed, they are particularly critical of those authors, such as LeCompte and Goetz (1982) and Miles and Huberman (1984), who attempt to transpose positivist procedural rules and criteria (such as validity and reliability) into an interpretivist framework in the hope that qualitative inquiry can thereby achieve the same standards of 'rigour' as quantitative inquiry (Smith and Heshusius 1986: 1–10).

By contrast, those authors, such as Bryman (1988) and Brannen (1992), who argue that quantitative and qualitative research can be combined, do so from the basis of practical achievements in carrying out mixed methods research. Read and Marsh (2002) also share this view. They argue that the dichotomy between quantitative and qualitative methodologies is 'false' and invoke 'evidence from research practice' in support of their argument:

> in our view while the distinction between quantitative and qualitative methods is useful heuristically, we must not overemphasize the differences between them. In particular, the link between epistemology and methodology is important, but far from determinant. We cannot say that positivists never use qualitative data or that all non-positivists reject quantitative analysis. Indeed, evidence from research practice suggests that the traditional philosophical division between quantitative and qualitative methods is increasingly becoming viewed as a false dichotomy.
>
> (Read and Marsh, 2002: 235)

However, it is not entirely clear from Read and Marsh's argument just what is the relationship between epistemology and choice of research methods. Indeed, this lack of clarity is characteristic of the arguments of compatibility theorists, who often seem unsure of the link between the philosophy of social research and the practice of social research. Bryman, for example, having noted the tendency for participants in this debate to confuse epistemological with technical issues, writes:

> while the apparent debate between quantitative and qualitative methodology may have some meaning at the epistemological level... in the context of research practice there is no direct link between these precepts and particular techniques, since research typically comprises both elements... *Indeed, there may be a case for saying that techniques are neutral in respect of epistemological issues and debates.*
>
> (Bryman, 1984: 88; emphasis added)

Johnson and Onwuegbuzie go further. They explicitly invoke the philosophy of pragmatism to justify the mixing of research methods, which they claim constitutes a 'third research paradigm' (2004: 22). They write (somewhat ironically given their view that the mixing of methods is now paradigmatic):

> By utilizing quantitative and qualitative techniques within the same framework, mixed methods research can incorporate the strengths of both methodologies. *Most importantly, investigators who conduct mixed methods research are more likely to select methods and approaches with respect to their underlying research questions, rather than with regard to some preconceived biases about which research paradigm should have hegemony in social science research.*
>
> (Johnson and Onwuegbuzie, 2004: 23–4; emphasis added)

However, as I argue throughout this book, the idea that we can choose research questions and research methods in the absence of epistemological 'precepts' – as Bryman puts it – or 'preconceived biases' about research paradigms – as Johnson and Onwuegbuzie have it – is fundamentally misleading. It is characteristic of methodologists operating from a pragmatist position to argue that researchers should ignore epistemological issues and simply match methods to research questions as appropriate. But, pragmatists forget that researchers can only make this decision with the help of a set of pre-existing intellectual resources, which define the nature of objects of inquiry and how they can be known and which researchers draw on (usually implicitly) when deciding what sorts of question to ask and how best to answer them. To this extent, Read and Marsh are right to argue that 'one's ontological and epistemological position affects all aspects of the research process' (2002: 241). For example, how one generates and interprets data will differ according to one's philosophical standpoint. Therefore, we must avoid the temptation of reducing philosophical theory to research practice, which is the implication of the pragmatist line of reasoning.

However, this does not mean – as incompatibility theorists tend to suggest – that our philosophical position *determines* what choices we make about research design. On one level, it is obvious that, even if we claim to be, say, an interpretivist, we will still have choices over what sorts of social objects to investigate and how – although our choices will fall within the range defined by the paradigm we are claiming to follow. However, on another level it is not obvious that our research practices always reflect the philosophical position we claim to hold. For example, we may claim to be following positivist philosophy in identifying an empirical regularity as a causal law but our research practices may in fact presuppose an alternative theory of causation of which we may be completely unaware. Such inconsistencies will usually become apparent in the form of practical anomalies. For example, we may think that, having identified an empirical regularity, we can use this law to predict how people will act in certain conditions and design policy on this basis. But, we may find in practice that people do not act as predicted, as a result of which we may decide to revise the understanding of science that informed our practice. Certainly, it would be incoherent for a researcher to claim to be following the tenets of both positivism and interpretivism at a purely theoretical level. But, even if the researcher followed Read and Marsh's injunction and used a combination of qualitative and quantitative methods in a way that the researcher believed was consistent either with a positivist or interpretivist paradigm (2002: 241), the researcher's practices might still be inconsistent with the researcher's understanding of science if that understanding derived from a philosophy that was already incoherent. In short, if our research practices imply a particular theory of science, so that we do not have direct knowledge of this theory, it cannot be the case that the theory of science we profess, and thus do know about, determines what we do. Another way of putting this is to say that it is in virtue of the partiality and fallibility of our understanding of science that we often make mistakes or that our research practices do not give us the results we anticipated. Therefore, we must avoid the temptation of reducing research practice to philosophical theory, which is the implication of the methodological purists' line of reasoning.

Now, what seems to have happened recently – and what has sparked the debate between the incompatibility and compatibility theorists – is that researchers, in reflecting more consciously on the process of research, have become much more aware of the inconsistencies between the theory and practice of social research. Recent debates about interpretation, theory generation and generalization in qualitative research have revealed the tacit acceptance of positivist philosophy (Bryman, 1988: 72–92), with the result that researchers are gradually changing their understanding of quantitative and qualitative research – at least to the extent that researchers are now acknowledging the theoretical commonalities between the two approaches. For example, interpretivist concerns about remaining faithful to the research subject's point of view and about what to do when interpretations of the same setting clash can only be understood in the context of a tacit commitment to positivism and to a correspondence theory of truth. From an interpretivist perspective, according to which social reality is constructed in the subject's thought and discourse, these are not problems at all because a difference of interpretation would not imply that one account was somehow more valid than another, just that different accounts reflected different (that is, incommensurable) realities. Similarly, interpretivist ambivalence towards the generation of theory can only be understood in the context of a tacit commitment to positivism and the associated notions of hypothesis testing and falsification. Thus, on the one hand, interpretivists claim that the practice of theorizing amounts to the 'thick description' of a particular culture (Geertz, 1993); yet, on the other hand, because contemporary positivists would regard such descriptions as 'atheoretical investigations' (Bryman, 1988: 86), reminiscent of the sort of blind empiricism that Popper (1959, 1963) criticized, interpretivists have sought to incorporate a notion of hypothesis testing into the logic of social inquiry, either at the beginning of the research process, as in analytic induction,[3] or right at the end, as in grounded theory.[4] Finally, although interpretivists claim that they can construct only local and particular understandings of the social world, the fact that they are now prepared to examine more than one case (Bryman, 1988: 87–9) and to consider analytical generalization (ibid: 90–1) suggests that they are equally concerned to develop universal and general knowledge – the characteristic concern of positivism.

Willis has called the tacit acceptance of positivist assumptions – in particular, an empiricist epistemology and inductivist logic of explanation – in qualitative research ‘covert positivism’ (1980: 89–90). That Willis should reach such a conclusion is unsurprising to critical realist philosophers, who argue that interpretivists ground the distinction between natural and social objects in the context of a tacit acceptance of the empirical realism and actualism of positivism. Hence, although interpretivists explicitly acknowledge that social objects are intrinsically meaningful, the tacit implication of their philosophical position is that understanding of these objects can only be reached through sensory experience and the constant conjunction form. In short, despite presenting itself as in radical opposition to positivism, interpretivism takes for granted a position of empirical realism and actualism and uses it as a platform on which to build a *conceptual* realism and actualism; or, as Bhaskar puts it, ‘upon analysis, anti-naturalist theories of social science may often be seen to consist entirely in, or at least depend essentially on, the inversion or displacement, transformation and/or condensation of characteristically positivist themes’ (1998: 19).[5] The opposition between positivism and interpretivism, then, is a pretence because both positions are complicit in accepting the same, mistaken ontology; as such, they constitute what critical realists call a *dialectical antagonism* or *pair*.

However, what is also interesting about the methodological reflections of qualitative researchers is that, although some accounts do indeed reveal a tacit commitment to positivism, others at the same time acknowledge tacitly the limitations of the positivist account of social research. For example, Ball realizes that his participant observation of a secondary school betrays a ‘selective’ focus:

> Access to a world of fleeting, overlapping, contradictory, murky, incoherent realities demands selective attention from the fieldworker. For everything that is noticed a multitude of other things go unseen, for everything that is written down a multitude of other things are forgotten. Great parts of the real world experienced by the participant observer, probably the greater part, is *selected out.*
>
> (Ball, 1984: 78, original emphasis; cited in Bryman, 1988: 73)

Now, if indeed the researcher is making such selections, the possibility of doing this presupposes a prior set of theoretical assumptions and value commitments. In other words, if observation is theory- and value-laden – not as interpretivists would have it, theory- and value-determined (which is implicit in Ball’s notion of ‘incoherent realities’) – the positivist injunction that theory and observation, and facts and values, are separate collapses. Moreover, as Bulmer (1979) has realized, if observation is theory dependent, the idea that the researcher can suspend theoretical reflection until the later stages of fieldwork must also be questioned. Woods (1985), in fact, argues that theory is not simply ‘revealed’ by the data but that theory construction involves the inference of a deeper level of meaning from the data through powers of creative insight and Hammersley *et al.* point to the role of ‘comparative analysis’ and the ‘selection of critical cases’ as of crucial importance in the development and testing of theory (1985: 56–8).

The preceding discussion of the philosophical reflections of qualitative researchers indicates that the way in which practitioners understand the nature of social science contradicts positivist and interpretivist conceptions of social science. Critical realist philosophers of science call this sort of contradiction a *theory–practice inconsistency* and it is also evident in mixed-methods researchers' anxieties about the possibility of inconsistent scientific results emerging. For example, Devine and Heath argue that social scientists have been left to make sense of inconsistencies between the results of 'quantitative' and 'qualitative' research on their own:

> Proper attention has yet to be devoted to making sense of some of the contradictory findings that frequently emerge from different methods and techniques. It is easy enough to select snippets from qualitative interviews to 'flesh out' the data from quantitative research. A more important issue arises, however, when qualitative material does not confirm or even challenges quantitative findings (and vice versa). Should one or other data source be conveniently discarded? How does a researcher try to reconcile contradictory findings? What criteria should be applied? Some of these issues are yet to be fully addressed in the welcome although not totally unproblematic shift towards methodological eclecticism.
>
> (Devine and Heath, 1999: 14)

Without an understanding of how to deal with contradictory findings, researchers may be tempted to treat one set of findings as being somehow more 'valid' than another, as Bryman points out in his comments on Newby's (1977) study of Suffolk farm workers. However, one cannot simply ignore an empirical anomaly, because that would be to invalidate the whole point of attempting to combine quantitative and qualitative methods.

Mixed-methods researchers clearly require philosophical assistance if they are to make sense of contradictory findings. Bryman observes that there are 'few rules of thumb for dealing with research strategies which combine the two research traditions' (1988: 155). However, in the last 30 years or so, a new intellectual paradigm has emerged, one that can help mixed methods researchers to reconcile contradictory findings. This paradigm, which is known as *critical realism*, overcomes the traditional dichotomy between positivism and interpretivism, and the associated dichotomy between quantitative and qualitative research, not by combining or juxtaposing these traditions but by incorporating the valid insights of each into a novel synthesis – in other words, by giving them a new meaning within the context of a single philosophical framework. Moreover, unlike pragmatism, critical realism overcomes such dichotomies through explicit ontological reflection so that it is able to provide a coherent explanation for the practically successful attempts to combine different research methods that Bryman has documented (1988: ch. 6).

Where the positivist and interpretivist traditions have gone wrong, critical realists argue, is in their continuing commitment to an *empiricist* epistemology and an *actualist* ontology. Thus, both traditions assume that sensory experience is the limit to what can be known about the world; and both assume that what can be known are particular events and states of affairs, the constant conjunctions of which constitute causal laws. Of course, as mentioned earlier, the interpretivist tradition parts company with the positivist tradition over the issue of naturalism. Positing a radical difference between the natural and social worlds, interpretivism reflects the empirical realism and actualism of positivism in its own *conceptual* realism and actualism, according to which the aim of social inquiry is not to explain events causally (since reasons supposedly cannot be causes) but to understand the meaning of social actions and thence to identify regularities of meaning. Hence, the interpretivist tradition is fundamentally *anti*-naturalist.

Now, it is the influence of empiricism, both overt in positivism and covert in interpretivism, I suspect, that explains the expectation among researchers that findings obtained through different research methods ought to be consistent. Indeed, the expectation that findings derived from the use of different research methods will be mutually confirmatory and will thereby enhance the validity of an investigation is enshrined in the notion of 'triangulation', as popularized by Denzin (1970: 308–10). Let us suppose, then, that a researcher expects the empirical patterns detected in a survey of a given population to match the conceptual patterns detected in an ethnographic study of a selection of members of the surveyed population but finds that the results of the survey and the ethnographic study are actually inconsistent. How could philosophers help the researcher to make sense of this state of affairs? As I argued above, neither interpretivists nor positivists could help the researcher. On the one hand, interpretivists would treat the survey results as invalid on the grounds that the objective search for causal laws in the social realm is impossible and that what patterns are detected are simply the effect of the researcher imposing a meaningless conceptual scheme on the population. On the other hand, positivists would treat the ethnographic interpretation as invalid on the grounds that its subjectivity and uniqueness render it unreliable as a form of knowledge. Yet, researchers have found that respondents both understand the questions asked of them – so that the interpretivist assumption that the meanings people develop are completely different is found to be misleading – and misunderstand the questions asked of them – so that the positivist assumption that the meanings people develop are entirely the same is also found to be misleading.

Why, then, do researchers find that the regularity they identify through survey research (and which they may implicitly assume is universal) is 'broken' when they carry out participant observation of a particular setting involving members of the surveyed population? Critical realists[6] have argued, from the possibility of successful scientific experimentation and from the possibility of social practices more generally, that to explain such a finding we must recognize the necessity of ontological depth; that is, we must recognize, *contra* empiricism, that the perceptual criterion for the ascription of reality is distinct from but can nevertheless establish the causal criterion for the ascription of reality. Thus, critical realists argue that reality can be understood as three overlapping domains, which reflect the vertical dimension, or *stratification*, of reality. The domain of the 'real' embraces the structures and mechanisms that generate actual events and states of affairs, which we may experience in different ways and which we may not experience at all. The domain of the 'actual', which embraces the events and states of affairs we may or may not experience, is therefore a subset of the 'real', and the domain of the 'empirical', which embraces what we do experience is therefore a subset of the 'actual'. But, in addition to the vertical dimension of reality, there is also an equally important horizontal dimension. The nature of some structures and mechanisms (for example, gravity) may be such that they can be isolated from their structural context by means of scientific experimentation. Activating the mechanism in a closed system will generate a regular pattern of events that will be the empirical ground for the identification of the mechanism as a real object. However, in the absence of human intervention in the causal order of nature, events and states of affairs will be generated by a multiplicity of different mechanisms (physical, chemical, biological, social, and so forth) in what is known as an 'open system',[7] so that the effect of the operation of one mechanism may not be manifest as an empirical regularity if, say, its operation is counteracted by the effects of the operation of another mechanism. The possibility of differentiating between open and closed systems, therefore, presupposes the second feature of ontological depth – the *transfactuality* of generative objects – that is, their existence independent of any particular sequence or pattern of events detected empirically. It follows that causal laws refer not to patterns of events detected at the level of the empirical but to the operation of structures and mechanisms at the level of the real and that these must be analyzed, not as regularities but as tendencies.

In short, we can make sense of the human intervention in nature required to produce a constant conjunction of events and state of affairs only if we assume that there is both vertical and horizontal ontological depth. Because the constant conjunction we produce is the empirical ground for the existence of a structure we have not produced, if we take constant conjunctions as given, as positivists do, we inevitably commit ourselves to the absurdity that, in scientific experiments, we are producing, rather than discovering, the laws of nature and, furthermore, we become unable to explain how we manage to apply our knowledge of nature in technological achievements.

Similarly, if we are to make sense of the possibility of social practices, we must assume that society also has both vertical and horizontal depth. As I argue in Chapter 3, social structures and casual mechanisms are the pre-existing and necessary conditions for the exercise of human agency but they exist only by virtue of human agency (which both reproduces and transforms them). Indeed, scientific inquiry (of which laboratory experimentation is but one aspect) is no different from any other social practice in this respect, for the production of knowledge would simply be impossible in the absence of a pre-existing social context. However, the interpretivist tradition, in assuming that social reality is entirely a construction of thought and discourse, once again denies the possibility of ontological depth and becomes embroiled in judgemental relativism. In other words, the interpretivist tradition denies the existence of a realm of social objects, which have causal powers and liabilities *sui generis* – that is, which are *real* – and of which we can have fallible knowledge *through* thought and discourse. The interpretivist tradition, then, in presupposing an ontology of empirical (and conceptual) realism, is unable to make sense of scientific – indeed, more generally, social – conflict, just as the positivist tradition is unable to do.

Now, the possibility of scientific conflict, which presupposes the possibility of intellectual error, points to the third feature of ontological depth: *intransitivity*. Critical realists argue that we need to distinguish clearly between the intransitive domain of science (which encompasses the objects of inquiry) and the transitive domain (which encompasses our knowledge of those objects); for, only if we see thought as contained within, yet emergent and so distinct from, being can we make sense of the possibility of changing knowledge of an unchanging reality, and *vice versa*, and so of reconciling epistemic relativism and fallibilism with judgemental rationalism (that is, rationally comparing rival theories). But, in collapsing the distinction between thought and being, positivism and interpretivism entail a series of related philosophical mistakes: the *empirical fallacy*, or the reduction of events and states of affairs to our experiences of them, which contains within it the *actualist fallacy* or the reduction of causal laws to constant conjunctions of events and states of affairs and which implies that statements about being can be reduced to statements about our knowledge of being – that is, the *epistemic fallacy*. The epistemic and actualist fallacies, in turn, presuppose and are presupposed by the *ontic fallacy* or the reduction of knowledge to natural things (manifest in the fetishism of constant conjunctions of events and states of affairs), which implies that our knowledge of being can be reduced to being alone. But, if what exists is equivalent to what we can know, not only must knowledge determine being but being must also determine knowledge. Hence, we can speak of the *epistemic–ontic fallacy*, which in the social domain also entails the *linguistic fallacy* or the reduction of being to our discourse about being and which is underpinned by a more fundamental error, the *anthropic fallacy* or the reduction of being to *human* being.

In turn, these errors support and are supported by a range of additional, more specific, errors. Thus, in assuming that scientific inquiry is limited to the passive recording of naturally occurring atomistic events and states of affairs, we are effectively assuming that knowledge is accumulated gradually; that is, that science is monistic in its development, that it has certain foundations (in sensory experience) and that it is absolute (since there is nothing more to do than record a scientific fact accurately). In other words, in treating facts as things, we reify, naturalize and eternalize science and turn it into an asocial (and atheoretical) process.

So far, we have seen that, if science is to be possible, there must be three different kinds of depth to reality: stratification, transfactuality and intransitivity. We have also seen that these ontological assumptions entail a set of epistemological assumptions: relativism, fallibilism and judgemental rationality. What, then, of the methodological position of critical realism? Now, positivism stands squarely in the tradition of naturalism: that is, it accepts that the method of inquiry across all the sciences is essentially the same,[8] whether it be through experimental control of variables, as in the physical sciences, or through statistical control of variables, as in the social sciences. In other words, there is literally only one way to do science, which amounts to the accurate recording of empirical regularities. Interpretivism, by contrast, sits firmly in the tradition of anti-naturalism; that is, it proposes that, in virtue of the radical differences between natural and social objects, the methods of inquiry used in the physical sciences (which positivists take to be examples of the scientific method) are inappropriate to the investigation of social objects, which cannot be controlled in the way that natural objects can because the former, unlike the latter, are intrinsically meaningful. Furthermore, given that the meanings possessed by social objects are inherently contextually variable, interpretivists argue that it is not possible to find universal laws of human behaviour and therefore propose that researchers immerse themselves in a particular culture so as to understand a particular lifeworld.[9]

Now, critical realism transcends the dichotomy between naturalism and anti-naturalism. It proposes that a *qualified* or *critical* naturalism, consistent with the assumptions of transcendental realism, is possible. This proposal stems from the assumption that there are important ontological differences between natural and social objects, which turn on the concept- and activity-dependence, and greater space–time specificity, of social objects and which impose certain limits on a naturalistic science of the social. For example, unlike natural objects, social objects cannot be identified by means of human intervention in the world but have to be isolated (that is, abstracted) entirely in thought (the epistemological limit);[10] unlike natural objects, social objects may be subject to explanatory critique – that is, the existence of false beliefs may be explained (the critical limit) and, unlike natural objects and natural scientific inquiry, social objects and social scientific inquiry may be causally interdependent (the relational limit). Hence, *contra* interpretivism, people's conceptions of reality may be both causal – in the sense that beliefs (as well as interests) motivate or constitute the reasons for action – and fallible, so that actions may have unintended consequences. The notion of concept- and activity-dependent social objects is therefore entirely consistent with the non-identity of being and thought assumed in transcendental realism. If, as in the conceptual actualism of the interpretivist tradition, social objects are assumed to be concept- and activity-*determined*, being and thought become an identity, an assumption that carries with it the implication that all conceptualizations are infallible and that the material world is either a by-product of, or radically divorced from, what is constructed in thought and discourse.

Now, the methodological implication of these ontological and epistemological assumptions is that, *contra* Kuhn and Feyerabend, there *is* something essential about the method of scientific inquiry, which is that it is characterized by a backwards movement from the discovery of objects lying at one stratum of reality to the discovery of objects lying at another, deeper, one. Thus, once phenomena at one level of reality have been identified and shown to explain something at a higher level, they in turn become something to be explained by phenomena lying at a lower level. The essence of the logic of scientific inquiry, therefore, is neither deductive (as assumed by the positivist tradition) nor inductive (as assumed by the interpretivist tradition); rather, it is retroductive, which is consistent with the emergent and therefore stratified nature of reality.

But, if there is a sense in which there is a unity of method across the sciences, there is also a sense in which there is a diversity of method. Critical realists argue that this diversity stems from ontological differences between objects of inquiry lying at different strata of reality. For example, while certain natural objects can be subject to experimental control, social and psychological objects cannot be (in virtue of their concept and activity dependence). But, even if social systems cannot be closed, their preinterpreted character – that is, the fact that they are conceptualized and linguistified – provides the starting point for social scientific inquiry. Hence, the subject matter of the social scientist must be understood – that is, adequately described by means of a range of methods involving formal observation of actions and elicitation of lay meanings through interviews – before being subject to possible critique as part of a causal explanation and thus redescribed *scientifically*. In short, the methodological position of critical realism, which is consistent with the epistemological and ontological positions previously elaborated, may be summed up by the phrase '*unity-in-diversity*'.[11]

We are now in a position to understand why mixed methods researchers often find that what they thought was an empirical regularity does not hold in a particular case study. If social systems are intrinsically open, social researchers should not expect to find regular successions of events and states of affairs that hold across time and space. Even though the researcher may find a statistically significant relationship between two or more variables, this relationship will not be universal because the actual events that are observed in the empirical domain of reality are the product of a complex conjunction of causal mechanisms. It is contingent whether or not an existing causal mechanism is first exercised and second actualized, in virtue of the possibility of causal mechanisms counteracting each other. But, if it is possible for the effects of causal mechanisms to cancel each other out – that is, to contradict each other – it is also possible for them to reinforce each other. Now, if such causal reinforcement proves relatively enduring, the effects of this must be described as a (robust) *tendency*, which may then be detected at the empirical level as a statistically significant relationship between variables. But, it is precisely because the causal process in question is a tendency that the observed relationship will be a partial, rather than universal, regularity. As Lawson explains:

> A demi-regularity, or *demi-reg* for short, is precisely a partial event regularity which *prima facie* indicates the occasional, but less than universal, actualization of a mechanism or tendency, over a definite region of time–space. The patterning observed will not be strict if countervailing factors sometimes dominate or frequently co-determine the outcomes in a variable manner. But where demi-regs are observed there is evidence of relatively enduring and identifiable tendencies in play.
>
> (Lawson, 1997: 204)

We can also now understand why the use of different methods of inquiry – whether or not they are called quantitative or qualitative – may generate seemingly contradictory results. When researchers carry out social surveys, what they are measuring are the *effects* of the operation of underlying causal mechanisms. Danermark *et al.* call this an 'extensive' empirical procedure (2002: 165) because the aim of such an investigation is to find out what are the distinguishing characteristics of a population and the data generated from the sample – on people's opinions, attitudes, intentions, demographics and so forth – is analyzed statistically with this aim in mind. However, when researchers carry out participant observation of individual members of that population, they may not necessarily observe the pattern of characteristics representative of the wider population because, in a case study, they will be confronting the *particular* outcome of a complex and contingent causal context and it is the elucidation of this context – the identification of a set of social structures – that is the primary aim of what Danermark *et al.* call an 'intensive' empirical procedure (2002: 165). But, even if the empirical findings from one particular case are not generalizable across other cases, the causal powers and liabilities of the social structures identified are generalizable across contexts (within a certain range) because they are *necessary* properties of the objects concerned; it is the particular combination of causal powers that is a contingent matter. In short, if 'extensive' empirical procedures allow us to generate empirical generalizations of different sorts, 'intensive' empirical procedures allow us to generate theoretical generalizations of different sorts.

From the perspective of critical realism, then, the positivist claim that empirical regularities can be detected in the social world has a certain degree of merit by virtue of the possibility of social processes establishing a high degree of similarity of meaning. However, the fact that such processes may also lead to differences of meaning implies that empirical regularities cannot be universal. Similarly, the interpretivist claim that social phenomena are context dependent has a certain degree of merit, to the extent that the complexity and contingency of social causation gives rise to variability of meaning. However, if the complexity and contingency of social causation means that some causal mechanisms, when activated, are more powerful in their effects than others, it will still be possible to detect partial generalities of meaning and action. Therefore, the inconsistencies that mixed-methods researchers claim to find are in fact merely observed differences in the outcomes of unobservable, complex and contingent processes of social causation; it is the task of social scientists to show how such differences are consistent with the same theoretical account of reality.

A further implication of my argument is that positivist-inspired hypothesis testing and falsification is likely to be highly problematic when it comes to theory assessment. According to the logic of the hypothetico-deductive method of inquiry, we should select appropriate indicators for the concepts related in our hypothesis. If we find insufficient empirical support for our hypothesis (assuming that we have chosen reliable indicators, that our sample is representative and so forth) either we reject or modify our hypothesis. Yet, this logic of inquiry presupposes that social systems can be completely closed: that, in measuring a range of dependent and independent variables, we are achieving something analogous to what the natural scientist achieves in the laboratory. But, if social systems cannot be completely closed and we continue to follow this logic, we may find ourselves rejecting a hypothesis on the grounds that there is insufficient evidence to support it, when it may be that the causal mechanisms to which the concepts in our hypothesis refer have failed to become actualized. In other words, just because the operation of causal mechanisms cannot be detected in the expected way – as a constant conjunction of events and states of affairs – does not mean that the casual mechanism in question does not exist. What is happening is that the operation of that causal mechanism is out of phase with the events and states of affairs observed. Following the logic of the hypothetico-deductive method, therefore, may lead us into making erroneous conclusions about the nature of reality. We can avoid making such mistakes if we remember that reality has both vertical and horizontal depth.

## Integrative pluralism

In the previous section we have seen that the concepts of vertical and horizontal depth lie at the core of transcendental realist philosophy. In this section, I want to explain how we can use these primary concepts and the secondary concepts deriving from them (that is, intransitivity, stratification and transfactuality), to justify scientific integration. In fact, we can use these concepts to justify scientific differentiation as well because, as I argue below, scientific integration and differentiation constitute a *duality*, exemplifying both dialectical distinction and dialectical connection.[12]

Let me start by considering two recently developed approaches to the understanding of interdisciplinary studies: one that draws implicitly, although incompletely, on transcendental realist philosophy, the other sympathetic to postmodernist concerns in its critique of disciplinary conventions. I maintain that both approaches are inadequate in their justification of scientific integration and differentiation. Let me explain the (implicitly) transcendental realist approach first and the postmodernist response to it second.

We saw in Chapter 1 that justifications for integrative, interdisciplinary research typically refer to the idea that society is a complex whole; that is, that its many parts are interdependent. We also saw that certain commentators took that understanding a stage further in claiming that society is an emergent whole – that is, that it possesses systemic properties irreducible to the properties of the parts of which it is composed and where the parts encompass both social and natural objects of inquiry. Hence, it was generally felt that integrative, interdisciplinary research was needed to understand the relationships between the parts of society but in a way that respected the emergent properties of society. However, I argued that such justifications for integrative interdisciplinarity were inadequate to the extent that they failed to examine in sufficient depth the exact nature of the different parts of reality and the exact nature of their interrelationships. I argued, in short, that existing justifications of integrative interdisciplinarity invoking the concept of complexity did not go far enough ontologically.

Newell has put forward a theory that goes some way towards deepening the ontological justification for interdisciplinarity. As many previous commentators have done, Newell argues that it is the complexity of reality that justifies interdisciplinarity:

> It is the contention of this paper that complex systems and phenomena are a necessary condition for interdisciplinary studies. An interdisciplinary approach is justified only by a complex system. So if a behavior is not produced by a system or the system is not complex, interdisciplinary study is not required.
>
> (Newell, 2001: 1)

However, in contrast to previous commentators, Newell works with a richer notion of complexity, a notion that draws explicitly on the insights of complexity theory, particularly the concept of nonlinearity:

> I believe the approach to complexity most fruitfully applied to interdisciplinary studies comes out of the study of complex systems, though my thinking is shaped by the entire set of theories. Specifically, the theory of interdisciplinary studies I am advocating focuses on the form of complexity that is a feature of the structure as well as the behavior of a complex system, or complexity generated by nonlinear relationships among a larger number of components, and on the influence of the components and relationships of the system on its overall pattern of behavior.
>
> (Newell, 2001: 7)

Moreover, in contrast to previous commentators, Newell's argument points towards the concepts of vertical and horizontal ontological depth in recognizing the possibility of synchronic emergent properties and positive and negative feedback effects:

> All systems (complex or otherwise) are made up of components that interact, either directly through mutual causation or indirectly through feedback loops, causing an overall pattern of behavior. Those feedback loops can be positive (enhancing the behavior) or negative (dampening or reducing the behavior). Because of those interaction effects, the system as a whole is more than the sum of its parts; indeed, it is different from the sum of its parts. In particular, the organization of components and their interaction produces a distinctive self-organizing, overall pattern or set of patterns of behavior that gives the system its identity. Each sub-system and... even each plane of a multi-dimensional system can have its own emergent properties as well.
>
> (Newell, 2001: 7)

Newell's understanding of complexity, then, at least in so far as it deals with the concepts of emergence and multiple causation, is clearly consistent with the philosophical ontology of transcendental realism that I discussed in the previous section. The possibility that a distinctive set of properties may emerge from a particular 'organization of components and their interaction' and the possibility that 'feedback loops can be positive...or negative' have clear parallels with the transcendental realist concepts of stratification (through emergence) and transfactuality (through differentiation), both of which allow for the reinforcement ('positive feedback') as well as the counteraction ('negative feedback') of the effect of causal mechanisms.

However, although there are clear similarities between Newell's ontological position and that of transcendental realism, there are also important differences. Indeed, it is because Newell's ontological position is less explicitly defined that he is unable to give a clear account of the precise ontological makeup of the complex systems to which he refers. In particular, Newell seems unsure about what is the exact nature of the 'components' that comprise the system. For example, early on in his article Newell identifies these components with 'variables':

> In the natural and social sciences, it is widely accepted that each discipline focuses on a set of interrelated variables observable from its perspective. Those variables can easily be seen as components of a system.
>
> (Newell, 2001: 2–3)

Later on, he gives us some examples of what the components of a system may be:

> A complex system is composed of components actively connected through predominantly nonlinear relationships. The components can be molecules, cells, organs, phenotypes, species, individual human beings, institutions, groups, nations, artistic movements, cultures – in short, the stuff of the system.
>
> (Newell, 2001: 9)

Now if, as Newell claims, the components of a system are 'observable' variables, it is difficult to see how he can sustain a theory of emergent properties because the possibility of emergence presupposes a clear distinction between, on the one hand, generative mechanisms and hence the causal powers and liabilities of the entities that such mechanisms presuppose, which are unobservable, and, on the other hand, the effects of those mechanisms when triggered, which are observable. For example, we can think of an institution as a set of (relatively enduring) properties (that is, causal powers and liabilities) emergent from a particular set of relations between positions occupied by people. It is emergent precisely in the sense that the properties inherent react on – that is, modify the properties of – the people who are its components. The observed actions of such people, then, are the outcomes of the exercise of the causal mechanisms pertaining to the institution. Furthermore, the interaction of these mechanisms is complex because the realization of the causal powers and liabilities of the institution may be affected by the exercise of additional causal mechanisms contingently related to it, so that observed behaviour will not be strictly regular or 'linear'. To say that the components of an institution are purely observable variables, therefore, would be to reduce the emergent properties of a particular structure to the emergent properties of people, so that an institution would become nothing more than the regular behaviour of people who possess the same set of preferences – the starting point of methodological individualism. In short, to claim, as Newell does, that scientific inquiry focuses only on things that are observable is to commit the epistemic fallacy.

Now, an important consequence of Newell's tendency to commit the epistemic fallacy is ambiguity concerning the meaning of the terms 'linear' and 'nonlinear'. On the one hand, he uses these terms to describe the nature of the relationships between the components of a complex system, where the properties of the components are distinguished from the emergent properties of the system. For example, he writes: 'A complex system links together combinations of components, simple systems, and even complicated systems using predominantly nonlinear connections' (Newell, 2001: 8). On the other hand, he uses the terms 'linear' and 'nonlinear' to describe the nature of the relationships between empirical variables:

> If there is any coherence to each discipline... the variables on which it focuses ought to be more closely and linearly related to each other than to the variables studied by other disciplines. If... interdisciplinary study draws on more than one discipline's perspective to synthesize a more comprehensive understanding, it must then of necessity encompass more nonlinear relationships (i.e. with squared terms or even higher powers) among the larger set of variables linked together.
>
> (Newell, 2001: 2–3)

Now, the implication of transcendental realism is that the terms 'linear' and 'nonlinear' ought to be used to describe differences in the empirical *outcomes* of the operation of underlying causal mechanisms, so that the second of the two meanings that Newell gives to these terms is to be preferred to the first. However, if this second meaning is to be preferred, the 'variables' to which Newell refers must be clearly distinguished from the underlying 'components' of the system. Having made this distinction, we can then use the transcendental realist distinction between closed and open systems to distinguish clearly between the meaning of a 'linear' and 'nonlinear' empirical outcome. Thus, if we have generated a closed system to identify and describe the working of a particular structure, the empirical variables we use as indicators of the existence of such a structure will be linearly related, because the structure will be working in isolation. However, in an open system, the operation of that structure will be subject to the influence of the operation of additional structures, so that the same set of empirical variables will be nonlinearly related. For example, in physical chemistry, the gas laws are defined by linear relationships between volume, pressure and thermodynamic temperature – three variables that are indicators of the operation of kinetic energy, the causal mechanism that explains such properties of gases as heat capacity and conduction. However, whether or not these laws hold depends on the influence of intermolecular forces, so that, under certain conditions, the behaviour of gases cannot be described in a linear way.

Newell's theory of interdisciplinarity, then, in drawing on the insights of complexity theory and in pointing to the importance of emergent properties and multiple causation, marks an important step forward towards a clearer ontological justification for scientific integration. However, his conceptions of emergence and of conjunctural causation are underdeveloped from the perspective of transcendental realism, so that his conception of nonlinearity, which is fundamental to his theory, is rather confusing. It appears that vestiges of empiricism in Newell's thinking are blocking a full understanding of vertical and horizontal ontological depth, because a complete understanding of these two concepts would allow him to distinguish clearly between empirical variables and non-empirical system components. But, without such an understanding, Newell's theory remains vulnerable to criticism from those invoking the terminology of complexity theory. Thus, Mackey criticizes Newell's theory on the grounds that it 'inappropriately borrows the concept nonlinear from chaos theory and fractal geometry, which it then uses as a mysterious *deus ex machina* to explain emergent self-organizing structures or behavior' (Mackey, 2001: 65); and Bailis criticizes it for lacking, firstly, 'a rigorously explicated formalism (e.g., graphic, formulaic, or axiomatic) that shows the structure and dynamics of a complex system to which interdisciplinarians ought to liken the phenomena that interest them' and, secondly, 'some thoroughly described exemplars that concretely show the pair of benefits he claims for modelling different phenomena in complex system terms – that *both* the phenomena *and* the process of interdisciplinary scholarship will be better understood' (Bailis, 2001: 30–1). Later in this section, I argue that the categorical grammar of transcendental realism can provide the sort of rigorous explication of complexity and interdisciplinarity that Bailis demands and that there are concrete examples of social scientific research that presuppose such an understanding of complexity and interdisciplinarity. In particular, I show how the concepts of stratification, entailing vertical ontological depth and transfactuality, entailing horizontal ontological depth, provide a coherent ontological grounding for scientific integration and differentiation.

But, before I embark on the task of enriching Newell's theory, I should also consider the postmodernist response to it because this challenges the transcendental realist justification for integrative interdisciplinarity. As expected, the starting point of the postmodernist critique is to question the very concept of disciplinary inquiry because, if this is found to be problematic, postmodernists argue, it will be unwise for scholars to assume that it can be an appropriate basis on which to develop *inter*disciplinary inquiry. Thus, Carp wants to question the 'hidden premise' (2001: 78) in Newell's argument, which is that interdisciplinarity necessarily presupposes the integration of disciplinary knowledge. In Carp's view, disciplined inquiry should not be regarded as a privileged site for knowing because, as particular (that is, socially and historically situated) points of knowing, the disciplines constitute one type of what Carp calls a 'knowledge formation'. Moreover – and this is crucial to the postmodernist case – the disciplines, as knowledge formations, do not reflect the study of an object existing independently of the knower; rather, they constitute that object. As Carp puts it:

> What if the so-called object of study is not the primary factor determining the coming into being, development, and primary content of a discipline? What if disciplines and disciplinarity play a role in constituting the very objects they study? What if we explore the disciplines as knowledge formations – historical and cultural artifacts embodying, participating in, and regenerating a complex of factors tied to psychological, economic, structural, and intercultural developments in Western Europe and the United States over the past two-and-a-half centuries? This may cause us to re-evaluate the *corpus* they present to us as knowledge. Understood this way, disciplines may be unreliable guides towards a knowledge capable of assisting human understanding and conduct toward personal and ecological well-being, individual and socio-cultural equity, or those most ineffable of human goods – wisdom and joy.
>
> (Carp, 2001: 78–9)

Given the 'normalizing pressures' of academic institutions, Carp argues, if we base our understanding of interdisciplinarity on existing academic disciplines, we are likely to restrict severely the possibility of the emergence of a 'plurality of interdisciplinarities'. Yet, in Carp's view, what we need are 'new institutional forms' that will allow scholars 'to participate in knowledge formations outside the academy' (ibid: 79), and which will help to emancipate mankind from the oppression it has created through disciplinary knowledge formations. In short, what Newell sees as an academic 'consensus' about the meaning of interdisciplinarity, Carp sees as an institutionally defined 'orthodoxy' to be interrogated and criticized (ibid: 83).

Yet, Carp's proposed alternative to orthodox notions of interdisciplinarity, which he calls 'integrative praxes that learn from multiple knowledge formations' (ibid: 109), is itself problematic, given Carp's assumption that reality is simply the product of ways of thinking and talking. For example, this is what Carp expects 'integrative praxes' to accomplish:

> One task of integrative praxes may be to bring new objects and new knowing selves into being, to query the world and our experience of it in ways that generate new problematics, new questions, new objects, and new knowledges, some of which may challenge existing knowledges, or even be incommensurate with them. One task of integrative praxes may be to listen carefully to learn from the excluded knowledge formations of the

> dispossessed – women, the poor, the internal colonies, the external colonies, webs of cultural trajectories outside Europe and the United States. If so, integrative praxes cannot begin by presuming or incorporating the disciplines, and Newell's trope of integration will not be helpful.
>
> (Carp, 2001: 93)

But how, we may ask, can we 'listen' and 'learn' from knowledge formations that may be 'incommensurate' with each other? If two or more knowledge formations have nothing in common, communication between members of each will be impossible and, if communication is impossible, how can we possibly integrate knowledge through 'integrative praxes'? Indeed, it is interesting to observe that by 'integrative praxes' Carp means a dynamic relationship between 'thoughtful practices and practical thoughtfulness' (ibid: 74). Yet, if Carp wants to sustain the idea that theory and practice constitute a (non-reducible) duality, which is implied in his concept of 'integrative praxes', he cannot also assume that thought, language and being are identical because to make such an assumption is to imply that theory determines practice and practice determines theory. To recall the argument of the previous section: if we assume that theory determines practice, we cannot then make sense of many of our practical experiences – of making mistakes and of unintended consequences – and, if we assume that practice determines theory, we cannot make sense of the contradictions and anomalies in our thinking, which reflect the existence of unacknowledged conditions and unconscious motivations for action. In short, if we want to maintain the assumption that theory and practice are dialectically distinct and dialectically connected (and so existentially interdependent) elements of a duality, we must assume that being and thought constitute the same sort of duality.[13]

The fundamental problem with the postmodernist conception of interdisciplinarity, therefore, is that it cannot sustain an intelligible conception of scientific integration and differentiation. If different forms of thought and language have no real basis – that is, they do not refer to objects existing independently of the observer – they can be sustained only through convention – the implication of which is that interdisciplinarity amounts to the deconstruction of existing disciplinary conventions and the reconstruction of new, interdisciplinary conventions. Yet, conventionalism begs the fundamental question of why scientists classify objects of inquiry in particular ways. To pose the problem in another way: if the classification of scientific objects has no real grounds, how can we make sense of the success of our scientifically informed practical interventions in the world? Only if we see the categories of scientific thought as attempts to express the truth of independently existing objects – which the possibility of *referential detachment*[14] establishes – can we start to understand the need for differentiation and integration in scientific inquiry. By distinguishing clearly between thought and reality (while recognizing that thought is constellationally contained within reality), we can come to understand how the differentiation and interconnection of reality is the condition for the possibility of differentiation and integration in science. It is the failure to sustain the idea of existential independence, therefore

– a failure rooted in the epistemic fallacy – that leads the postmodernist to a conception of interdisciplinarity as one of intellectual *dis*integration and to an ontology defined by contingency and indeterminacy to the exclusion of natural necessity and determinacy.[15] However, this absence comes back to haunt the postmodernist in the form of theory–practice inconsistency.[16]

It is worth noting at this point that positivism is also unable to sustain a coherent conception of scientific integration and specialization. Like postmodernism, positivism is an example of irrealism; that is, it denies the possibility of natural necessity (or at least reduces it to logical necessity).[17] Unlike postmodernism, which implies an ontology of difference, positivism implies an ontology of non-difference. Yet, if reality is undifferentiated, it is unclear why science should be differentiated and why scientific integration is desirable at all. Like the postmodernists, then, positivists are driven towards conventionalism in their understanding of the differentiation of scientific inquiry. Moreover, if reality and science are undifferentiated, interdisciplinarity can only mean the unification of science by method – which finds expression in the view, propagated by orthodox economists, that man is everywhere rational and can be analyzed as such.

Yet, as we saw in the first section of this chapter, science is characterized by both methodological diversity and methodological similarity so that the essentialist methodological position of positivism and the radical pluralist methodological position of postmodernism are both misplaced theses.[18] Moreover, methodological diversity and similarity in science implies ontological diversity and similarity. Clearly, then, we need to develop an ontological framework that can show that it is by virtue of the similarities of the properties of different objects of inquiry that the integration of knowledge from specialized sciences is possible and that it is by virtue of the differences in the properties of similar objects that specialized modes of inquiry are possible. I argue that critical realism offers such a framework; that the concepts of vertical and horizontal ontological depth and the concepts of stratification (through emergence) and transfactuality (through differentiation) deriving from them can justify scientific differentiation and integration. However, I argue that the meaning of these concepts must be refined if we are to understand the difference between *social* scientific and *natural* scientific differentiation and integration.

Let me start with the stratification of reality. Bhaskar (1975) has argued from the practical successes of science that the logic of scientific discovery is characteristically open ended, in the sense that it involves a continual backwards movement in which structures and causal mechanisms lying at successively deeper layers or strata of reality are discovered. Hence, once one set of objects lying at one level of reality has been identified and shown to explain objects lying at a higher level, it in turn becomes something to be explained at a lower level. Bhaskar gives as an example of this process the 'historical development of chemistry', which has involved the discovery of structures and causal mechanisms lying at progressively lower levels of reality:

| | | |
|---|---|---|
| Stratum I | $2Na + 2HCl = 2NaCl + H_2$ | |
| | explained by | |
| Stratum II | theory of atomic number and valency | Mechanism 1 |
| | explained by | |
| Stratum III | theory of electrons and atomic structure | Mechanism 2 |
| | explained by | |
| Stratum IV | [competing theories of sub-atomic structure] | [Mechanism 3] |

> It should be noted that the historical order of the development of our knowledge of strata is opposite to the causal order of their dependence in being. No end to this process of successive discovery and description of new and ever deeper, and explanatorily more basic, strata can be envisaged.
>
> (Bhaskar, 1978: 168–9)

From this example, we can see that the strata of reality are vertically ordered in the sense that the lower levels are the preconditions for the higher levels – the 'causal order of their dependence in being'. But, the causal order is the reverse of the order of discovery, so that what is a lower level from an ontological perspective is a higher level from an epistemological perspective. For example, although atoms are ontologically lower and so more fundamental entities than molecules, they are epistemologically higher than molecules because the understanding of the structure of the atom presupposed the prior discovery of molecular forms, such as solids, liquids and gases. However, social entities are an exception in the sense that they are both ontologically higher than what they presuppose – that is, human agency – *and* epistemologically higher, because knowledge of social forms can come about only through the prior conceptualization of human agency. (To avoid confusion I refer henceforth to higher and lower levels only in the ontological sense.)

How exactly, then, are the strata of reality related? Critical realists argue that, if one stratum is to explain another stratum without explaining it away, each stratum must be rooted in, emergent from, and so irreducible to and unpredictable from, the one below it. (Collier's account of stratification is fairly typical in this respect [1994: 110–15].) Let us consider this idea in more detail because it is the concept of emergence that gives us a way of understanding how levels of reality may be both differentiated and interconnected and hence how the sciences may be both differentiated and interconnected. Now, Elder-Vass has attempted to clear up an ambiguity concerning the concept of emergence, which he detects in the work of Collier and Bhaskar, and which turns on the question of whether or not the relations between strata are relations of composition (Elder-Vass, 2005: 326–31). He argues that:

> the concept of emergence is inherently compositional. By this I mean that any higher-level entity (and its emergent properties) is dependent upon a collection of lower-level entities in the sense that (a) they are the necessary component parts of the higher-level entity; (b) the emergent property is dependent upon (but not eliminatively reducible to) the properties of these

> parts; and (c) the emergent property, in the sense of a power or tendency, is not dependent upon the properties of other entities that are not such parts (although it may be so dependent for its realisation).
>
> (Elder-Vass, 2005: 325–6)

For example, a water molecule can be considered to be a higher-level entity in the sense that its lower-level parts are hydrogen and oxygen atoms, which, in turn, can be considered to be higher-level entities in the sense that *their* lower-level parts are electrons, protons and neutrons. However, it is crucial to recognize that it is only from a *particular structure* of hydrogen and oxygen atoms that water (or hydrogen oxide) emerges (just as it is only from particular organizations of electrons, protons and neutrons that oxygen and hydrogen atoms emerge). Chemical bonding is the mechanism that describes the way the structure of oxygen and hydrogen atoms works, such that the water molecule possesses properties, that is, causal powers and liabilities, dependent on, yet irreducible to, the properties of hydrogen and oxygen. Hence, it is the fact that hydrogen and oxygen atoms have the power to combine in a certain way – that is, that they can form covalent bonds – that explains why hydrogen oxide possesses its own set of causal powers and liabilities, such as solvency, electrical conductivity, non-combustibility, and so forth. But the properties of water could not have been predicted from knowledge of the properties of oxygen and hydrogen considered separately because oxygen and hydrogen – as gases, for example – are highly combustible whereas water, in any state, is not. In short, the properties of water amount to something more than the sum of the properties of its parts.

Yet, Elder-Vass, having cleared up one ambiguity, leaves another unresolved, which is how the concept of causation relates to the concept of emergence. He is quite explicit that the relationship between parts and whole is compositional and *not* causal because causal relations between entities are diachronic relations, whereas compositional relations between entities are synchronic relations:

> My argument, then, is that it is because a higher-level entity is composed of a *particular stable organisation* or configuration of lower-level entities that it may be able to exert causal influence in its own right. This does *not* mean that an emergent property of a higher level entity is *caused* by its parts or by their powers in the usual sense of the term; emergence is a synchronic relationship between a whole and its parts, whereas cause is a diachronic relation in which the powers of a group of entities at one moment *causally* determine the events which follow at the next. The point of emergence is that it is the way that a set of entities is related to each other at a *given* point of time that determines the joint effect they have on the world at that moment. Emergence, then, is a synchronic relation amongst the parts of an entity that gives the entity as a whole the ability to have a particular (diachronic) causal impact. The relation between a whole and its parts is thus a relation of composition, and not of causation.
>
> (Elder-Vass, 2005: 321)

Distinguishing between the concepts of emergence and causation in this way allows Elder-Vass to invoke the possibility of 'morphogenetic causes' – that is, entities whose causal powers when activated bring about or trigger the emergence of a new entity – and 'morphostatic causes' – that is, entities whose causal powers when activated help to sustain the existence of the new entity – in diachronic accounts of the emergence of a new entity (ibid: 324–5). For example, if we consider water again, we would need to postulate a stimulus for the reaction between hydrogen and oxygen gases – the 'morphogenetic cause' – and certain ambient conditions – the 'morphostatic cause' – if we were to show how water continues to exist.

Collier, too, seems to take the view that causation can only be diachronic in nature. Having reminded us that one stratum of reality explains the one immediately above it, he argues:

> Here we have a problem of ambiguity in the word 'explains', which has to serve to refer both to the relation between one theory and another, and to that between the real strata to which the theories refer. If we lived in the Middle Ages it would be natural to refer to the real relation between the mechanisms at different strata as one of cause; the more basic mechanism causes the less. But in modern usage that would be misleading. The two mechanisms are simultaneous, not successive; neither is an event or action; there is no question of one's being the other's *efficient cause* – the only kind of cause with which most modern philosophy is happy. It is important to distinguish the way in which one mechanism explains another (which we may call *vertical explanation*) from the way in which a mechanism plus a stimulus explain an event (*horizontal explanation*).
>
> (Collier, 1994: 109)

Yet, *contra* Collier and Elder-Vass, I cannot see why the synchronic relationship between two adjacent strata of reality cannot involve causation as well as composition. Collier argues that, given that vertically related causal mechanisms are 'simultaneous, not successive', we have no licence to talk of the lower-level mechanism *causing* the higher-level mechanism because causes can only be 'efficient' causes in the sense of triggering actions. But, if that were so, the whole notion of causal mechanism, which critical realists – Collier included – routinely invoke, would not make sense. Consider once more the emergence of water. The conditions for the emergence of water, as we saw above, are oxygen and hydrogen gases, a stimulus that causes them to react and ambient conditions. Now, if the two gases react successfully, water molecules will form; in other words, the oxygen and hydrogen atoms will bond together in a particular arrangement. But, can we say that it was *only* the stimulus for the reaction that caused water to emerge? No, because the oxygen and hydrogen atoms had to possess the property that they could combine – the property they possess in virtue of their sub-atomic structure. However, when this causal power is activated in a reaction such that chemical bonding occurs, it does not stop operating after bonding is complete.

Even though a new substance that possesses its own causal powers and liabilities has emerged, the combining power of the oxygen and hydrogen atoms continues to be exercised; that is, the oxygen and hydrogen atoms continue to be attracted to each other. What has happened, in short, is that the properties of the hydrogen and oxygen atoms have changed. Before they react with each other, they are highly unstable so that, as gases, they are combustible but, after they react, they become stable so that, as the components of water, they are no longer combustible. Yet, the oxygen and hydrogen atoms still possess the power to combine, which must continue to be exercised if water is to exist.

If we accept the preceding argument, we can now say that an emergent property pertaining to a higher-level entity is caused by the emergent properties of its lower-level parts. But, as should now be clear, there will also be additional causal conditions that bring the new entity into existence – what Collier would call an 'efficient' cause and Elder-Vass a 'morphogenetic cause' – and that allow the new entity to continue to exist – what Elder-Vass would call a 'morphostatic cause'. Therefore, we need no longer restrict the meaning of 'cause' to diachronic accounts of emergence; causation is involved in the emergence of entities, whether we analyze this phenomenon from either a synchronic or a diachronic perspective.

But, it is interesting to note that, even though Collier claims that causation can only be diachronic in nature, he implies throughout much of his discussion of stratification and emergence that it can be synchronic too. This is particularly clear in the following two passages, in which Collier argues that the relations between lower-level and higher-level strata are asymmetric. By this, he means that a given stratum of reality presupposes ontologically and is thus 'governed' by, all the strata lying beneath it, whereas the reverse does not hold (that is, a given stratum does not depend for its existence on strata lying above it):

> It is tempting to think that the mineral kingdom is governed by the laws of physics and chemistry, the vegetable and animal kingdoms by the laws of botany and zoology, and so on. But in the first place, animals do not break the laws of physics and chemistry. They are after all composed of atoms, and those atoms obey the same laws whether or not they are parts of living organisms. So animals are necessarily governed by *both* kinds of law, physico-chemical and biological.
>
> (Collier, 1994: 47)

> The relations between the more basic and less basic domains are one-way relations of inclusion: all animals are composed of chemical substances but not all chemical substances are parts of animals, and so on.
>
> This means that animals are governed both by biological and by chemical laws. An animal can do all sorts of things which the chemicals of which it is composed could not do were they obeying not the biological laws governing the organism but only 'their own' chemical laws. But of course the animal is not able to *break* the laws of chemistry or physics . . .

> Anything belonging to a higher stratum of nature will be governed by more than one kind of law, which is as much as to say more than one kind of mechanism is operating in it.
>
> (ibid: 107–8)

Elder-Vass, too, in a discussion of the meaning of 'cause' also seems to accept that causation can be synchronic in nature. Consider, for example, the meaning of the following passage in which Elder-Vass twice refers to the 'causal impacts' of lower-level parts of an entity:

> it is also important to recognise . . . that the various entities that are parts of the distinct higher-level entities involved also have causal powers. Any given higher-level entity, then, can be seen as a 'pyramid' of successively lower-level parts, and the causal impact of the higher-level entity as a whole includes the causal impacts of those parts. At each level, the entities formed from the lower-level parts have causal powers in their own right by virtue of how those parts are organised. The total causal impact of a higher-level entity conceived of in these pyramidal terms, then, includes the impact of all its lower-level parts as well as the causal powers that are emergent at its highest level.
>
> (Elder-Vass, 2005: 332)

In short, there does seem to be an ambiguity in the work of both Collier and Elder-Vass concerning the relationship between causation and emergence. On the one hand, both claim that causal explanation can only be horizontal explanation; on the other hand, both appear to accept that causal explanation can be vertical explanation as well – an acceptance that is implicit in Collier's claim that 'more than one kind of mechanism is operating' in concrete entities and in Elder-Vass's use of the term 'total causal impact' to describe the effects of the exercise of mechanisms at different levels. It seems strange, therefore, to deny that vertical explanation involves causation when the exercise of the causal powers of the parts of an emergent entity is one of the conditions for its emergence.

Moreover, a conception of emergence as involving the principles of both composition and causation seems to be in accordance with Bhaskar's own conception of emergence and multiple determination, which, following Bunge (1973: 162), Bhaskar calls a theory of '*integrative* or structured *pluralism*' (1986: 106). He summarizes this theory as follows:

> On this conception, reality consists of partially interconnected hierarchies of levels, in which any element e at a level L is in principle subject to the possibilities of causal determination by and of higher-order, lower-order and extra-order (extraneous) effects, besides those defining it as an element of L (including those individuating it as an e).
>
> (Bhaskar, 1986: 106)

Let us explore the meaning of 'causal determination' further because it is crucial to understanding both the differentiation and interconnection of objects of scientific inquiry. Now, in light of the theory of emergence that I have revised above, I suggest that causal determination encompasses two distinct types of causal process. The first type I call *causal interdependence*, which refers to the internal relationship between causal objects lying at: (a) different yet adjacent levels of reality; and (b) the same level of reality. Consider once more the emergent entity, water. The oxygen and hydrogen atoms of which water is composed are subject to lower-order determination by sub-atomic particles and are subject to higher-order determination by their very arrangement or structure (which is what gives rise to water). Now, the fact that the causal powers of oxygen and hydrogen atoms are modified by the structure in which they are arranged means that there is *intra*-order causal determination – that is, an internal relationship between causal objects lying at the same level of reality (because the oxygen and hydrogen atoms mutually determine each other) and that there is *inter*-order causal determination – that is, an internal relationship between causal objects lying at different yet adjacent levels of reality (because the causal powers of water depend on the exercise of the modified causal powers of oxygen and hydrogen and *vice versa*). Similarly, if we move down a level, we can see that the higher-level, modified causal powers of oxygen and hydrogen depend on the lower-level modified causal powers of sub-atomic particles and, *vice versa*, that the sub-atomic particles mutually determine each other.

We also find causal interdependence when we consider the relationship between social structure and human agency. By virtue of their biological constitution, people possess causal powers and liabilities – what we call human agency. But, the fact that the causal powers which people possess are modified by the structure of which they are part means that the (modified) causal powers of human agents – the lower-level parts – depend on the causal powers of social structure – the higher-level entity; while the causal powers of social structure depend on the causal powers of human agents because it is only by virtue of the particular way in which people are related that a higher-level entity – that is, social structure – emerges.

The concept of causal interdependence, therefore, describes the internal relationship between different causal objects. It involves both *inter*-order causal determination – that is, causal determination between entities lying at different yet adjacent levels of reality – and *intra*-order causal determination – that is, causal determination between entities lying at the same level of reality. In short, causal interdependence may have a vertical as well as a horizontal dimension.[19]

The second type of causal process I call *causal influence*, which refers to the external relationship between causal objects lying at any level of reality. Collier uses the colour of moths as an example of this sort of causal determination (1989: 48–9). Although the colour of moths is a biological property, it is nevertheless affected by social mechanisms – such as industrial production – whose effects interfere with the mechanism of natural selection. This is an example, not of causal interdependence but of causal influence, because the social mechanisms, even though they exist 'higher up' the order of being than biological mechanisms, are not emergent from moths: they are emergent from relations between people. Similarly, changes to the climate are affecting human habitation on earth but, although the causal powers and liabilities of human beings depend on the causal powers and liabilities of biological, chemical and physical entities, these mechanisms are not necessarily the same as the ones involved in generating climate patterns so that, in this case, we can speak of 'extra-order' causal influence. Causal influence, then, presupposes that the relations between causal objects lying at different levels are external; when the direction of causal influence is two-way, we have a process of *causal interaction*.[20]

Finally, I should make it clear that the concept of causal determination is different from the concept of ontological dependence, which refers to the way in which the existence of a given entity at a given level of reality presupposes the existence of all the entities lying in the strata below it. This is what Collier means when he says that mechanisms lying at one stratum are 'governed' by those lying at strata further down (see the quotations from Collier reproduced above). But, the concept of ontological dependence involves a one-way relation of necessity, because the entities lying at a given level do not depend for their existence on higher-order entities – only on lower-order entities. It may be objected, therefore, that the concept of ontological dependence contradicts the concept of causal interdependence. However, there is no contradiction. When we examine entities at a given level of reality, either we can look at how they become the parts of higher-order emergent entities – that is, by considering how their causal powers and liabilities are modified through the principle of multiple causal determination – or we can treat the entities at our chosen level as wholes – that is, in abstraction from any entities they may constitute as parts – and ask what must be the conditions of their existence.

A refined theory of integrative pluralism, therefore, offers us a way of understanding how it is that the sciences can be different – *contra* the theses of 'ontological monism (or holism) and epistemological reductionism (e.g. physicalism, biologism, individualism)' – yet still connected – *contra* the theses of 'ontological (monadic) pluralism (or atomism) and epistemological meta-empiricism, "separatism" or "eclecticism"' (Bhaskar, 1986: 106).[21] As we have seen, reductionism is an untenable thesis because, given the stratification of reality, it is impossible to explain the nature of an emergent entity solely in terms of the properties of more fundamental entities and to deny its status as a causal object in its own right. For example, we cannot explain why water extinguishes fire by referring only to the properties of hydrogen and oxygen, because these elements, when they exist as gases, are combustible; we have to refer to the properties of the water molecule as a particular chemical structure possessing properties – such as non-flammability – distinct from those of oxygen and hydrogen. For the same reason, eclecticism is untenable. If the levels of reality were completely unconnected, so that we could not in fact talk of a hierarchy of 'levels', scientists would not be able to explain the properties of one entity (the whole) as the outcome of the operation of the properties of another set of entities (the parts). In other words, the historical pattern of discovery in science as one of increasing ontological depth would not make sense, if reality were simply a random flux of diverse things having no relationship to each other.

We can represent the stratification of the sciences as shown in Figure 2.1. A movement down the ladder of the sciences represents an increase in ontological depth as scientists discover entities lying at successively deeper levels of reality, whereas a movement up the ladder represents an increase in ontological complexity, in the sense that entities higher up ontologically presuppose a greater range of types of causal mechanism. Thus, social structures and mechanisms are governed not only by biological but also by chemical and physical mechanisms. We can now appreciate why many concrete entities – such as people – are so complex; for a person is not only a 'structuratum' – that is, a 'structured entity' (Collier, 1989: 193) – but also a 'laminated system' – that is, an entity 'whose elements are necessarily bonded by an irreducible plurality of structures' (ibid: 194).

Now, Figure 2.1 is of course a highly simplified representation of the stratification of the sciences. It must be recognized, for example, that there is stratification within each science as well as between sciences. Thus, the 'chemical sciences' will reflect more than one level of reality – as the subdivisions of biochemistry and physical chemistry demonstrate. Similarly, each of the subdivisions within the 'biological sciences' – molecular biology, cell biology, physiology, anatomy, and so on – deals with a different level of reality. What, though, of the social sciences? Given that social science is subdivided into various disciplines – economics, political science, sociology and anthropology are the ones usually identified – can we explain these subdivisions in the same way that we can explain the subdivisions within biology and chemistry? In other words, can we identify *vertical* relations between the social sciences such that they constitute distinct, emergent levels of reality? Bhaskar offers little in the way of clarity on this issue, apart from arguing that 'the predicates "natural", "social", "human", "physical", "chemical", "aerodynamical", "biological", "economic", etc. ought not to be regarded as differentiating distinct kinds of events, but as differentiating distinct kinds of *mechanisms*' (1978: 119).

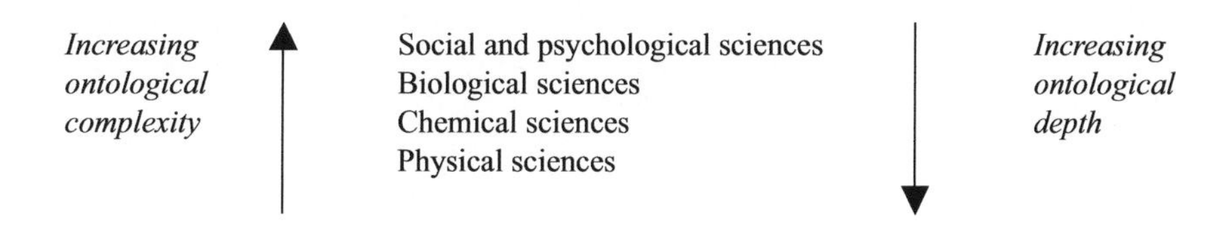


*Figure 2.1* The ladder of the sciences[22]

Source: based on Collier, 1989: 45

The question remains, though, whether or not predicates such as 'social', 'economic' and 'political' refer to *distinct layers of reality* in the same way as predicates such as 'physical', 'chemical' and 'biological'. I am not so sure that we can relate the former predicates to each other in the same way as we can relate the latter, for it is not at all clear to me that 'social', 'economic' and 'political' mechanisms do constitute distinct, emergent levels of reality. Both Lawson and Hay, for example, have proposed that the category 'social' be differentiated according to 'aspect' rather level of reality. Thus, Lawson has argued that the 'economic' is just one type of aspect of social activity:

> I cannot think of a single sphere of human activity – from lending support to a football team, to listening to music, or even to making love – that does not (or could not) have an economic aspect . . . These and all other activities take place in space and time, both of which can have alternative uses. All human activities require material conditions . . . But at the same time very few activities, if any, have *merely* an economic aspect.
>
> (Lawson, 2003: 162)

Similarly, Hay describes the 'political' as one amongst a range of different types of aspect of social activity:

> Though all social relations may also be political relations, this does not imply that they are only political relations, nor that they can be adequately understood in such terms . . . The political is perhaps best seen as an aspect or moment of the social, articulated with other moments (such as the economic or the cultural). Though politics may be everywhere, nothing is exhaustively political.
>
> (Hay, 2002: 256 – 67)

Furthermore, we must also recognize that the political and economic aspects of the social are ontologically interdependent. Consider, for example, the relationship between landlord and tenant. This relationship is a social structure because the two component positions are internally related. As such, it is an emergent entity because the people who occupy the positions of landlord and tenant have powers which they would not have were they not occupying those positions. Thus, a person who occupies the position of tenant can only pay rent to a landlord by virtue of occupying this position. Hence, the causal powers and liabilities pertaining to the landlord and tenant are not simply the sum of the causal powers and liabilities pertaining to people because, when people occupy societal positions, they retain their basic, biological powers and liabilities yet gain a set of *social* powers and liabilities as well. Because the landlord–tenant relation is concerned with the allocation of a particular material resource – that is, housing – it has an economic aspect. Because landlords and tenants possess different rights and must follow different obligations, it also has a political aspect. Moreover, because these obligations and rights may be enforced in law, it has a 'legal' aspect, and because the provision of housing within society is subject to argument and debate (by virtue of the struggle over resources within a predominantly capitalist society), it has an 'ideological' aspect. It follows that:

- the political aspect depends on the economic, in the sense that the economic aspect constitutes the material conditions for the political aspect – that is, the exercise of human agency – (for people would not be able to act as landlords and tenants unless there were houses for them to act in relation to);
- the economic aspect depends on the political aspect, in the sense that the provision of housing through tenancy arrangements would not be possible without landlords and tenants exercising their legal rights and fulfilling their legal obligations – for example, to maintain the property to an agreed standard and to pay rent at an agreed time;
- both the economic and political aspects depend on the legal aspect in the sense that it is through courts of law that tenancy agreements are (ultimately) enforced, if such agreements are to continue to exist;
- the economic, political and legal aspects depend on the ideological aspect, in the sense that the provision of housing through renting and its legal enforcement must receive a sufficient degree of legitimacy throughout society for it to continue to exist.

We can see from this line of argument that the economic and political aspects of the social are closely related in the sense that they are ontologically interdependent; that is, the one constitutes the conditions for the other and *vice versa*. By contrast, the ideological and legal aspects are less closely related to the economic and political because they constitute sustaining conditions for the economic and political and thus stand to the economic and political in relations of ontological dependence rather than ontological interdependence. Finally and crucially, we can also that the different aspects of social structure are not emergent from each other; rather, the categories economic, political, legal and ideological refer to entities emergent at the same level of reality; therefore, they must be regarded as designating particular types of horizontal ontological depth.

So far, I have argued that we can differentiate social structure by aspect and that the relations between the different aspects of social structure are relations of ontological dependence and interdependence (or existential constitution).[23] However, we must also recognize that higher-order social entities, such as totalities,[24] can be differentiated according to the types of social (and natural) structures constituting them; for it is by virtue of the possibility that social and natural structures may be internally related to each other that higher-order entities may emerge. Consider again the social structure of tenancy. This structure will be causally dependent on other types of structure. For example, the landlord's right to demand rent from the tenant for occupation of the property presupposes a structure of property ownership because the landlord must be the owner of the residence if he is to accept tenants. In turn, the structure of property ownership (in this case housing) is internally related to the market for owner-occupied housing because such a market could not exist without it. The structure of tenancy is internally related to the market for rented housing because, again, such a market could not exist in the absence of tenancy agreements. We can summarize these relationships as shown in Figure 2.2.

What makes a particular set or *conjuncture*[25] of relations between structures a totality is that the internal relations between the structures give rise to holistic causal properties. For example, in the last 30 years or so in the UK, the sort of holistic effect we have seen in the provision of housing is a tendency for the average price level of privately owned houses and the average rent level for privately owned accommodation to increase much more rapidly than the increase in the average level of income, as the demand for privately owned housing has exceeded its supply. These holistic properties are the conditions for the operation of the constitutive structures – the various forms of market, ownership and tenancy – which mediate their causal influence and which, in turn, is mediated via human agents – in this case, house buyers and sellers, landlords and tenants, estate agents, and so on. But, it is only through the exercise of human agency that the

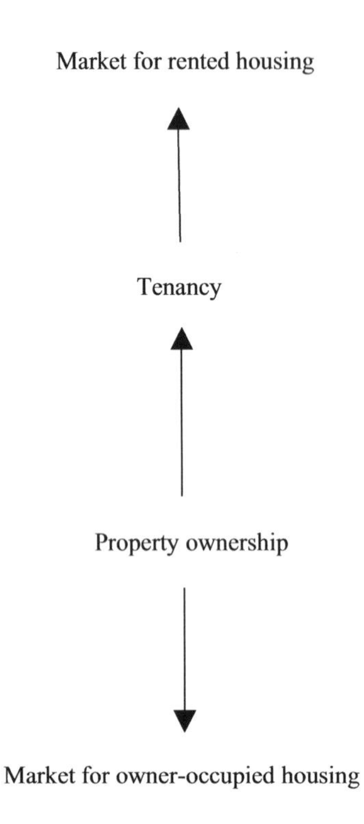


*Figure 2.2* Causal dependence between social structures

constitutive structures and hence the conjuncture are reproduced. Therefore, we have here an example of 'holistic causality' (Bhaskar, 1993: 127), where structures mediate the causal effect of the (partial) totality that they constitute and where the structures mediate the exercise of human agency, by means of which they and the conjuncture of which they are determinative, continue to exist.

Now, to say that an entity is characterized by holistic causality is to say that it is characterized by *multiple control* because it involves interconnected causal processes at multiple levels of reality. But, multiple control is only a species of what Bhaskar calls 'multiple determination' (1993: 131) because different types of structure may simply interact with each other (that is, may be externally related) – in which case the combination of structures will be determinative of actual events and states of affairs but will not have emergent properties.[26] Consider, for example, the relationship between the market for owner-occupied housing and the market for credit. It is possible – indeed common in the UK – for non-property-owners to become property owners by borrowing money to purchase a fixed asset – in this case a house. During a credit expansion, when interest rates are relatively low, prospective buyers will find it relatively easy to repay a mortgage and so demand in the market for owner-occupied housing will tend to increase. Now, if the demand for housing exceeds supply, the price of housing will also tend to increase, thereby adding fuel to the demand for credit as existing owner-occupiers attempt to take advantage of the increase in the average value of housing. However, if the demand for credit starts to exceed the supply of credit, the rate of interest will tend to rise, leading to a credit contraction. In this situation, owner-occupiers may find it more difficult to meet their debt repayment obligations so that house repossessions may rise. As the demand for housing falls, so does the price. Hence, the relationship between the credit and housing markets is one of causal interaction. Of course, the situation is typically more complex than this, in the sense that other types of social structure are usually involved. For example, potential homeowners may decide not to enter the market for owner-occupied housing, even though credit is relatively cheap, if there is a shortage in the supply of housing and the average price of housing is too high. In this situation, where there is upward pressure on the price level, entrepreneurs will find it relatively more profitable to build houses and will take on skilled labour so that the demand for skilled labour in the labour market will increase. Now, if the demand for skilled labour exceeds supply, wages will tend to rise, leading to a corresponding increase in the demand for housing and credit. So, we can think of the causal mechanisms pertaining to the labour, housing and credit markets as mutually reinforcing.

We also have to consider the possibility of contradictory, in the sense of countervailing, causal effects. For example, if the government were to change the rules on immigration such that the supply of skilled workers increased, the wage rises of skilled workers in the construction sector would tend to be relatively smaller as the production of new homes increased and so the increase in the number of skilled workers able to afford a mortgage might not be so great. Similarly, if the government were to change the rules on credit such that it became more difficult for non-property-owners to meet the conditions of obtaining a mortgage, the increase in the demand for, and price of, housing might be relatively lower as interest rates fell and, if the government were to change the planning rules so as to make it easier for construction companies to find land on which to build new houses, the increase in the price of housing following an increase in demand might be relatively lower.

We can summarize the preceding argument in Figure 2.3, which shows the causal relations between the labour, housing and credit markets and different types of government regulation (including taxation of house purchases and sales).

The form of multiple determination wherein relations between the structures of a conjuncture are only external we may say characterizes 'mechanical complexes' (as opposed to 'organic totalities', where structures are internally related; Bhaskar, 1986: 110).[27] However, because the structures within a conjuncture may be internally as well as externally related and because reality is always changing, we need to think of totalities as being 'open, incomplete and partial' (Norrie, 2010: 90–1).[28] Indeed, we must also recognize the possibility of internal and external relations between totalities and thus the possibility of new, higher-order entities emerging – an example of 'recursive embeddedness' (Bhaskar, 1993: 142).[29] Consider the complexity of the causal relationships between marriage, the family, the labour market, employment and education/training.

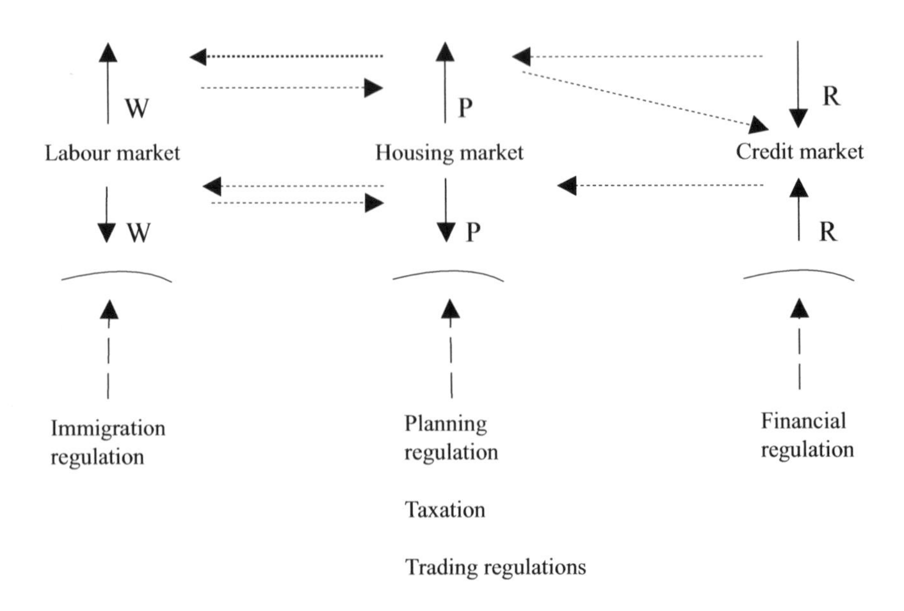


*Figure 2.3* Causal interaction between the labour, housing and credit markets: P = price of housing; R = rate of interest; W = wage

- The relationship between the labour market and marriage is external because what is necessary for the existence of a labour market is a supply of labour power and it is contingent upon whether or not the people who supply their labour power are married. Thus, one could imagine a scenario in which married people opted out of the structure of paid employment and lived by self-subsistence while only single people entered paid employment. Indeed, in the past, it was expected that husbands would enter paid employment while wives would engage in unpaid work at home. However, as the demand for particular types of worker has increased over time (for example, part-time workers) so more and more married women have entered the labour market. Hence, today it is generally expected that both husbands and wives will be in paid employment. Therefore, we have a relationship of *causal interaction* between marriage and the labour market.
- Marriage affects the working of the family in the sense that changing expectations about the length of marriages and the acceptability of divorce have influenced the structure of the family; for example, the increase in the number of remarriages has led to an increase in the number of extended families involving 'step children' and 'step parents'. So, the relationship between marriage and the family is one of *causal influence*.
- Changes in the nature of employment may also affect the working of the family in the sense that increases in work intensity may have an adverse effect on parents' ability to raise their children well. So, the relationship between employment and the family is one of *causal influence*.
- Because a supply of labour power is essential to the existence of a labour market and because the family is the means by which new labour power is created (through human reproduction), the labour market is *causally dependent* on the structure of the family. But, the working of the labour market also *affects* the working of the family in the sense that changes in the availability of paid employment may influence people's decisions about whether or not to have children and may affect the ability of existing parents to ensure an adequate upbringing for their children. So, the relationship between the family and the labour market is one of both *causal dependence* and *causal influence*.
- The labour market is *causally dependent* on the structure of paid employment because the different instances of the employment relationship are the basis on which people compete against each other as buyers and sellers of labour power.
- Relationships of both *causal dependence* and *causal interaction* also exist between the labour market and education and training. For example, a supply of *skilled* labour power presupposes a structure of education and training, while changes in the demand for skilled workers of different types may affect how people are educated and trained.
- Similarly, the relationship between education and training and the family is one of both *causal dependence* and *causal interaction*. For example, the existence of the teacher–student relationship depends on a supply of people to be

taught, which the family provides, while changes in the education curriculum, for example through the introduction of parenting classes and comprehensive education, may affect people's ability to be good parents and their view of marriage and family life.

We can summarize these relationships in a diagram (Figure 2.4). What we have in Figure 2.4, therefore, is an example of a partial totality. The structures identified as its parts are by no means exhaustive of the range of structures that may be connected to it; indeed, the inclusion of the structure of employment and the labour market points to connections with structures of ownership, production and exchange so that (from a Marxian perspective) we may speak of a (capitalist) *social formation*.[30] The point of this example, though, is to illustrate the complexity of social objects, such as (partial) totalities, and the need to think carefully of the distinctions as well as the connections between their parts – the individuation of structures as well as mode(s) of articulation.[31] Of course, it is the work of science to uncover specific configurations of structures. Herein lies the justification for the integration as well as the differentiation of science, for we need specialized forms of scientific inquiry to understand the essential nature of different types of causal object – whether these different types of object pertain to the vertical or horizontal stratification of reality – and integrative forms of scientific inquiry to understand the precise connections between the different types of causal object. 'Abstract' social sciences (such as political science and economics), therefore, can take us only so far in our understanding of social objects: we also need 'intermediate' abstract sciences, such as political economy,[32] if we are to understand the connection(s) between the political and economic aspects of social reality (Bhaskar, 1986: 112–13).[33]

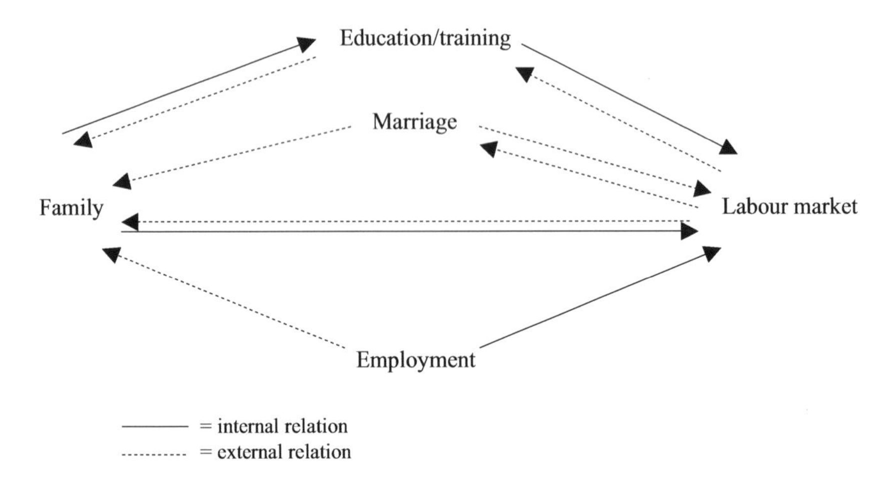


*Figure 2.4* Causal dependence and causal interaction between social structures

The multiple determination of events and states of affairs, then, implies that we need to draw on theories from different scientific fields to understand how different types of causal object work together to generate phenomena of interest. Consider Danermark's example of a 'noise-induced hearing impairment'. This phenomenon involves physiological structures, which determine a person's ability to hear; psychological structures, which determine a person's experience of the hearing impairment; and sociocultural structures, which determine how deaf people are received in society (2002: 57–8). We can represent the relationships between these different mechanisms and the particular aspect of human agency of interest – that is, the ability to hear – as shown in Figure 2.5.

In Figure 2.5, we have three different types of structure, all of which are the preconditions for human agency. The sociocultural and psychological structures presuppose each other – that is, they are existentially interdependent – and so emerge at the same level of reality. Sociocultural mechanisms enable us to use our minds because they give specific content to human consciousness and it is through our consciousness of the social and cultural world that we can act. Hence, human agency is causally dependent, via the operation of psychological mechanisms, on sociocultural mechanisms. However, sociocultural mechanisms are causally dependent, via the operation of psychological mechanisms, on human agency because it is through the exercise of human agency that we reproduce and transform the social and cultural world.

Yet, human agency also depends on the operation of physiological structures – for example, the delicate apparatuses that give us the power of sensory perception and the ability to move – while human consciousness also depends on the operation of the brain; and, *vice versa*, the operation of physiological mechanisms

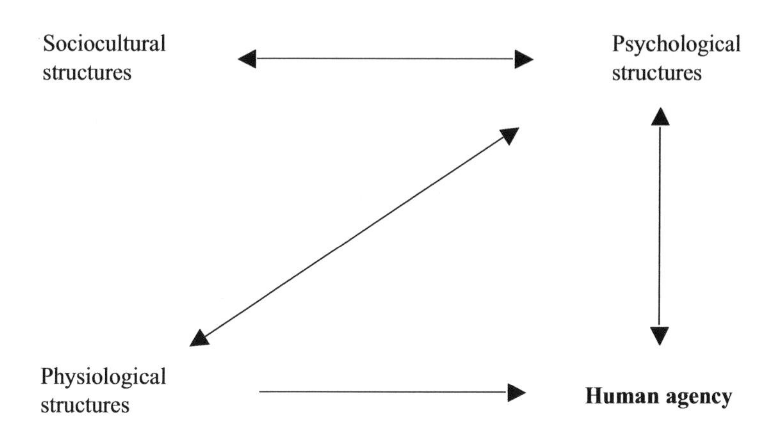


*Figure 2.5* Preconditions for human agency

depends on the exercise of human agency in the sense that we must feed ourselves to survive. So, we can see that human agency is embedded in, and so emergent from, a (partial) totality of causal mechanisms of different types – social, psychological and physiological.[34]

If, then, a person is exposed to a sufficiently high level of noise for a sufficient length of time that they suffer hearing loss, that person will not be a fully conscious human being because, as we have just seen, full consciousness depends on the existence of fully functioning physiological mechanisms. The damage to human agency will also have sociocultural and psychological implications. Given that social interaction requires the use of language, deaf people may be able to participate in social life, to a certain extent at least, if they learn to lip read, if they learn to use sign language and if they are supplied with a hearing aid. However, even if deaf people regain some of the functions they have lost, this does not mean that they will not be disabled because the very fact that they cannot communicate in the normal way or find it difficult to communicate with able-bodied people, will mark them out as different and may set off a sociocultural process of stigmatisation; and the lack of understanding that deaf people receive from able-bodied people may trigger psychological mechanisms causing deaf people to become depressed. In other words, a physiological impairment, such as hearing loss, is mediated socioculturally and psychologically.

Hence, if we want to understand the problems that disabled people face in society, we need to understand the relationships between the different types of causal mechanism relevant to their disability and its effects and so we will have to draw on and integrate knowledge of biology, psychology and sociology. As Danermark (2002: 62–3) argues, if we try to overcome the problem of hearing loss simply by supplying a hearing aid, we will be implicitly assuming that deafness is a biological problem and thus will be guilty of scientific reductionism – of assuming that concrete phenomena can be explained by the theories of only one branch of knowledge. But, if phenomena in open systems are subject to multiple determination, we will need to use different methods of inquiry and we will need to develop different theories of causal mechanisms in respect of the range of causal objects that may be involved in the generation of the phenomenon in question. We will also have to understand how the different causal mechanisms involved are interrelated – how they form a (partial) totality. Of course, we may not know which causal mechanisms are involved so that we may have to begin our inquiry from the perspective of one science. However, the results of practical experience – that is, the unintended consequences of our investigations of, and practical interventions in, the world – will help us to determine whether or not we need to draw on the knowledge of more than one science. For example, if we find that deaf people do not use the hearing aid they have been given, and if we find that they appear withdrawn or aggressive, we will be alerted to the possibility that deafness may be a social and psychological as well as a biological problem.

## Social scientific integration in practice

Having developed a coherent philosophical justification for integration and specialization in scientific inquiry, I now want to show how social scientists' failure to sustain such a theory undermines, firstly, their ability to achieve social scientific integration and, secondly, their ability to understand the potential for interdisciplinary integration within social science. Given this objective, it is appropriate that I should examine the works of the classical political economists of the eighteenth and nineteenth centuries because it is widely acknowledged that the classical political economists were implicitly committed to integrative, interdisciplinary social science.[35] However, it is less widely acknowledged that the scientific works of the classical political economists often presuppose contradictory philosophical assumptions and that it is by virtue of such contradictions that the classical political economists failed to achieve coherent social scientific integration. Moreover, I argue that the methodological writings of the later classical political economists are characterized by similar contradictions and that it is by virtue of these contradictions that the classical political economists were unable to understand explicitly the integrative, interdisciplinary *nature* of political economy and hence the *potential* for interdisciplinary integration within the social sciences.

It is perhaps unsurprising, given the intellectual aims of the classical political economists, that most contemporary academics – for example, historians of economic thought – should have examined the social scientific contributions that the classical political economists made (Barber, 1991; Heilbroner, 2000; Hunt, 2002; Stilwell, 2006). Indeed, it is argued that what made the contributions of the classical political economists distinctive was their understanding of the emerging capitalist order as a social 'system' wherein different types of social structure – for example, market exchange and capitalist production – are interrelated (O'Brien, 1975: 29; Skinner, 1979: 111; Gamble, 1995: 518).

However, few contemporary academics have examined in sufficient depth the ontological presuppositions of classical political economy. Where they have addressed this subject, they have argued that classical political economy is characterized by an underlying coherence and unity in its ontological foundations. Watson's argument is typical in this respect:

> It is true that the classical political economists were divided over the relative importance of logical deduction versus inductive theory building based on direct observation. However, this dispute does not concern me here. Much more important for current purposes is that the classical political economists shared a common ontology. They agreed on what the economy was, as well as on what it was about the economy that warranted study from a social scientific perspective. It is on basic ontological propositions that the classical political economists are united, and it is this that recommends the classical tradition as a suitable basis for IPE, despite its differences within that tradition on how best to develop specific economic theories.
>
> (Watson, 2005: 69)

Similarly, when Dow argues that, despite its many theoretical inconsistencies, Smith's political economy betrays a theoretical unity when considered from the point of view of its 'object of study' – that is, social relationships – she is implying that it betrays a unity at an ontological level as well (Dow, 1987: 343–4). Yet, I want to argue that the existence of theoretical inconsistencies in the works of the classical political economists is indicative, not of unity but of disunity at an ontological level; that is, theoretical inconsistencies are manifestations of a contradictory ontological position. We may understand these inconsistencies in three different ways: firstly, as inconsistencies at the level of social scientific practice or *practice–practice inconsistencies*; secondly, as inconsistencies between the philosophical presuppositions of social scientific practice and professed philosophies of social science or *theory–practice inconsistencies*; and, thirdly, inconsistencies at the level of (professed) philosophy of social science or *theory–theory inconsistencies*. Using excerpts from the social scientific arguments and methodological reflections of the classical political economists, I demonstrate the existence of these three types of inconsistency and discuss their implications for the ability of the classical political economists to achieve integration at the level of social scientific practice and to understand the nature of, and potential for, social scientific integration at the level of philosophical theory.

Let me start with practice–practice inconsistencies in the political economy of Adam Smith. Unlike his successors, Smith did not leave any explicit reflections on the nature of political economy other than to state in the introduction to the fourth book of *An Inquiry into the Nature and Causes of the Wealth of Nations* that:

> Political œconomy, considered as a branch of the science of a statesman or legislator, proposes two distinct objects; first, to provide a plentiful revenue or subsistence for the people, or more properly to enable them to provide such a revenue or subsistence for themselves; and secondly, to supply the state or commonwealth with a revenue sufficient for the publick services. It proposes to enrich both the people and the sovereign.
>
> (Smith [1776] 1976: 428)

What is immediately striking about Smith's definition, especially when it is compared with contemporary, positivist conceptions of social science, is that it presupposes that social science has ethical and practical implications, in the sense that theoretical claims, value judgements and policy proposals are necessarily related. By stating explicitly that political economy is 'a branch of the science of a statesman or legislator' – that is, a science that policymakers can draw upon – rather than just a branch of social science, Smith is presupposing that policy objectives – in this case, enriching 'both the people and the sovereign' – cannot be divorced from theoretical means, and that these objectives are worthy.

When we turn to Smith's scientific discourse, a similar picture emerges: we find a combination of theoretical claims, value judgements and policy guidance, as the following extract from the second chapter of the fourth book demonstrates:

> What is prudence in the conduct of every private family, can scarce be folly in that of a great kingdom. If a foreign country can supply us with a commodity cheaper than we ourselves can make it, better buy it of them with some part of the produce of our own industry, employed in a way in which we have some advantage. The general industry of the country, being always in proportion to the capital which employs it, will not thereby be diminished, no more than that of the above-mentioned artificers; but only left to find out the way in which it can be employed with the greatest advantage.
>
> (Smith [1776] 1976: 457)

In addition to its ethical and practical implications, Smith's social scientific discourse quite obviously reveals an economic aspect. This particular aspect is the focus of the first book of his *Inquiry*, in which Smith analyzes individual economic categories such as the division of labour, exchange, money and prices.[36] Yet, although Smith's *Inquiry* does focus on the economic aspect in its analytic moment, in its synthetic moment it shows how the economic is related to other aspects of the social such as the political and to other aspects of reality in general such as natural objects. Consider, for example, the following extracts from the seventh chapter of the first book, in which Smith explains the relationship between market and natural prices:

> The natural price, therefore, is, as it were, the central price, to which the prices of all commodities are continually gravitating. Different accidents may sometimes keep them suspended a good deal above it, and sometimes force them down even somewhat below it. But whatever may be the obstacles which hinder them from settling in this center of repose and continuance, they are constantly tending towards it.
>
> (ibid: 75)

> But though the market price of every particular commodity is in this manner continually gravitating, if one may say so, towards the natural price, yet sometimes particular accidents, sometimes natural causes, and sometimes particular regulations of police, may, in many commodities, keep up the market price, for a long time together, a good deal above the natural price.
>
> (ibid: 77)

In allowing for the possibility of 'particular accidents', 'natural causes' and 'particular regulations of police' interfering with the mechanism of competition, Smith's social scientific theorizing – at least in this part of his study – presupposes a philosophical theory of causal contingency – that is, a theory that different types of causal mechanism may either counteract or reinforce each other – so that the effect of the activation of the causal mechanism of interest – in Smith's case, competition – must be described as a *tendency*.

If, however, the focus of the fourth book is on explaining the accidental effects that different sorts of causal powers and liabilities may have on the operation of markets, the focus of the fifth book is on demonstrating that other types of social structure and, hence, other types of causal mechanism, are necessary to support the operation of the market. Thus, Smith explains how markets and production cannot operate without such institutions as law, defence and education. In doing so, Smith presupposes a theory of causal necessity and his argument embraces other aspects of the social such as the political and the legal.

When interpreted from the perspective of the current division of labour in social science, therefore, Smith's object of inquiry, in embracing different aspects of the social, is quintessentially interdisciplinary. It is true that Smith gives most weight to the political and economic aspects of the social in his *Inquiry* – after all, that is why he refers to 'political œconomy'. But, Smith is no reductionist, at least in this part of his argument, because at the back of his mind is the idea that the political and economic are connected to other aspects of the social and that they have to be understood in the wider, social context. Smith's method was to understand the economic aspect first in isolation and second in conjunction with the political and other aspects of the social – the method of analysis and synthesis that Redman argues was so familiar to the Scottish moral philosophers of the eighteenth century (1997: 128–31).

I suggest, therefore, that, to the extent that Smith's political economy presupposes relationships between theory, values and practice and presupposes a structural theory of causation incorporating both contingency and necessity, it is consistent with the philosophy of transcendental realism that I defined in the previous section of this chapter.[37] I suggest that, given the argument of the previous section (that transcendental realism can justify both specialization and integration in scientific inquiry), it is in virtue of this way of thinking about reality that Smith is able to embrace both social scientific specialization – that is, understanding the meaning of individual economic categories – and social scientific integration – that is, understanding how individual economic categories are connected as a system and how that system both interacts with natural causes and depends on government regulations and other types of social structure for its existence.[38]

I now want to show that the philosophical position implicit in Smith's social scientific theorizing is altogether more complicated because it involves a fundamental tension between transcendental realist and empirical realist thinking and that this philosophical complexity is manifest in contradictions between different parts of Smith's overall argument.

In the second chapter of the first book of his *Inquiry*, Smith argues that the division of labour is the 'very slow and gradual consequence of a certain propensity in human nature . . . the propensity to truck, barter, and exchange one thing for another' ([1776] 1976: 25). Smith is not sure how to account for this principle and speculates as to whether it is 'one of those original principles in human nature' or is 'the necessary consequence of the faculties of reason and speech' (ibid.). However, in the third chapter of the same book, Smith argues that the extent of the division of labour depends on the extent of the market and he describes exchange, not as a universal principle of human nature but as a 'power' – a description that suggests that exchange is not a property of people but is a property of social structure:

> As it is the power of exchanging that gives occasion to the division of labour, so the extent of this division must always be limited by the extent of that power, or, in other words, by the extent of the market. When the market is very small, no person can have any encouragement to dedicate himself entirely to one employment, for want of the power to exchange all that surplus part of the produce of his own labour, which is over and above his own consumption, for such parts of the produce of other men's labour as he has occasion for.
>
> (ibid: 31)

Smith goes on to describe how, in the Highlands of Scotland, people must live by self-subsistence because there is no market to allow them to exchange their produce. As Smith puts it, 'every farmer must be butcher, baker and brewer for his own family' (ibid: 31). In short, Smith's argument implies that it is only in virtue of the existence of the market that people have the power to exchange produce. If that is the case, though, the trucking and bartering involved in exchange cannot be something that is natural and so permanent but must be something that is *social* and so geo-historically specific.

The tendency to confuse the properties of social objects with the properties of natural objects – which I call naturalization (because the implicit assumption is that social laws cannot be changed by man just as natural laws cannot be changed by man)[39] – is characteristic of Smith's work. When Smith deals with capital accumulation, for example, he tells us that 'the principle which prompts to save, is the desire of bettering our condition, a desire which, though generally calm and dispassionate, comes with us from the womb, and never leaves us till we go into the grave' (ibid: 341). Again, Smith's explanation here leads us to believe that saving is somehow a natural property of people; yet, it is only in virtue of the structure of a particular form of society that saving is encouraged – as Smith's frequent reference to 'that rude state of society in which there is no division of labour' suggests (ibid: 276). Naturalization also permeates Smith's historical narrative in the first chapter of the third book, in which he describes the 'natural Progress of Opulence' and reminds us continually how 'human institutions' disturb the 'natural course of things' (ibid: 376–80), all of which suggests that the course of human history is somehow predetermined, that things could not have turned out differently.

What explains the tendency toward naturalization in Smith's arguments is, I suggest, the influence of empiricist thinking. According to empiricism, the objects of scientific thinking – scientific 'facts' – can be the objects only of sensory experience and so take the form of given, atomistic events and states of affairs – the constant conjunctions of which constitute the basis for Humean causal laws. If such facts are taken as given to the observer – that is, they do not depend on human activity for their existence – and, if such facts are assumed to be value-free, they take on the qualities of *natural things*. In other words, empiricism logically entails the naturalization and reification of knowledge and hence the naturalization and reification of reality (because in empiricism being determines knowledge – the ontic fallacy – at the same time as knowledge determines being – the epistemic fallacy). We can now understand how the influence of such a way of thinking about the nature of knowledge encourages the view that social objects – such as the market – are naturally occurring and so permanent and unchangeable. Moreover, if this way of thinking restricts social science to the investigation of individuals' actions and effects – because only individuals' actions and effects can be known through sensory experience – we can understand how social scientists who have been influenced by such thinking may come to the view that the observed actions of, say, individual buyers and sellers are not only natural but also the result of human agency alone (rather than being the effect of an unobservable social structure). In short, empiricism and the empirical realist ontology it presupposes has the overall effect of making the current organization of society appear normal and legitimate by concealing its underlying generative context and the particular set of values that accompanies it.

A contradiction between transcendental and empirical realist thinking is also evident in Smith's theory of value and of production through the division of labour. In the opening chapter of his *Inquiry*, Smith recognizes explicitly that human labour is a causal power: that human beings, in virtue of their natural constitution, have the capacity to produce – to turn raw materials into finished goods that are of use to their owners. The explicit recognition that human labour is a causal power is reflected in the title of the opening of the first book: 'Of the Causes of Improvement in the productive Powers of Labour, and of the Order according to which its Produce is naturally distributed among the different Ranks of the People' ([1776] 1976: 13). However, when Smith explains what determines the value of commodities, he mixes up the idea that value is determined by the quantity of labour power expended in the production of the commodity with the idea that its value is determined by the quantity of labour that it will command through exchange. For example, in the first paragraph of the fifth chapter, he argues that the value of a commodity is determined by the amount of labour that may be exchanged for it:

> The value of any commodity... to the person who possesses it, and who means not to use or consume it himself, but to exchange it for other commodities, is equal to the quantity of labour which it enables him to purchase or command. Labour, therefore, is the real measure of the exchangeable value of all commodities.
>
> (ibid: 47)

Yet, at the start of the second paragraph of the same chapter, Smith suddenly introduces the idea that the value of a commodity depends on the quantity of labour embodied in it before reverting to the idea that value depends on the quantity of labour commanded:

> The real price of every thing, what every thing really costs to the man who wants to acquire it, is the toil and trouble of acquiring it. What every thing is really worth to the man who has acquired it, and who wants to dispose of it or exchange it for something else, is the toil and trouble which it can save to himself, and which it can impose upon other people. What is bought with money or with goods is purchased by labour as much as what we acquire by the toil of our own body. That money or those goods indeed save us this toil. They contain the value of a certain quantity of labour which we exchange for what is supposed at the time to contain the value of an equal quantity. Labour was the first price, the original purchase money that was paid for all things. It was not by gold or by silver, but by labour, that all the wealth of the world was originally purchased; and its value, to those who possess it and who want to exchange it for some new productions, is precisely equal to the quantity of labour which it can enable them to purchase or command.
>
> (ibid: 47–8)

> the person who either acquires, or succeeds to a great fortune, does not necessarily acquire or succeed to any political power, either civil or military... The power which that possession immediately and directly conveys to him, is the power of purchasing; a certain command over all the labour, or over all the produce of labour which is then in the market. His fortune is greater or less, precisely in proportion to the extent of this power; or to the quantity either of other men's labour, *or, what is the same thing, of the produce of other men's labour, which it enables him to purchase or command.* The exchangeable value of every thing must always be precisely equal to the extent of this power which it conveys to its owner.
>
> (ibid: 48; emphasis added)

And in the seventh paragraph of the same chapter, we find the two different conceptions of value jumbled up:

> The discovery of the abundant mines of America reduced, in the sixteenth century, the value of gold and silver in Europe to about a third of what it had been before. As it cost less labour to bring those metals from the mine to the market, so when they were brought thither they could purchase or command less labour... Equal quantities of labour, at all times and places, may be said to be of equal value to the labourer. In his ordinary state of health, strength and spirits; in the ordinary degree of his skill and dexterity, he must always lay down the same portion of his ease, his liberty, and his happiness. The price which he pays must always be the same, whatever may be the quantity of goods which he receives in return for it. Of these, indeed, it may sometimes purchase a greater and sometimes a smaller quantity; but it is their value which varies, not that of the labour which purchases them. At all times and places that is dear which it is difficult to come at, or which costs much labour to acquire; and that cheap which is to be had easily, or with very little

> labour. Labour alone, therefore, never varying in its own value, is alone the ultimate and real standard by which the value of all commodities can at all times and places be estimated and compared. It is their real price; money is their nominal price only.
>
> (ibid: 50–1)

What we have in these extracts is a theoretical inconsistency – an inconsistency at the level of social scientific practice, or *practice–practice inconsistency*. On the one hand, Smith is offering an explanation of value – that is, he is telling us that value is created through the exercise of human labour power; on the other hand, he is simply defining value – that is, he is telling us that the value of a commodity is equal to the quantity of expended labour power given in exchange for the commodity. In the former idea, the emphasis is on the origin or source of value; in the latter, the emphasis is on the measurement of value. Yet, to maintain theoretical consistency between the theory of production as set out in the opening chapter and the theory of value as set out in the fifth chapter, Smith should have sustained the idea that it is the exercise of human labour power that generates value and that the appropriate measure of value, therefore, should be labour time and thus increasing the productive power of human labour by extending the division of labour and introducing new machinery will save labour time and thereby reduce the value of the commodities being produced.

What explains the theoretical confusion in Smith's argument, I suggest, is the influence, once again, of empiricist thinking. Smith refers continually to the quantity of expended labour power for which a commodity will exchange, because he is thinking that the relationship between the product of human labour and the labourer's reward is the same as the exchange between two commodities; in other words, Smith is thinking that the wage that the labourer receives is equal to the value of the product of his labour. This way of thinking reflects what I call an 'empirical bias' – that is, a focus on what can be observed, which in this particular theoretical context means a focus on acts of exchange. Since human labour, as a causal power, is not something that can be observed directly, it is understandable that an empirical bias in his thinking should lead Smith to reduce human labour power to the product of the exercise of human labour power when he considers the relationship between labourers and those who employ them.

In fact, the empirical bias continues to prevail in the sixth chapter, where Smith sets out his famous components theory of price and where it leads, once more, to theoretical inconsistencies. So, in the first paragraph, Smith introduces the concept of labour time as the measure of value and thereby presupposes that the value of a commodity in exchange is determined by the quantity of labour embodied in it. However, after he has told us why, in commercial society, the labourer has to give up part of the product of his labour to his employer and to the landowner, Smith tells us that the value of each of the three components of the price of a commodity – wages, profit and rent – is determined by the quantity of labour that they will command in exchange:

> The real value of all the different component parts of price, it must be observed, is measured by the quantity of labour which they can, each of them, purchase or command. Labour measures the value not only of that part of price which resolves itself into labour, but of that which resolves itself into rent, and of that which resolves itself into profit.
>
> (ibid: 68)

Moreover, further on, Smith creates more theoretical confusion when he appears to conflate the two different ideas about value:

> As the price or exchangeable value of every particular commodity, taken separately, resolves itself into some one or other or all of those three parts; so that of all the commodities which compose the whole annual produce of the labour of every country, taken complexly, must resolve itself into the same three parts... Wages, profit, and rent, are the three original sources of all revenue as well as of all exchangeable value. All other revenue is ultimately derived from some one or other of these.
>
> (ibid: 69)

Wages, profits and rent are indeed sources of revenue but they cannot at the same time be sources of value. In writing this sentence, Smith appears to be thinking back to the earlier section, where he argued that profits and rent are deductions from the total produce of the labourer and thus to the idea that value is created by the quantity of labour expended in production. So we have, once again, a practice–practice inconsistency.

The significance of the inconsistencies in Smith's social scientific work is that they undermine the claim that Smith was an integrative, interdisciplinary social scientist. I argued in the previous section of this chapter that, to be coherent, social scientific integration must presuppose a transcendental realist ontology; so it is not surprising that, in those parts of his work that are overtly interdisciplinary – such as his theory of the market – Smith should presuppose such an ontology. Yet, Smith's empiricist way of thinking, as revealed in his understanding of value, cuts across his transcendental realist way of thinking. Because it presupposes that we can know about only the effects of the exercise of causal powers, empiricism presupposes an empirical realist ontology and reduces the existence of unobservable causal powers (such as human labour) to the observable effects of their exercise (the product of labour). Consequently, the lack of vertical ontological depth makes it impossible to understand the meaning of categories such as political and economic; for, if the social scientist thinks purely at the level of observable events, he or she will not be able to say why one event is political and another economic (because he or she will have no independent grounds for doing so). By contrast, if we accept that social reality constitutes a domain of causal objects lying beyond what we can experience directly, we can start to find independent reasons for describing one thing as economic and another as political, so that these concepts will no longer be defined according to convention but will express – however imperfectly – some feature or other of social reality.

However, the practical achievement of social scientific integration may be undermined not only by empiricist but also by rationalist thinking. The political economy of David Ricardo provides a clear example of this. When we examine Ricardo's theory of value, as set out in the first section of the first chapter of his *Principles*, we find a clear recognition that the value of commodities in exchange is regulated by the exercise of human labour power:

> In speaking then of commodities, of their exchangeable value, and of the laws which regulate their relative prices, we mean always such commodities only as can be increased in quantity by the exertion of human industry, and on the production of which competition operates without restraint.
>
> In the early stages of society, the exchangeable value of these commodities, or the rule which determines how much of one shall be given in exchange for another, depends almost exclusively on the comparative quantity of labour expended on each.
>
> (Ricardo, [1821] 1951: 21)

When we examine Ricardo's theory of market exchange, we find a similar understanding of causal powers. For example, in the fourth chapter of his *Principles*, Ricardo explains how imbalances in the supply and demand for commodities lead to competition among buyers and sellers, which, in turn, causes the market price of commodities to deviate from the natural price. The difference between market and natural prices leads to a change in capital flows between different sectors of industry and causes the market price to move back towards the natural price. Implicit in this theory is a conception of the market as a social structure and of competition as the causal mechanism regulating the movements of market prices. Indeed, Ricardo acknowledges that other causal powers – what he calls 'accidental causes' – may, when triggered, interfere with the mechanism of competition:

> Having fully acknowledged the temporary effects which, in particular employments of capital, may be produced on the prices of commodities, as well as on the wages of labour, and the profits of stock, by accidental causes, without influencing the general price of commodities, wages, or profits, since these effects are equally operative in all stages of society, we will leave them entirely out of our consideration, whilst we are treating of the laws which regulate natural prices, natural wages and natural profits, effects totally independent of these accidental causes. In speaking then of the exchangeable value of commodities, or the power of purchasing possessed by any one commodity, I mean always that power which it would possess, if not disturbed by any temporary or accidental cause, and which is its natural price.
>
> (ibid: 91–2)

In leaving contingent causes 'out of our consideration' Ricardo is not assuming them out of existence; that is, he is not supposing that the movements of prices, wages and profits will be manifest as empirical regularities; rather, he supposes that the movements of prices, wages and profits are the effects that competition tends to have when it is triggered – that is, that they are real tendencies, as his description of the movements of both market and natural prices in the fifth chapter makes clear:

> With the progress of society the natural price of labour has always a tendency to rise, because one of the principal commodities by which its natural price is regulated, has a tendency to become dearer, from the greater difficulty of producing it. As, however, the improvements in agriculture, the discovery of new markets, whence provisions may be imported, may for a time counteract the tendency to a rise in the price of necessaries, and may even occasion their natural price to fall, so will the same causes produce the correspondent effects on the natural price of labour.
>
> The natural price of all commodities, excepting raw produce and labour, has a tendency to fall, in the progress of wealth and population; for though, on one hand, they are enhanced in real value, from the rise in the natural price of the raw material of which they are made, this is more than counterbalanced by the improvements in machinery, by the better division and distribution of labour, and by the increasing skill, both in science and art, of the producers.
>
> The market price of labour is the price which is really paid for it, from the natural operation of the proportion of the supply to the demand; labour is dear when it is scarce, and cheap when it is plentiful. However much the market price of labour may deviate from its natural price, it has, like commodities, a tendency to conform to it.
>
> (ibid: 93–4)

> The natural tendency of profits then is to fall; for, in the progress of society and wealth, the additional quantity of food required is obtained by the sacrifice of more and more labour. This tendency, this gravitation as it were of profits, is happily checked at repeated intervals by the improvements in machinery, connected with the production of necessaries, as well as by discoveries in the science of agriculture which enable us to relinquish a portion of labour before required, and therefore to lower the price of the prime necessary of the labourer.
>
> (ibid: 120)

However, when Ricardo deals with profit, his argument becomes inconsistent with his previous argument about the determination of value. For example, in the fourth section of the first chapter, Ricardo explains why profits must fall when the value of labour power rises:

> There can be no rise in the value of labour without a fall of profits. If the corn is to be divided between the farmer and the labourer, the larger the proportion that is given to the latter, the less will remain for the former... Suppose, then, that owing to a rise of wages, profits fall from 10 to 9 per cent., instead of adding 550l. to the common price of their goods (to 5,500l.) for the profits on their fixed capital, the manufacturers would add only 9 per cent. on that sum, or 495l., consequently the price would be 5,995l. instead of 6,050l. As the corn would continue to sell for 5,500l., the manufactured goods in which more fixed capital was employed, would fall relatively to corn or to any other goods in which a less portion of fixed capital entered.
>
> (ibid: 35)

The problem here is that profit enters this example as an *unexplained variable*; that is, Ricardo simply assumes an initial rate of profit of ten per cent. He makes the same assumption later on in this section, when arguing that commodities are more valuable the longer they take to bring to market:

> Suppose I employ twenty men at an expense of 1000l. for a year in the production of a commodity, and at the end of the year I employ twenty men again for another year, at a further expense of 1000l. in finishing or perfecting the same commodity, and that I bring it to market at the end of two years, if profits be 10 per cent., my commodity must sell for 2,310l.; for I have employed 1000l. capital for one year, and 2,100l. capital for one year more. Another man employs precisely the same quantity of labour, but he employs it all in the first year; he employs forty men at an expense of 2000l., and at the end of the first year he sells it with 10 per cent. profit, or for 2,200l. Here then are two commodities having precisely the same quantity of labour bestowed on them, one of which sells for 2,310l. – the other for 2,200l.
>
> (ibid: 37)

Nowhere in his *Principles* does Ricardo explain explicitly what profit is and where it comes from. When he tells us in the fourth section of the first chapter that the greater the proportion of corn given to the labourer, the smaller is the proportion given to the farmer, he is suggesting that profits and wages constitute deductions from the total product of the labourer. But, Ricardo does not see – as Marx recognizes[40] – that what he thinks is profit in the extracts above is actually surplus value. Hence, instead of linking profit to the exercise of human labour power, Ricardo treats profit as a kind of surcharge on the necessary value of a commodity (that is, the value that the labourer must produce for his subsistence). The further consequence of this error is that the inverse relationship between wages and profits that Ricardo repeatedly stipulates (especially when he discusses profits explicitly in the sixth chapter) becomes not a real tendency but an empirical *regularity*. By contrast, if Ricardo had shown that the rate of profit depends on the ratio between the surplus value created and the total capital advanced, as

Marx does, he would have understood that it is possible for the rate of profit to change while the wage remains constant.

I suggest that what prevents Ricardo from *explaining* profit is the influence of rationalism in his thinking. Ricardo is implicitly assuming that the deductive logic of his examples guarantees the truth of the proposition that he wishes to demonstrate. In doing so, Ricardo reduces natural necessity to logical necessity, so that the causal power of human labour becomes fixed and predetermined when, in fact, human labour power is liable to produce greater value the longer it is exercised and the more intensely it is exercised (up to a certain limit) and, moreover, that people's power to produce is magnified when they are combined with machines. In short, human labour, as a causal power and as an example of natural necessity, is subject to the influence of the exercise of contingent causal powers and liabilities. The influence of rationalist thinking, therefore, which presupposes a conceptual realist ontology, interferes with the transcendental realist element of Ricardo's thinking and generates inconsistencies in Ricardo's social scientific reasoning.

However, Ricardo's ontological position is made more complicated by the influence of empiricism in his thinking, which supports the rationalist influence in his thinking and which, again, generates theoretical inconsistencies. Recall that Ricardo argues in the first section of the first chapter of his *Principles* that the value of a commodity will fall only when less labour power is expended in its production. However, in the example given above, where Ricardo compares what happens to the price of corn and cloth when profits fall from ten to nine per cent, Ricardo is now arguing that the value of a commodity – in this case cloth – can fall even though the quantity of labour expended in its production has remained constant. Here is the continuation of the passage quoted above:

> The degree of alteration in the relative value of goods, on account of a rise or fall of labour, would depend on the proportion which the fixed capital bore to the whole capital employed. All commodities which are produced by very valuable machinery, or in very valuable buildings, or which require a great length of time before they can be brought to market, would fall in relative value, while all those which were chiefly produced by labour, or which would be speedily brought to market would rise in relative value.
>
> (ibid: 35)

What is happening in this passage and elsewhere is that Ricardo is forming an identity between the value of a commodity in exchange and its *cost price*. In fact, he admits this in a footnote at the end of the sixth section of the first chapter: 'Mr. Malthus appears to think that it is a part of my doctrine, that the cost and value of a thing should be the same; – it is, if he means by cost, "cost of production" including profits' (ibid: 47). But, in forming an identity between exchangeable value and cost price, Ricardo is making the mistake that Smith makes when he sets out his components theory of price; that is, Ricardo is presupposing that profits are a source of exchangeable value, despite insisting that variations in exchangeable value depend only on the expenditure of labour power. It is once again the influence of empiricism in his thinking that prevents him from understanding that exchangeable value is not something that can be perceived directly. We can observe the price of a commodity but, if we think that price and value are the same, how are we to explain the existence of profit? Ricardo's postulation of an inverse relationship between wages and profits should have made him realize that the value that the labourer produces in exchange for his wages is not the same as the cost price, because the labourer produces an extra amount of value for which he is not paid – a surplus – and that it is the existence of this surplus that makes possible the existence of profit.

The empiricist influence in Ricardo's thinking reinforces the rationalist influence in his thinking because both have the effect of leading Ricardo to reduce the existence of unobservable causal powers – in this case, human labour – to their effects – the product of labour – and both thereby entail the actualist fallacy. Of course, the difference between them is that in the one case, empiricism, the domain of events is reduced further to the domain of experiences and, in the other case, rationalism, the domain of events is reduced further to the domain of concepts. We have seen that the influence of both forms of thought is manifest in the social scientific theorizing of Smith and Ricardo as confusion between the measurement of value by means of various empirical categories – such as different sorts of price – and the generation of value by means of non-empirical causal powers, and further confusion between regularities in relationships between empirical categories and (non-empirical) tendencies.

That contradictions at the level of social scientific practice should presuppose contradictions at the level of epistemology and ontology indicates the possibility of a second type of contradiction: that between social scientific practice and professed conceptions of social scientific practice – or *theory–practice inconsistencies*. With practice–practice inconsistencies, the contradictions at the level of social scientific practice are explicit, whereas the contradictory philosophical presuppositions of social scientific practice are implicit and have to be revealed through philosophical inquiry – as we have just seen. By contrast, with theory–practice inconsistencies, the contradiction of interest is between the philosophical presuppositions of social scientific practice and the practitioner's *professed* conception of his or her practice. With theory–practice inconsistencies, then, philosophical inquiry will still be needed to reveal the philosophical presuppositions of social scientific practice but the extent to which it will be required to reveal further the practitioner's conception of science will depend on the extent to which the practitioner has *explicitly* reflected on the nature of his or her practice. For example, some practitioners may have thought about their practice at only a methodological level, whereas others may have engaged in deeper reflections at an ontological level.

We can find examples of theory–practice inconsistencies in the work of Ricardo and his contemporary, Malthus. We have just seen that much of Ricardo's social scientific practice is consistent with a transcendental realist ontology; in particular, a theory of complex and contingent causation. However, when we examine Ricardo's brief reflections on the nature of political economy, we find a different conception of social science emerging – one that is more in line with the rationalist element in his thinking. For example, in a letter to James Mill, Ricardo comments on some discussions he has had with Malthus about the nature of political economy:

> Malthus has been staying with me for a few days... We had plenty of discussion... Political Economy he says is not a strict science like the mathematics, and therefore he thinks he may use words in a vague way, sometimes attaching one meaning to them, sometimes another and quite different. No proposition can surely be more absurd.
>
> (Ricardo, [1821] 1952: 331)

By contrast, in a letter to Malthus, Ricardo attempts to explain the method of reasoning he adopted in his *Principles* in a way that is more consistent with transcendental realist thinking:

> My object was to elucidate principles, and to do this I imagined strong cases that I might shew the operation of those principles. I never thought for example that practically any improvements took place on the land which would at once double its produce, but to shew what the effect of improvements would be undisturbed by any other operating cause.
>
> (Ricardo, [1820] 1952: 184)

The 'strong cases' that Ricardo refers to are abstractions. In making these abstractions, Ricardo intends to understand how particular causal mechanisms, such as human labour power and market exchange, work in isolation of the wider social context in which they are embedded. Indeed, in this respect, Ricardo's work can be seen as a more specialized form of social scientific inquiry than Smith's work. But, as I argued in the previous section of this chapter, specializing in the study of a particular aspect of the social – in Ricardo's case, the economic – does not preclude the possibility of integrating this understanding into a broader understanding of the precise modes of connection between the economic and other aspects of the social.

Moreover, in making these abstractions, Ricardo employs a deductive logic, which can still be consistent with transcendental realism as long as the social scientist understands that, by employing deductive reasoning, he is showing how a particular causal mechanism works in isolation of countervailing causal mechanisms. An isolated causal mechanism, when triggered, will produce a constant conjunction of events – in which case it becomes possible to show by deduction what will be the actual consequence of activating the mechanism. However, if we used deductive reasoning as an end in itself, perhaps because we believe – as at one point Ricardo seems to – that mathematical logic is essential to social scientific inquiry, our practice would not be consistent with the principles of transcendental realism.

We can find further examples of theory–practice inconsistencies in the work of Thomas Malthus. In the introduction to his *Principles of Political Economy*, Malthus reflects explicitly on the nature of the subject matter of his inquiry. At various points in the introduction, his reflections betray the influence of transcendental realist thinking, particularly in his explicit recognition of the possibility of complex causation and in his explicit recognition of the need for empirical assessment of theory:

> In political economy the desire to simplify has occasioned an unwillingness to acknowledge the operation of more causes than one in the production of particular effects; and if one cause would account for a considerable portion of a certain class of phenomena, the whole has been ascribed to it without sufficient attention to the facts, which would not admit of being so solved.
>
> (Malthus, [1836] 1986: 8)

> Where unforeseen causes may possibly be in operation, and the causes that are foreseen are liable to great variations in their strength and efficacy, an accurate yet comprehensive attention to facts is necessary, both to prevent the multiplication of erroneous theories, and to confirm and sanction those that are just.
>
> (ibid: 11)

In recognizing explicitly in these passages the possibility of multiple causation and the possibility of differential causal force, Malthus is presupposing that reality has vertical depth – in the sense that there is a domain of causal objects lying beyond what can be immediately observed – and horizontal depth – in the sense that events are determined by multiple causal objects, some of which may be more powerful in their effects than others.

When we turn to Malthus' social scientific work, we find certain concepts and theories that presuppose a transcendental realist ontology and are thus consistent with the conception of social science that Malthus set out in the introduction to his *Principles*. This is most apparent in the second section of the first chapter, where Malthus follows and develops Smith's definition of productive labour:

> Labour may then be distinguished into two kinds, productive labour, and personal services, meaning by productive labour that labour which is so directly productive of material wealth as to be capable of estimation in the quantity or value of the object produced.
>
> (ibid: 30)

However, when we examine Malthus' theory of value, we find the same preoccupation with the measurement of value as we find in Smith's work. For example, in one of his earlier works, *The Measure of Value*, Malthus argues, as does Smith, that the quantity of labour embodied in a commodity can be a measure of its value in exchange only when the commodity is produced by labour alone. However, once we allow for profits, we can no longer measure value in this way and have to measure the value of a commodity by the quantity of labour that the commodity will command, which is equal to the sum of the quantity of labour 'worked up' in the commodity and the 'profits on all the advances estimated in labour'. As Malthus puts it:

> It appears, then, that in the same country, and at the same time, the exchangeable value of those commodities which can be resolved into labour and profits alone, would be accurately measured by the quantity of labour which would result from adding to the accumulated and immediate labour actually worked up in them the varying amount of the profits on all the advances estimated in labour. But this must necessarily be the same as the quantity of labour which they will command.
>
> (Malthus, [1823] 1986: 188)

In focusing on the question of how to measure value, Malthus' work betrays the same empirical bias that afflicts Smith's work. The result is that Malthus overlooks the significance of human labour as a causal power that can be exercised for varying lengths of time and in varying degrees of intensity; in so doing, he reduces the causal power of human labour to the product of its exercise and treats wages as representing the value of the product of labour rather than as the value of labour power: 'We may also consider as a postulate which will be readily granted, that any given quantity of labour must be of the same value as the wages which command it, or for which it actually exchanges' (ibid: 183). As we saw above, if we treat wages as representing the value of the product of human labour, we cannot explain where profits come from. Hence, profit enters Malthus' argument as an unexplained assumption, just as it does in Ricardo's work.

To the extent, then, that Malthus' theory of value betrays the dual influence of empiricist and rationalist thinking, it contradicts his theory of production, which betrays the (weaker) influence of transcendental realist thinking; it also contradicts his explicit acknowledgement of the reality of underlying causal powers in the introduction to his *Principles*. In short, we can see that Malthus' work is characterized by both theory–practice and practice–practice inconsistencies.

What is interesting about Malthus' reflections on the nature of political economy in the introduction to his *Principles* is that they too are contradictory. We have seen that, in allowing for the possibility of conjunctural causation, Malthus recognizes that a distinction must be made between the existence of causal powers and their effects. The implication of making this distinction is that we cannot assess theories according to their degree of predictive power because we cannot isolate causal objects in the social sciences in the way that we can in the natural sciences. In the social sciences, because we have to confront the reality of an open system, we have to assess our theories according to their degree of explanatory power – that is, according to how many empirically detected events and patterns of interest they can explain. Yet, we find in the introduction to his

*Principles* that Malthus refers continually to the importance of predicting results. In fact, he often seems to combine acknowledgement of the reality of conjunctural causation with a preference for scientific prediction:

> yet there is no truth of which I feel a stronger conviction than that there are many important propositions in political economy which absolutely require limitations and exceptions; and it may be confidently stated that the frequent combination of complicated causes, the action and reaction of cause and effect on each other, and the necessity of limitations and exceptions in a considerable number of important propositions, form the main difficulties of the science, and occasion those frequent mistakes which it must be allowed are made in the prediction of results.
>
> (Malthus, [1836] 1986: 8–9)

> I should be the last person to lay an undue stress upon isolated facts, or to think that a consistent theory, which would account for the great mass of phenomena observable, was immediately invalidated by a few discordant appearances, the reality and the bearings of which there might not have been an opportunity of fully examining. But certainly no theory can have any pretension to be accepted as correct, which is inconsistent with general experience. Such inconsistency appears to me at once a full and sufficient reason of its rejection. Under such circumstances it must be either radically false, or essentially incomplete; and in either case, it can neither be adopted as a satisfactory solution of existing phenomena, nor acted upon with any degree of safety for the future.
>
> (ibid: 10)

> To trace distinctly the operations of that circle of causes and effects in political economy which are acting and reacting on each other, so as to foresee their results, and lay down general rules accordingly, is, in many cases, a task of very great difficulty.
>
> (ibid: 13–14)

> In many cases, indeed, it may not be possible to predict results with certainty, on account of the complication of the causes in action, the different degrees of strength and efficacy with which they may operate, and the number of unforeseen circumstances which are likely to interfere; but it is surely knowledge of the highest importance to be able to draw a line, with tolerable precision, between those cases where the expected results are certain, and those where they are doubtful; and further to be able satisfactorily to explain, in the latter case, the reasons of such uncertainty.
>
> (ibid: 14)

I suggest that it is the influence of empiricism in his thinking about the nature of social science that prevents Malthus from understanding the epistemological implications of the ontology of transcendental realism that he presupposes when acknowledging the reality of complex and contingent causation. In retaining a role for prediction, Malthus presupposes that the objects of social scientific inquiry are constant conjunctions of events manifest as empirical regularities, whereas the implication of a theory of complex and contingent causation is that the social scientist will detect at best only partial regularities. It is in the same empiricist spirit that Malthus claims that a theory's inconsistency with experience is 'at once a full and sufficient reason of its rejection', even though the implication of a theory of complex and contingent causation is that an inconsistency of this sort may well be the result of a defect in the theory – perhaps a misplaced or inadequate abstraction – or be the result of an unforeseen causal force – as Malthus himself acknowledges – in which case we should revise the theory rather than simply reject it. In short, Malthus' reflections on the nature of political economy in the introduction to his *Principles* constitute a classic case of contradiction at the level of philosophical theory – or *theory–theory inconsistency*.

We can find other examples of theory–theory inconsistencies in the works of later political economists who reflected at length on an appropriate methodology for political economy. John Stuart Mill's essay, 'On the Definition of Political Economy; and on the Method of Investigation Proper to It' is a classic example. Mill begins his essay by distinguishing between two modes of reasoning, one of which is induction, the other of which is deduction or what Mill calls 'ratiocination':

> those who are called practical men require *specific* experience, and argue wholly *upwards* from particular facts to a general conclusion; while those who are called theorists aim at embracing a wider field of experience, and, having argued upwards from particular facts to a general principle including a much wider range than that of the question under discussion, then argue *downwards* from that general principle to a variety of specific conclusions...
>
> The first of these methods is a method of induction, merely; the last a mixed method of induction and ratiocination. The first may be called the method *à posteriori*; the latter, the method *à priori*... By the method *à posteriori* we mean that which requires, as the basis of its conclusions, not experience merely, but specific experience. By the method *à priori* we mean (what has commonly been meant) reasoning from an assumed hypothesis; which is not a practice confined to mathematics, but is of the essence of all science which admits of general reasoning at all. To verify the hypothesis itself *à posteriori*, that is, to examine whether the facts of any actual case are in accordance with it, is no part of the business of science at all, but of the *application* of science.
>
> (Mill [1844] 1967: 324–5)

Mill continues by arguing that it is the 'method *à priori*' that is characteristic of political economy and, like Ricardo, makes an analogy with mathematics:

> It reasons . . . from assumptions, not from facts. It is built upon hypotheses, strictly analogous to those which, under the name of definitions, are the foundation of the other abstract sciences. Geometry presupposes an arbitrary definition of a line . . . Just in the same manner does Political Economy presuppose an arbitrary definition of man, as a being who invariably does that by which he may obtain the greatest amount of necessaries, conveniences, and luxuries, with the smallest quantity of labour and physical self-denial with which they can be obtained in the existing state of knowledge.
>
> (ibid: 325–6)

What is most interesting about Mill's account is that it is far from clear what he means by 'assumptions' and how we arrive at them. When Mill explains that the 'method *à priori*' is a 'mixed method of induction and ratiocination', we are led to believe that the assumptions of political economy derive purely from experience. Indeed, at particular points in his essay, Mill tells us that 'The desires of man, and the nature of the conduct to which they prompt him, are within the reach of our observation', and that 'We can also observe what are the objects which excite those desires' (ibid: 329). At another point he tells us:

> If the knowledge what are the particular causes operating in any given instance were revealed to us by infallible authority, then, if our abstract science were perfect, we should become prophets. But the causes are not so revealed: they are to be collected by observation; and observation in circumstances of complexity is apt to be imperfect . . . it is only the habit of long and accurate observation which can give us so correct a preconception what causes we are likely to find, as shall induce us to look for them in the right quarter.
>
> (ibid: 332)

To the extent, therefore, that Mill thinks that the premises of political economy are nothing more than statements about what can be observed, he is implicitly drawing on an empiricist epistemology.

However, when Mill reminds us continually that 'assumptions' are not the same as 'facts', he appears to be suggesting that the premises of political economy may derive from what exists beyond experience. For example, in the following two extracts from his essay, Mill's thinking presupposes a theory of complex and contingent causation, which, in turn, presupposes that causes are irreducible to the level of events and states of affairs. Mill writes of the political economist:

> In proportion as the actual facts recede from the hypothesis, he must allow a corresponding deviation from the strict letter of his conclusion; otherwise it will be true only of things such as he has arbitrarily supposed, not of such things as really exist. That which is true in the abstract, is always true in the concrete with proper *allowances*. When a certain cause really exists, and if

left to itself would infallibly produce a certain effect, that same effect, *modified* by all the other concurrent causes, will correctly correspond to the result really produced.

(ibid: 326–7)

When the principles of Political Economy are to be applied to a particular case, then it is necessary to take account all the individual circumstances of that case; not only examining to which of the sets of circumstances contemplated by the abstract science the circumstances of the case in question correspond, but likewise what other circumstances may exist in that case, which not being common to it with any large and strongly-marked class of cases, have not fallen under the cognizance of the science. These circumstances have been called *disturbing causes*.

(ibid: 330)

Now, if actual events and states of affairs are the product of complex and contingent causal processes lying beyond the realm of experience, it follows that we cannot acquire knowledge of such causal processes directly through observation. Yet, that is what Mill assumes when he claims that the 'method *à priori*' is essential to scientific inquiry.[41] He is assuming that the premises of political economy are not statements about the ways of working of unobservable causal objects but are simply statements about what has been observed and, since what is observed must be a regularity – at least if the political economist is to deduce explanations and predictions – he is assuming that the effects of unobservable causal objects are *always actualized* – in short, that social systems are always closed. But, to assume that causal powers and liabilities are always actualized as constant event conjunctions is to render redundant the philosophical idea that such patterns are the result of the exercise of causal objects lying beyond experience; for, if we accept that causal processes operate not in isolation from but in conjunction with each other, so that the exercise of causal powers and liabilities will *not* always be actualized as a regularity, we have to distinguish between causal laws, which are statements about the effects that causal objects *tend* to have when in exercise, and the actual events and states of affairs that we may observe. In fact, right at the end of his essay, where Mill discusses the nature of generalization, he suggests that causal laws should be thought of as tendencies on the grounds that causal powers may modify each other's effects:

The error, when there is error, does *not* arise from generalizing too extensively... but in making the wrong *kind* of assertion: he predicated an actual result, when he should only have predicated a *tendency* to that result – a power acting with a certain intensity in that direction. With regard to *exceptions*... What is thought to be an exception to a principle is always some other and distinct principle cutting into the former: some other force which impinges against the first force, and deflects it from its direction.

(ibid: 337–8)

The problem with Mill's account of the nature and method of political economy, therefore, is that it is philosophically contradictory. On the one hand, it suggests that the premises of political economy are merely statements about empirical regularities; on the other, it suggests that they are statements about the way political economic causal processes tend to work. A similar sort of philosophical contradiction may be detected in the methodological reflections of J. E. Cairnes. In a series of lectures on *The Character and Logical Method of Political Economy*, Cairnes follows Mill in arguing that political economy is essentially an abstract science that employs the deductive method. But, whereas Mill assumes that the premises of political economy derive from experience, Cairnes offers a more complex – if contradictory – account of the origins of the premises of political economy. Against those who argued that induction was 'the true path of economic inquiry' Cairnes argues that it is not: induction can only be employed in the experimental sciences and political economy is not an experimental science (1875: 63–5). Now, to a certain extent, Cairnes is right to argue that induction is involved in the experimental sciences: when we set up an experiment to isolate a particular causal mechanism, we have produced a closed system and can with good reason make a general claim about how the mechanism we have isolated works from observation of its effects when its causal powers or liabilities are triggered. However, when Cairnes describes how certain physical principles, such as gravity and motion, were discovered, what he is describing is not an inductive logic – which is what he thinks he is describing – but a retroductive logic:

> But the point to be attended to here is that the necessity for the method of induction as the path to physical discovery arose entirely from the fact that *mankind have no direct knowledge of ultimate physical principles*. The law of gravitation and the laws of motion are amongst the best established and most certain of such principles; but what is the evidence on which they rest? We do not find them in our consciousness, by reflecting on what passes in our minds; nor can they be made apparent to our senses... They are not statements of any actual experiences, but, in the words of Mr. Herbert Spencer, 'truths drawn from our actual experiences, but never presented to us in any of them.'... And what is true of the laws of gravitation and of motion is true equally of all the ultimate principles of physical knowledge... all... elude direct observation, and are only known to us through their physical effects.
>
> (ibid: 70–1)

In this extract, Cairnes argues quite clearly that we can only acquire knowledge of causal objects indirectly; that is, we have to infer their existence from observation of their effects. But, to make such an inference, we cannot be reasoning from observation in the particular to observation in general; rather, we must be reasoning 'backwards' from the events we observe to the (un)observable object(s) that caused them. Cairnes is wrong, therefore, to conclude that the 'inductive method... formed the necessary and inevitable path by which, having regard to the limitation of the human faculties, physical investigation was bound, in the outset of its career to proceed' (ibid: 71).

Cairnes adds to the sense of methodological confusion when he discusses how we arrive at knowledge of economic laws. He argues that we do not need to employ an 'elaborate process of induction' to arrive at the premises of political economy because we already have 'direct knowledge' of them 'in our consciousness of what passes in our own minds, and in the information which our senses convey...to us of external facts' (ibid: 75–6). Quite what Cairnes means by acquiring knowledge through 'consciousness' is not clear but this is what he has to say:

> Everyone who embarks in any industrial pursuit is conscious of the motives which actuate him in doing so. He knows that he does so from a desire, for whatever purpose, to possess himself of wealth; he knows that, according to his lights, he will proceed towards his end in the shortest way open to him; that, if not prevented by artificial restrictions, he will buy such materials as he requires in the cheapest market, and sell the commodities which he produces in the dearest. Everyone feels that in selecting an industrial pursuit, where the advantages are equal in other respects, he will select that in which he may hope to obtain the largest remuneration in proportion to the sacrifices he undergoes; or that in seeking for an instrument for what he has realized, he will, where the security is equal, choose those stocks in which the rate of interest to be obtained is highest. With respect to the other causes on which the production and distribution of wealth depend – the physical properties of natural agents, and the physiological character of human beings in regard to their capacity for increase – for these also direct proof, though of a different kind, is available; proof which appeals not indeed to our consciousness, but to our senses.
>
> (ibid: 76–7)

Now, although Cairnes appears to be suggesting at the end of this extract that our 'consciousness' and 'senses' can give us 'direct knowledge' of the world, the main body of the extract presupposes that knowledge of society can be acquired only indirectly; for the sort of knowledge that he claims that 'everyone' has is tacit knowledge of unobservable social causes. The fact that it is tacit, and therefore usually taken for granted, may explain why Cairnes thinks it is 'direct', but it is not. Knowledge of social causes is not simply given to us in our minds but has to be worked out. Indeed, in this case it is a form of practical knowledge that we acquire through 'learning by doing' – through realizing that we have made a mistake and through reflecting on why things did not turn out the way we expected them to. In short, the (fallible) knowledge that constitutes the grounds for our reasons for acting is constructed indirectly from observation and experience of the consequences of our actions. Similarly, when it comes to working out the 'physical properties of natural agents' and 'the physiological character of human beings in regard to their capacity for increase', we can only acquire knowledge of such properties and capacities indirectly by inferring their existence from observation of their effects.

The same sense of methodological confusion crops up again when Cairnes discusses the different ways that hypotheses are used in the physical and social sciences. Having argued that the political economist can conduct experiments 'mentally', by which he means that the political economist can imagine what effects an economic cause would have if it were operating in isolation (ibid: 77–82), Cairnes claims that in physics we develop hypotheses to arrive at knowledge of 'ultimate causes and laws' because these are not 'susceptible of direct proof, through an appeal to the consciousness or senses', whereas in political economy we do not need to develop hypotheses because economic principles *can* be known from consciousness and the senses. As regards political economy,

> Conjecture here would manifestly be out of place, inasmuch as we possess in our consciousness and in the testimony of our senses . . . direct and easy proof of that which we desire to know. In Political Economy, accordingly, hypothesis is never used as a help towards the discovery of ultimate causes and laws.
>
> (ibid: 83–4)

Yet, to suppose that the principles of political economy can be given to us through the 'testimony of our senses', on the one hand, and to suppose that they can be acquired through a process of introspection, perhaps involving 'mental experimentation', on the other, is clearly philosophically contradictory. In the former case, we are supposing that we can have direct knowledge of economic causes, that such causes are always actualized and that they are therefore always observable to us as constant conjunctions of events and states of affairs. In the latter case, we are supposing that knowledge of economic causes cannot be given in experience, that in an open system economic causes take effect in conjunction with a range of other social (and natural) causes and that the observable result cannot be reduced to the effect of the operation of any one cause. In short, Cairnes' methodological position is hopelessly muddled and confused, torn between an implicit empirical realist ontology on the one hand and an implicit transcendental realist ontology on the other. It is surprising that it has attracted so little attention in the contemporary literature on classical social scientific methodology.[42]

## Conclusion

My aim in this chapter was to show how critical realist philosophy of science can justify integrative, interdisciplinary research. In the first section I introduced some of the key primary concepts of critical realism, namely vertical and horizontal ontological depth, and the key secondary concepts of intransitivity, stratification and transfactuality, and showed how these concepts can resolve the dichotomy between the so-called quantitative and qualitative research paradigms.

In the second section, I showed how a revised theory of integrative pluralism, deriving from the concepts of original and dialectical critical realism, offers a more coherent justification for scientific differentiation and integration than either positivism or postmodernism. I defined and exemplified two key types of causal process: (inter)dependence and influence (or interaction). I argued that the former process is an essential characteristic of emergent wholes, such as structures and totalities, and that the latter process establishes the openness and partiality of such entities. I then argued that it is in virtue of the possibility of multiple determination that scientists must decide which entities at which levels of reality generate the event(s) or state(s) of affairs of interest and therefore need to be able to identify different types of causal object as well as understand their mode(s) of articulation – hence the need for scientific specialization (to understand the differentiation of reality) and scientific integration (to understand its interconnection).

In the third section, I showed, through a case study of classical political economy, how a failure to sustain a transcendental realist ontology undermines the ability of social scientists to produce integrative, interdisciplinary research within the social sciences and their ability to understand the potential to produce this sort of research. I argued that this failure is revealed through practice–practice, theory–practice and theory–theory inconsistencies and that it is explained by the dual, reinforcing influences of empiricism and rationalism, which interfere with, and thereby distort, the transcendental realist basis of social scientists' thinking.[43]

How, though, do empiricism and rationalism undermine the transcendental realist basis of social scientists' thinking? It may seem *prima facie* that these two epistemological positions are in direct opposition to one another: whereas the one privileges and so fetishizes human experience, the other privileges and so fetishizes human thought. However, their opposition is in fact a pretence because the two positions are necessary to one another. For example, both positions presuppose an actualist ontology and epistemology, by which I mean that both reduce the reality of natural necessity and possibility to the actuality of events and states of affairs – as in empiricism – and of concepts – as in rationalism. Hence, the empiricist searches for regularity in observation and finds this in constant conjunctions of events and states of affairs, while the rationalist searches for regularity in thought and finds this in formal logic. Both imply a denial of the independent existence and transfactual efficacy of causal powers and liabilities and in this they complement one another: empiricism conceals the reality of natural necessity and possibility by ensuring that the objects of scientific inquiry are the objects only of experience; while rationalism conceals the reality of natural necessity and possibility by ensuring that the object of scientific inquiry is only logical necessity. Both positions, then, are necessary to one another: rationalism assumes that causal powers and liabilities are always exercised as regularities, while empiricism assumes that nothing beyond observed (and observable) regularities exists. Accordingly, although they may appear to be 'dialectical antagonists', in actual fact they are 'dialectical counterparts' (Bhaskar, 1993: 88) and we should not be surprised to find – as we did in the work of the classical political economists – their joint influence.

The key point, though, is that empiricism and rationalism are negative forces – that is, they tend to prevent scientists from thinking about ontological depth (both vertical and horizontal); for, as soon as we fall into the trap of the actualist fallacy, we become unable to make sense of the differentiation and interconnection of reality and hence the necessity for scientific differentiation and integration. The empiricist attempts to make sense of the differentiation of the social sciences at the level of events and states of affairs but is unable to say why we should use categories such as economic, political and cultural when re-describing and explaining events of interest; the rationalist attempts to make sense of the differentiation of the social sciences at the level of logical reason but is unable to say why some concepts are economic and others political. Hence, both empiricists and rationalists must appeal to convention to make sense of the classification of science.

However, empiricists and rationalists have turned the problem of scientific differentiation and integration into an opportunity. By incorporating the specific categories of the social sciences into the method of rational choice theory and re-defining them as different types of rational man – for example, rational economic man – they have created a form of interdisciplinarity that is purely methodological in nature – a form of interdisciplinarity that has been called 'economics imperialism' (Fine and Milonakis, 2009). It should be clear by now that this sort of interdisciplinarity does not amount to the integration of knowledge from different disciplines: it is simply the methodological unification of the social sciences masquerading as social scientific integration – a topic I return to at the end of Chapter 5.

# 3 Towards a theory of knowledge production

In the previous chapter, I presented an ontological justification for the integration of knowledge from different academic disciplines. In this chapter, I move from ontology to science; that is, I present a social scientific theory about the nature of knowledge production.

In Chapter 1, I argued that the traditional understanding of a scientific discipline, in presupposing a positivistic conception of science, was inadequate for the task of explaining the difficulty of producing integrative, interdisciplinary research. Clearly, then, we need to find a more adequate conception of a scientific discipline if we are to develop a solution to the problem of integrating knowledge.

The essence of my argument in this chapter is that disciplined, scientific inquiry presupposes an underlying context of (interdependent) social structures – such as recognition and reward, academic employment, the scientific division of labour, and so forth – and (logically related) ideas – namely, philosophical and scientific theories. I argue that these structures and ideas are the real (even if unobservable) conditions for scientific inquiry and, as such, facilitate the differentiation of knowledge production through disciplinary-based inquiry, yet constrain the production of integrative forms of knowledge through interdisciplinary scientific inquiry. It is the failure to comprehend the reality of this context – in all its complexity – that explains – at least in part – why attempts to encourage the integration of knowledge through the establishment of interdisciplinary research centres and institutes have not had the expected success.

Of course, in developing a theory of knowledge production, I am not starting from scratch because philosophers and sociologists of science have already attempted to develop theories of scientific development. I take these theories as my starting point in the first section of the chapter. Much of the argument of this section relates to the work of Thomas Kuhn (1962), who attempted to overcome the separation of the philosophy of science from the sociology of science. The latter discipline has tended to treat the context of scientific discovery as problematic and to take the context of scientific justification for granted, while the former has tended to do the opposite. However, in forging a relationship between the socio-psychological and intellectual conditions of science, Kuhn's work shows that the problem of scientific discovery is implicated in, and so cannot be divorced from, the problem of scientific justification, and *vice versa*. However,

Kuhn's theory is not without its limitations. Therefore, in the second section, I attempt to build a theory of knowledge production that overcomes these limitations and I do so by drawing on work in the sociology of science, particularly that of Richard Whitley (1984).

The key to understanding my theory of knowledge production is to recognize, firstly, that the social organization of science depends on the existence of a set of ideas, which may be divided into scientific and philosophical categories, and, secondly, that it is by virtue of the social organization of science that these ideas continue to exist and to be developed, because it is through the social practices associated with scientific inquiry that scientific fields are reproduced and transformed. Hence, there is an important relationship between the social and intellectual conditions of scientific inquiry. Moreover, when we examine each set of conditions separately we see two highly complex entities: a system or totality of ideas related to each other by logical necessity and a system or totality of materially based structures related to each other by natural necessity – both of which may be subject to internal and external contradictions.

In the third section, I apply my theory to the discipline of economics. Why choose economics? There has been an upsurge of criticism of the lack of intellectual pluralism within and the lack of practical relevance of modern economics, especially from the so-called post-autistic economics movement (Fullbrook, 2003, 2004, 2007). Although this movement has presented a thoroughgoing critique of the scientific and philosophical assumptions of orthodox economics, it has largely ignored the question of how the dominance of positivist ideas in economics is sustained. This is an important question to answer, not least if the movement is to achieve its aim of transforming the discipline of economics. What is needed, therefore, is a clearer understanding of the social and intellectual conditions for the hegemony of economic orthodoxy. The argument of the third section attempts to meet this need by applying the theory of knowledge production developed in the second section to the case of economics. In the concluding section, I consider the implications of my argument for the possibility of integrating knowledge through interdisciplinary research and set out the hypotheses that informed the empirical investigation of the (collaborative) interdisciplinary research projects discussed in Chapters 4 and 5.

## Theories of scientific development: philosophical and sociological perspectives

The explanation of scientific continuity and change has been a perplexing issue for philosophers and sociologists of science. Positivist philosophers have characteristically argued that scientific development is a cumulative process in which incorrigible facts about the world – that is, atomistic events and states of affairs, the constant conjunctions of which constitute causal laws – are recorded passively through observation and experience (Von Mises, 1951; Ayer, 1959; Hempel, 1966). In other words, positivist philosophy presents a picture of scientific continuity in which any scientific change that does occur is simply the result of the more accurate recording of empirical regularities. Early sociologists of science in America largely accepted this monistic account of scientific development, incorporating it into structural-functional explanations of scientists' behaviour. Thus, Merton argued that particular sociocultural norms were functional to 'the extension of certified knowledge' (1973: 270), an argument that Merton's followers, Hagstrom (1965) and Storer (1966), tacitly accepted.[1] However, having defined knowledge by the activity that produced it, so that science was simply the result of what scientists did, sociologists left themselves unable to explain how scientific ideas were produced – what Merton took for granted as the 'extension' of knowledge – and how they became socially validated – what Merton took for granted as the certification of knowledge. But, most important of all, the determinism built into the structural-functional approach left it unclear how scientific ideas changed. In short, in tacitly reducing the cognitive dimension of science to the social, Merton and his followers operated with a 'black box theory of knowledge' (Whitley, 1972: 63) and thus an inadequate theory of scientific development.

By contrast, Thomas Kuhn (1962) treated the cognitive dimension of science, and thus the nature of scientific ideas, as problematic and, in doing so, attempted to overcome the deficiencies of Merton's approach. Scientific development, Kuhn argued, is not a continuous but a discontinuous process, characterized by 'revolutions' in the 'paradigm' that makes possible the observation and interpretation of phenomena. During periods of 'normal science', scientists do not question the validity of the prevailing paradigm but refine and articulate it by solving intellectual puzzles or 'anomalies'. It is only when scientists are no longer able to generate problem–solutions (a period of scientific crisis or 'exceptional science') that they will replace the existing paradigm with one that can make sense of the persistent anomalies. The new paradigm is then codified and reproduced through the education system and 'normal science' resumes.

Undoubtedly, in treating both the cognitive and social conditions of scientific inquiry as problematic, Kuhn's theory helped to recast the relationship between the sociology, philosophy and the history of science. In particular, the theory pointed towards the possibility that the nature of scientific ideas might have something to do with the organization of science and *vice versa*. But, Kuhn could not explore this possibility because his conception of a scientific paradigm could not cope with the reality of philosophical contradictions and status differentials of forms of knowledge within a given scientific community. According to Kuhn's theory, such features were simply characteristic of scientific immaturity or pre-paradigmatic science.

What, then, is problematic about Kuhn's conception of a scientific paradigm? Martins (1972) has argued that Kuhn implicitly assumes that paradigms are independent, perfectly integrated and equally causally influential wholes, when in fact they may be interdependent, integrated and causally influential to different degrees. Indeed, Martins argues that, through the interaction of paradigms, which are subdisciplinary and so equivalent to research specialties, there may emerge 'cognitive orientations' and that the two sorts of intellectual structure are thereby mutually influential (ibid: 21). In this respect, Martins is pointing to the possibility that the intellectual frameworks upon which scientists draw may be differentiated by type of idea, such that some ideas are more fundamental than others. I say more about this in the following section. For now, the important point to take from this critique is that cognitive development in science is a much more complicated process than Kuhn imagined.

Critics have also identified confusion in the way that Kuhn uses the concept of scientific paradigm. It is important to consider this line of criticism because it has implications for the relationship between sociocultural structure and human agency (which is an issue that I address explicitly in the following section). The critic in this case is Masterman, who identifies 'not less than twenty-one different senses' in which Kuhn uses the concept of paradigm. Masterman argues that these can be categorized into 'metaphysical', 'sociological', and 'construct' or 'artefact' paradigms (1970: 61–6). Now, clearly, the existence of multiple meanings of 'paradigm' is problematic for those who ask what one is. For example, Shapere has argued that 'the breadth of definition of the term "paradigm"' reduces its 'explanatory value'; when Kuhn refers to the term in a concrete sense 'it is too easy to identify a paradigm' and when Kuhn refers to it in a metaphysical sense, 'it is not easy to determine . . . what the paradigm is supposed to have been'. Of course, as a positivist, Shapere is sceptical that paradigms – at least those of a metaphysical sort – even exist; that, in short, there really is anything going on 'behind-the-scenes' that might 'compel us to adopt a mystique regarding a single paradigm' (1964: 385–8).

Yet, as Masterman rightly points out, without accepting the existence of a paradigm, positivist philosophers 'cannot account for how any new research line suddenly starts up'; in other words, they cannot explain where – to use Popper's term – theoretical 'conjectures' come from (Masterman, 1970: 71). Thus, positivist philosophers are guilty of reducing scientific thinking to philosophical thinking: what Masterman calls 'philosophy-of-science aetherialism'. Kuhn has not committed this error in her view, because his theory is rooted in 'the actual set of habits which, in fact, characterize any new science' (ibid: 72). In other words, it is the 'construct' paradigm – 'the trick, or device, which starts off any new science or research line', which, in Masterman's view, makes normal science possible and which 'has to be Kuhn's primary sense of paradigm' (ibid: 73). The construct paradigm is a 'way of seeing' one thing in terms of another; it presents 'a concrete "picture" of something, A, which is used analogically to describe a concrete something else, B' (ibid: 77).

However, even if the construct paradigm is Kuhn's 'primary sense of paradigm', the difficulty remains of explaining this sort of paradigm; that is, of explaining how it is possible to make a 'crude analogy' in the first place and, moreover, one that is 'incomparable with any other crude analogy' (ibid: 79). As we have just seen, Masterman argues that Kuhn's construct paradigm is a correction to the positivist reduction of science to philosophy. The danger is that, in making this claim, Masterman has gone too far and has committed the opposite error, that of reducing philosophy to science. For example, when Kuhn asks why 'the concrete scientific achievement' is 'prior to the various concepts, laws, theories, and points of view that may be abstracted from it' (Kuhn, 1996: 11), Masterman argues that Kuhn has 'made clear that... something sociologically describable, and above all, concrete, already exists in actual science, at the early stages, *when the theory is not there*' (Masterman, 1970: 66; emphasis added).

Moreover, Masterman emphasizes that Kuhn:

> never, in fact, equates 'paradigm', in any of its senses, with 'scientific theory'. For his metaparadigm is something far wider than, and ideologically prior to, theory... His sociological paradigm... is also *prior to theory*, and *other than theory*, since it is something concrete and observable: i.e. a set of habits. And his construct-paradigm is less than a theory, since it can be something as little theoretic as a single piece of apparatus: i.e. anything which can cause actual puzzle-solving to occur.
>
> (Masterman, 1970: 66–7; emphasis added)

Can a sociological paradigm be 'prior to' and 'other than' a scientific theory? Bhaskar (1975) has argued that scientific experiments are the means by which scientists isolate hitherto unknown structures and mechanisms thought to be responsible for generating empirical phenomena. Being able to identify a causal mechanism in this way presupposes having a hunch about, or rough idea of, the object in question, because the point of a scientific experiment is to isolate the effect of one particular causal mechanism from the effects of others. Hence, a sociological paradigm cannot be 'prior to' and 'other than' a scientific theory because the latter is implicit in the very possibility of the former. It is theory that has temporal priority over concrete scientific activity because it is the hypothesis that makes possible the 'set of habits' scientists adopt when solving puzzles. It is the 'metaphysical' paradigm that is the source of hypotheses because, as Kuhn has made clear, a paradigm is a way of seeing – a 'world view' – as much as a 'concrete scientific achievement'. Indeed, Masterman admits as much when she writes that Kuhn's 'metaparadigm is something far wider than, and ideologically prior to, theory'.

What is also interesting is that Masterman admits that any attempt to define a paradigm in a 'purely sociological sense' will become trapped in circular reasoning:

> For, to establish the paradigm's (temporal) priority to theory in scientific action, we have to define it, sociologically, as an *already known* concrete scientific achievement, an *already established* set of habits. But how does the scientist himself, in a new science, first find out that what he is following is going to become a concrete scientific achievement, unless he already knows that he is following a paradigm?
>
> (Masterman, 1970: 69)

Masterman attempts to get out of this trap by forcing a distinction between what a paradigm 'is' and what one 'does':

> if we ask what a Kuhnian paradigm is, Kuhn's habit of multiple definition poses a problem. If we ask, however, what a paradigm *does*, it becomes clear at once (assuming always the existence of normal science) that the construct sense of 'paradigm', and not the metaphysical sense or metaparadigm, is the fundamental one. For only with an artefact can you solve puzzles.
>
> (ibid: 70)

But, surely, explaining what a paradigm 'does' presupposes knowing what one 'is'? Moreover, if it is not possible to define a paradigm in either the construct or sociological sense alone, how is it possible to solve puzzles 'only with an artefact'? While it may be the case that the 'explicit metaphysics' follows 'long after' the establishment of the construct paradigm (ibid: 69–70), the point remains that the very existence of a construct or artefact presupposes an implicit metaphysics. If this is the case, it does not make sense to argue that the construct or artefact paradigm is 'primary' or 'fundamental' if this means that it exists before a philosophy. Scientists may not be fully cognizant of the philosophical assumptions they are making when they work with a construct or artefact – as I argue below – but those assumptions are always implicit in any scientific inquiry. It usually falls to philosophers to render them explicit.

Of course, Kuhn's assumption that paradigms are incommensurable has also come under fire and has generated a heated debate between Kuhn and revisionist positivists such as Popper and Lakatos (Lakatos and Musgrave, 1970). Positivists argue that Kuhn cannot sustain the idea of scientific progress as the rational extension of knowledge while at the same time maintaining that paradigms are incommensurable because the assumption of incommensurability implies that it is not possible to compare the truth content of paradigms – so that scientists appear epistemologically irrational. Yet, if scientists are to be considered epistemologically rational, positivists argue, they must be able to make such comparisons (Popper, 1970; Lakatos, 1970). Kuhn's reply (1970a: 21), that, by scientific progress, he meant the continuation of the tradition of puzzle solving – one of the 'paramount' values of science – rather than the closer approximation of scientific inquiry to the truth, fails to deal with this criticism. On the one hand, to claim that scientific progress amounts to the continuation of puzzle solving is a rather strange notion of progress. As King has observed, it takes Kuhn away from trying to explain scientific change, which is supposed to be one of the key features of his argument and back towards an emphasis on scientific continuity (King, 1971: 29–32). Indeed, the value of puzzle solving that Kuhn invokes seems eerily reminiscent of the normative approach Merton used to explain scientific development. On the other hand, in arguing that there is a standard of science of one sort or another that guarantees scientific progress, Kuhn accepts implicitly that paradigms do have something in common – even if this is a basic conception of puzzle solving – and so can be compared – an acceptance that contradicts his commitment to incommensurability and his scepticism about truth.

From the perspective of critical realism, the assumption of paradigm incommensurability involves two mistakes: the epistemic fallacy and the sociological fallacy.[2] The epistemic fallacy (or the reduction of ontological questions to epistemological questions), which positivists also commit when they reduce reality to what can be known through sensory experience, makes it difficult to understand how knowledge changes while reality remains unchanged and of how knowledge remains unchanged while reality changes. However, if we accept that paradigms may be in competition with each other, as Einstein's was with Newton's, we cannot assume that they are incommensurable because the possibility of scientific competition presupposes that the paradigms have something in common – that there are similarities as well as differences between them – so that they can be rationally compared. If Einstein's theories of relativity can explain everything that Newton's mechanics can and more, then we have good reason to believe that Einstein's theories represent scientific progress. Yet, Newton and Einstein were not living in different worlds; they were trying to make sense of the *same* world. Therefore, we have to make a clear distinction between the *intransitive* objects of scientific inquiry, which constitute the reality independent of our knowledge, and the *transitive* objects of scientific inquiry – the socially and historically specific forms of knowledge of reality – if we are to make sense of scientific progress (Bhaskar, 1975).[3]

The reality of scientific competition suggests that scientific change – or 'revolutionary science' as Kuhn has it – is not a simple matter of scientific elites manipulating the prevailing scientific paradigm at will and that continuity – or 'normal science' – is not a simple matter of socialization and internalization of scientific norms, so that there is complete scientific consensus – all of which is the implication of the sociological fallacy (or the reduction of epistemological questions to sociological questions). Rather, it seems that scientific change is inherently contested – as the multiple paradigm conflicts in the social sciences indicate. According to their position in the social hierarchy, some scientists will be more able either to resist or promote change than others, so that we cannot assume that what happens in the cognitive context of knowledge production is determined by what happens in the social context. If scientists either exploit or conceal intellectual contradictions and inconsistencies, this implies that what happens in the cognitive context of science has implications for what happens in the social context and *vice versa*. It is important, therefore, that we recognize the complexity of intellectual conflict and that this has implications for the possibility of scientific continuity and change. (Below I show how intellectual conflict characterizes the present state of economics while, in Chapters 4 and 5, I show how attempts to achieve intellectual integration through interdisciplinary research are in conflict with the prevailing norm of disciplinary specialization.)

The possibility of scientific conflict means that we have to make a clear analytical distinction not only between the social and cognitive contexts of knowledge production but also between scientific activity and the social and cognitive contexts that pre-exist it. Indeed, this is one of the key points of Archer's account of the dynamic interplay between sociocultural systems and sociocultural action (Archer, 1995). We must assiduously avoid reducing one to the other; for, if we make scientific inquiry a by-product of the socio-intellectual context, we can understand scientific continuity but not change and, if we make the socio-intellectual context the by-product of scientific inquiry, we can understand scientific change but not continuity. We must also avoid conflating the two. Only if we examine the interplay between human agency and socio-intellectual structure through time can we start to explore the possibility of a more complex set of dynamics in which scientific change and continuity and conflict and consensus are in continual, symbiotic tension. The use of concepts such as 'sociological rationality' and epistemological rationality' (Whitley, 1972: 87, fn. 4) should be avoided, then – at least if this usage encourages the view that scientists act either in a sociological sense or in an epistemological sense. Such concepts confuse the underlying conditions of scientific inquiry with the actual practice of scientific inquiry; for human rationality, which is a property of the people who occupy the position of scientist, is conditioned by social as well as intellectual structures. Hence, the challenge for sociologists of science is to determine empirically what Martins (1972: 45) calls the 'relative potencies' of different aspects of scientific activity, social and intellectual or, as King puts it, the challenge is to determine the relationships between 'modes of thought, work-styles, and the social positions of scientific men' (1971: 31). But, to do this, we need to understand more clearly the nature of the elements King describes.

## The social and intellectual conditions of knowledge production

Before we can start to address the relationship between the social and intellectual conditions of knowledge production, we need to examine the nature of the two sets of conditions separately. As we saw above, Kuhn's thesis implies that there are social mechanisms reproducing cognitive norms. Although it points to the role played by the education and training system in the codification and reproduction of scientific paradigms, it has less to say about the relative importance of other sorts of social structure involved in the reproduction and transformation of scientific paradigms, such as the academic career hierarchy and the peer review system. Moreover, what sorts of ideas are the bases for cognitive and technical norms in science and how are these ideas related to each other? Again, the different meanings Kuhn attaches to the concept of paradigm do not help us to answer such questions. Therefore, we need to clarify the nature of the constituents of the social and intellectual conditions of science.[4]

Sociologists of science have attempted to elaborate explicitly upon the nature of the social and intellectual contexts of science (Whitley, 1974a; Knorr *et al.*, 1975; Mendelsohn *et al.*, 1977; Knorr *et al.*, 1980; Elias *et al.*, 1982). Perhaps the most significant line of inquiry – at least for our purposes – is that developed by Richard Whitley, who has attempted to understand different aspects of the relationship between the social and intellectual conditions of science. For example, Whitley has analyzed differences in the degree of social and cognitive institutionalization of scientific fields (1974b), differences in the organization of work, training and authority between 'unrestricted' and 'restricted' sciences (1977a) and, more broadly, has shown how differences in the institutionalization of 'intellectual resources', through education, training, employment and recognition and reward structures, imply differences in patterns of scientific development (1980). In short, the significance of this line of inquiry, which culminates in *The Intellectual and Social Organisation of the Sciences* (1984), is that it demonstrates how the nature of scientific ideas influences the social structuring of scientific fields and *vice versa*.

Let us take a closer look at one of Whitley's arguments. Whitley claims that a particular form of knowledge – what he calls the '"arithmetic" ideal' – has become institutionalized in 'restricted' sciences, such as physics, and is also becoming institutionalized in 'unrestricted sciences' such as biology and economics (1977b). Now, in restricted sciences, where arithmetization is dominant, there is a clear division of labour between theoretical and applied work, which is reinforced socially through a status differential so that theoreticians, who concentrate on mathematical modelling, are more prestigious and have greater authority than experimenters, whose work cannot be formalized in the same way. In other words, because theoretical scientists' claims to higher prestige and authority derive from the nature of mathematical formalism, which represents knowledge in a complete, perfect and final form, their work must be clearly separated from that of applied scientists, which is much more uncertain and incomplete. Once arithmetic reasoning becomes the benchmark for science, though, all sciences whether restricted or unrestricted, are obliged to trade mathematical formalism for respectability and recognition.

However, although this sort of argument about the relationship between the social and intellectual conditions of science takes us towards an explanation of how and why sciences differ in their organization, it is perhaps less able to deal with the reality of scientific conflict and change. For example, in later work, Whitley has argued that theoretical economics – that is, mathematical modelling – dominates applied economics because the uncertainty deriving from the results of the application of formal models – manifest most obviously in predictive failures – challenges the alleged certainties of mathematical models. Claiming and winning higher prestige, therefore, is one way in which mathematical modellers can continue their line of work, insulated from the vagaries and uncertainties associated with its application (1986, 1991). I say more about how well this argument applies to the current state of economics in the third section below. For now, I want to consider a question that arises from this argument, which is why it is so important that mathematical modelling in economics should survive. I want to suggest that, to answer this question, we need to look more closely at the philosophical presuppositions of formal modelling and the relationship between these presuppositions and the society in which they are reproduced; for it may be that the philosophical assumptions implicit in mathematical modelling of *social* phenomena justify and so negate challenges to the social conditions for the reproduction of mathematical models. It may be that the dominance of mathematical modelling in certain social sciences reflects the dominance of a particular set of philosophical assumptions throughout society. In short, if we introduce explicitly a philosophical category into our understanding of the intellectual context of science, we can start to understand more clearly how scientific ideas can become a force blocking changes to the organization of society and so of science. But, before we do this, we need to understand in greater detail *how* it is possible for particular forms of knowledge to become dominant within scientific disciplines. We must therefore examine the nature of the social context of knowledge production.

### *The social context*

An appropriate point of entry to examining the social context of knowledge production is to consider more generally the meaning of the term 'social'. Critical realist philosophers and social theorists (Bhaskar, 1998; Archer, 1995; Lawson, 1997; Lewis, 2000) have argued that social reality is neither simply the intentional creation of autonomous individuals nor somehow external to, and so determining of, individuals' actions. They argue that social reality is inherently relational – comprising both internal and external relations between positions – and emergent, in the sense that it is only from internal relations that social structures arise and have causal powers *sui generis*. Human agents – that is, people who have the capacity to formulate and execute plans of action – occupy or slot into societal positions, which pre-exist them, because current positions are the outcomes of the actions of previous occupants of societal positions. In following the rules or norms, formal or informal, associated with the occupancy of such positions, human agents carry out various social practices. In this way, social structure modifies human agency. But, since different sorts of rules and different sets of resources may be invested in different structural positions, some occupants may have more power and so may be less constrained than others. In other words, structural relations may be hierarchical.

Critical realists emphasize that social structures and human agency, although distinct entities, do not exist apart from one another – rather, that they are ontologically interdependent and so irreducible to one another. For example, social practices such as talking and driving would not be possible without pre-existing rules of grammar and rules of the road, respectively, but the rules of grammar and rules of the road would not exist without the social practices that either reproduce or transform them. Hence, actors cannot be creating social structures *ex nihilo* and as they wish, which is the error of voluntarism, because intentional human action presupposes the existence of social structures; social structures cannot be coercive of human agency, which is the error of determinism, because human actions, such as breaking rules, may have unintended consequences. In other words, it is because human agents may not be fully cognizant of the conditions for their motivated productions that they may unintentionally reproduce and transform those conditions through their intentional actions.

However, although it is usual for human agents to be only partially aware of the social context confronting them, the unequal distribution of power, wealth and status characteristic of that context gives rise to vested interests, so that some occupants of structural positions will be predisposed to social change, while others will be concerned to preserve the status quo. Hence, the hierarchical nature of social structures gives rise to the possibility of social conflict and it is at times of social conflict that people may become much more aware of the social conditions of their existence. Indeed, individuals in the same position in society may develop a common consciousness and join forces in the hope of prosecuting their interests more successfully. However, if the understanding of society that motivates collective acts of social transformation is incomplete or inadequate, such attempts may fail – at least to the extent that they have unintended and undesired consequences. Certain cultural forms, by presenting a misleading or false view of society, often have a crucial role to play in generating such failures and thereby helping to protect the status quo (as I discuss below).

If we think of society, therefore, as an ensemble of different sorts of social structure, such that systems or totalities of social structures may emerge, we should expect that the social context of science will also constitute a system or totality of social structures and, following the argument of Chapter 2, will be *complex*. But which social structures do scientists draw upon? Existing research in the sociology of science suggests that the following categories of social structures must be considered as particularly important influences on scientists' decision making: the structure of employment, the structure of recognition and reward, the structure of education and training, and the structure of scientific work (Whitley, 1980: 308–18). Now, given that these concepts designate different categories of social structure, there will of course be different *instances* of each category. Thus, scientists work in different institutional settings – in private industry, in government, as well as in the academic sector – and, in each setting, the way the structure of employment works will be slightly different, in the sense that the positions in the career hierarchy will differ, along with the research tasks, training, rewards and status associated with each position. Consequently, the context scientists work in may have important implications for the definition and reproduction of scientific fields. In academic contexts, scientists largely determine their own tasks and goals and it is their reputation among their peers that determines their employment ranking and the rewards they receive. Moreover, because academic scientists may also take on a teaching as well as a research role, they can influence the direction of scientific development and the reproduction of scientific fields. By contrast, in the employment context of private industry and government, scientists' work goals are determined largely by their employers and their employment status and rewards will depend on their contribution to the goals of the organization for which they work. But, because the needs of private industry and government may conflict with the scientific community's need to reproduce the field of knowledge, scientists working in non-academic sectors may find it more difficult to influence the direction of scientific development than their academic counterparts (Whitley, 1982: 313–28).

The connections between the different social structures pertaining to the production of knowledge are set out in Figure 3.1. They consist of both internal and external relations, both symmetrical and asymmetrical, so that we have relations of causal dependence and interdependence on the one hand and relations of causal influence and interaction on the other. Looking at pairs of structures in turn, we can say the following.

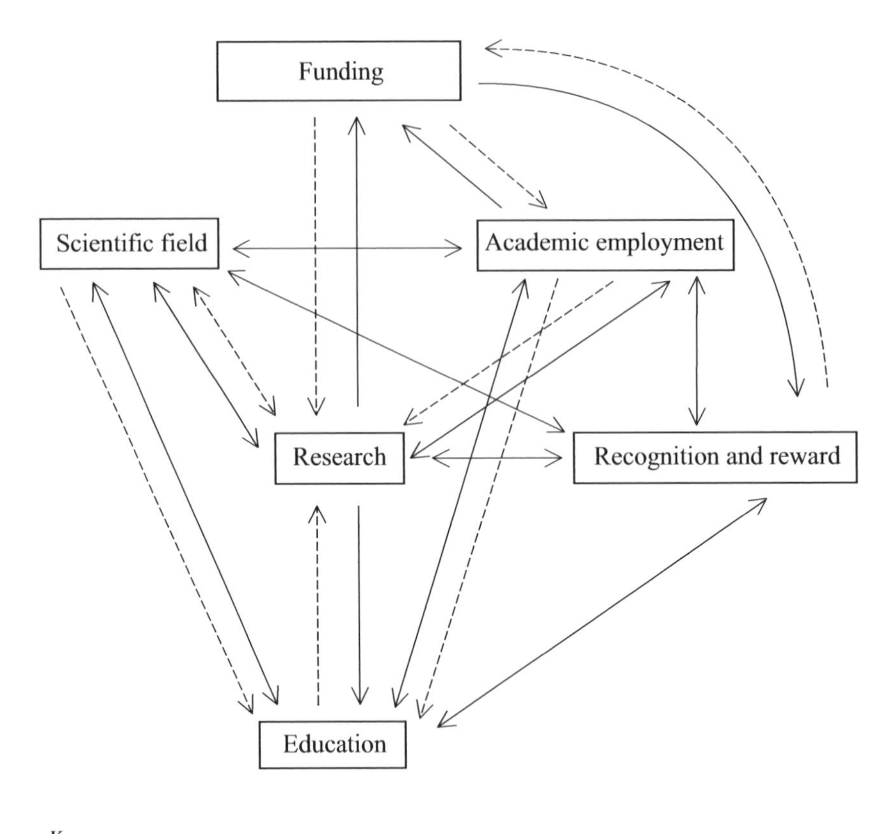


*Figure 3.1* The social system of knowledge production

- Academic employment and scientific fields:
  The reproduction of scientific fields would not be possible without academic employment because, as employees, scientists obtain the resources they need to undertake scientific inquiry, while their employment as academics would not be possible without a scientific field in which to practise. Hence, the structures of science and academic employment are interdependent.
- Scientific fields and recognition–reward:
  The reproduction of scientific fields also depends on the practice of peer review because the products of scientific inquiry have to be evaluated by the scientific community before they can be certified as genuine contributions to

knowledge. However, the practice of peer review would not be possible without an existing body of knowledge against which to compare new contributions to knowledge within a particular field. Hence, the structures of scientific fields and recognition–reward are interdependent.

- Academic employment and recognition–reward:
  Scientists compete among their peers to win reputations for contributions to knowledge and to acquire greater control over the direction of science. Hence, their entry to, and progression through, the academic career ladder depends on the results of the practice of peer review. Yet, the evaluation of new contributions to knowledge would not be possible unless the scientific community had the resources required to review new work. Hence, the structures of recognition–reward and academic employment are interdependent.
- Academic employment and research:
  The structure of research refers to the particular ways in which research projects are organized (and is thus distinct from the structure of scientific fields). For example, one often finds research teams led by a principal investigator who is responsible for managing the work carried out by research fellows, officers and assistants.[5] But, the prosecution of research projects would not be possible without a supporting academic employment context, while the practice of research is what (in part) defines the employment structure as academic. Hence, the structures of academic employment and research are interdependent. However, the way the academic employment structure works may also affect the way structures of research work. For example, university managers may expect employees to prepare collaborative, interdisciplinary research project proposals in response to demands from external research funders (such as the UK Research Councils).
- Academic employment and education:
  The structure of (higher) education refers to the way in which teaching, learning and assessment is organized – typically through relations between teachers and students, examiners and examinees, course leaders and tutors, and so on.[6] Higher education depends on the structure of academic employment because as employees academics acquire the resources needed to practice as teachers and examiners, while the practices of education are what define (in part) the employment structure as academic. Hence, the structures of academic employment and education are interdependent. However, the way in which the academic employment structure works may also affect the way the structure of education works. For example, university managers may expect employees to take on larger teaching loads in response to changes in levels of government funding for universities.
- Scientific fields and research:
  The practice of research would not be possible without a pre-existing scientific field, while scientific fields would not continue to exist without researchers working in them. Hence, the structures of science and research are interdependent. However, the two structures also interact in the sense that it is through the practices of research that new discoveries are made and new

problems emerge so that the content of scientific fields may change in response to the work of researchers. Equally, changes in the content of scientific fields may affect the nature of the research undertaken in research project teams.

- Research and education:
  It is through the structures of education that students acquire research skills and experience that enable them to work as researchers in project teams. Hence, the structure of research is dependent on the structures of education. Yet, the structures of education may also affect the structure of research in the sense that the quality of the education and training of new researchers may affect the quality of the products of research.
- Scientific fields and education:
  The reproduction of scientific fields also depends on the structures of education because it is through the practices of teaching, learning and assessment that scientists enable students to acquire knowledge of scientific fields. Equally, the education and training of new scientists would not be possible without a pre-existing scientific field. Hence, the structures of science and education are interdependent. At the same time, changes in the content of scientific fields may lead to changes in the higher education curriculum.
- Research and recognition–reward:
  Because peer reviewers are experienced researchers, the structure of recognition and reward depends on the structure of research and, because it is through the practice of research that new contributions to knowledge emerge, the structure of recognition and reward depends on the structure of research. Hence, the structures of research and recognition and reward are interdependent.
- Education and recognition–reward:
  Peer reviewers will be experts in their field and so will have acquired qualifications that certify them as such. Hence, the structure of recognition and reward depends on the structures of education. But, scientists would not be able to educate students in a field unless peer reviewers had certified contributions to knowledge in that field. Hence, the structures of education depend on the structure of recognition and reward.
- Funding and academic employment:
  Academic employment depends on funding because universities would not be in a position to employ academics unless they received grants for research and teaching. But, at the same time and as I have already indicated, funding decisions affect levels of academic employment, with knock-on effects for teaching levels and the type of research projects undertaken.
- Funding and research:
  The practice of research would not be possible without material resources. Researchers can acquire such resources in virtue of their position as academic employees (internal funding). However, they can also acquire material resources directly from the UK Research Councils (external funding). So, the structure of research depends on the structure of funding. But,

at the same time research funders can influence what sort of research is undertaken because, as the funders of research, they can set the research agenda.

- Funding and recognition–reward:
  The Higher Education Funding Councils make their decisions about the size of university research grants on the basis of the results of a national process of peer review – the Research Excellence Framework (formerly the Research Assessment Exercise). So, the structure of funding depends on the structure of recognition and reward, while the structure of recognition and reward, in turn, affects how funding decisions are made.

The picture that emerges from the preceding analysis is of a system or totality of interlocking social structures.[7] Given this complexity, which entails that academic employees will be occupying multiple positions within the system at the same time – for example, researcher, educator and peer reviewer – we can understand why Whitley should argue that academics have dominated scientific development (1982: 323–5). When we start to consider the way in which scientific fields are defined and reproduced through a multiplicity of causal mechanisms, we can understand why it may be difficult for scientists to produce integrative research if this means challenging the scientific norm of specialization. If peer review, academic employment, research and education all work on the basis that scientific fields are specialized, it is perhaps not surprising that the conditions of knowledge production militate against efforts to integrate knowledge through interdisciplinary forms of inquiry. I return to this problem later because we must now examine the cognitive or intellectual conditions of knowledge production.

***The intellectual context***

A useful starting point in considering the nature of the intellectual or cognitive context of knowledge production is Whitley's definition:

> The intellectual context of research is here considered as that abstracted set of norms and procedures which both govern and constitute what is done to what phenomena, in which cognitive setting, and how it is understood. It consists of the cognitive structures which, on the one hand, represent what is known and, on the other hand, constitute the resources with which to change and develop what is known. A particular scientific field, in this view, is constituted by the procedures which are required to develop knowledge in it so that rather than seeing scientific knowledge as a static structure which is fixed and permanent, it is viewed as a process of acquiring and changing understandings. To do research in a given field is therefore to use the procedures and intellectual resources that constitute it.
>
> (Whitley, 1980: 302)

Now, this definition is slightly ambiguous because, on the one hand, cognitive 'norms and procedures' are supposed to 'govern' what scientists do and, on the other hand, they are supposed to 'constitute' what scientists do. However, just as social structures are ontologically irreducible to human agency, so are intellectual structures. This means that cognitive norms and procedures do indeed 'govern' human agency, because they cannot exist apart from it. However, they cannot also 'constitute' human agency because that would imply that the intellectual context is simply the by-product or creation of what scientists do, when, as Whitley acknowledges, the intellectual context is the pre-condition for what scientists do – 'the resources with which to change and develop what is known'. This does not mean that cognitive norms and procedures *determine* what scientists do because, just as academic scientists have the option of breaking social rules – for example, by boycotting student assessment, so they have the option of breaking cognitive rules that define the field in which they work – for example, by refusing to follow the mathematical methodology dominant in their field. In both cases, the fact that such courses of action may incur material penalties – in the former case withdrawal of pay, in the latter case rejection of work for publication – establishes the ontological irreducibility of rules to the practices they govern.

Whitley goes on to identify four different sets of cognitive norms that govern scientific inquiry: 'domain assumptions', 'formative procedures', 'techniques' and 'interpretative procedures' (ibid: 303–5); and he argues that 'the degree of formalization of intellectual norms and procedures . . . and the degree of their interdependency and integration' vary across scientific fields (ibid: 307). The former concept refers to the degree to which intellectual norms and procedures are definite, the latter the degree to which they are connected. Thus, in highly formalized fields, which are also highly interdependent, the use of methods is highly restrictive and *vice versa*. However, I suggest that we should also emphasize the different degrees to which cognitive norms and procedures are tacitly or implicitly understood. It is likely, for example, that the domain assumptions, which define the boundaries of the field, may be much more implicit in the understanding of researchers than technical norms or what are usually thought of as 'research methods',[8] if only because, in designing a research project, researchers are forced to think explicitly about what sorts of methods are normally used given the type of question they have formulated. (Conceptualization of the research problem, or question formulation, will be governed by the 'formative procedures' specific to the field they are working in.)

Finally, to return to Whitley's initial definition of the cognitive context of science, I suggest that it is also problematic to define 'scientific knowledge' as a 'process of acquiring and changing understandings'. Certainly, we do acquire knowledge and transform it. But, we must qualify this statement by emphasizing, firstly, that knowledge is the pre-existing resource that we transform and is thus distinct from, although not ontologically inseparable from, the practices involved in its transformation and, secondly, that we need not limit our understanding of the term 'knowledge' to scientific concepts and theories because philosophy can give us knowledge too – albeit knowledge that is immanent to, and conditional upon, science (as I argued in Chapter 2). Indeed, it is through philosophical inquiry that we can identify and understand the cognitive norms referred to above. If a broader definition of knowledge is accepted, we should be able to discern differences in the extent to which the scientific elements and the philosophical elements of the intellectual context vary during the process of scientific inquiry, so that, as our understanding of specific phenomena deepens, the philosophical concepts on which our understanding of science depends may not change or at least not change to the same degree as the scientific concepts that are the basis of our scientific claims.

What, though, do I mean by 'philosophical elements' and how do these relate to scientific concepts and theories? It follows from the argument of Chapter 2 that all scientific claims about the world presuppose philosophical assumptions, which we can divide into three categories: ontological, epistemological and methodological. Let me deal with each briefly in turn. A philosophical ontology is a theory of what all the objects scientists investigate have in common. As there are different types of science, such as social and natural science, so there are different types of philosophical ontology. Thus, a *social* philosophical ontology would be theory of what all the objects social scientists investigate have in common, whereas a *natural* philosophical ontology would be a theory of what all the objects natural scientists investigate have in common (usually philosophical ontological inquiry encompasses both, as in critical realism, so that differences and commonalities between natural and social objects can be identified). A specific social philosophical ontological position, then, would define a specific theory of the nature of social reality. For example, according to social atomism the social pertains to the actions and effects of individual people; by contrast, according to social holism, the social designates entities above and beyond the actions and effects of individual people.

Any theory of the nature of social reality logically entails a theory of the nature of knowledge of social reality or an epistemology. A key question with which we are concerned in this domain of philosophical inquiry is what is the source of truth. For example, according to the doctrine of empiricism, knowledge derives entirely from sensory experience; hence, statements that are not capable of empirical assessment cannot be regarded as valid descriptions of reality. By contrast, according to the doctrine of rationalism, reason is the sole source of knowledge, so that statements that do not accord with the principles of formal logic cannot be regarded as true.

Finally, a theory of the nature of reality and of the nature of knowledge of that reality also entails a methodology or a theory of how we can best arrive at valid statements about the world. For example, if one of the methodological implications of empiricism is that we should 'induce' scientific laws from repeated observations of regular successions of events and states of affairs, we may employ a survey and statistical techniques to help us to do this. Alternatively, we may make assumptions about the world and deduce scientific laws from them using the techniques of mathematics – the methodological implication of rationalism. In other words, methodology is concerned with justifying the use of particular methods or procedures for generating and interpreting data, given the nature of the object to be investigated, the question(s) posed, the sources of data available, and so on. It is this part of the philosophical framework into which Whitley's formative, technical and interpretative norms fit.

There is one important element of the intellectual context of knowledge production that we have yet to consider but that is implied by the meaning of 'domain assumptions' referred to earlier. These assumptions, the reader will recall, refer to the boundaries of scientific fields; they demarcate a particular cognitive space in which relevant pieces of research can be located. The 'social' is one such cognitive domain and may be defined by the entities or objects considered to be most basic – for example, markets, firms, institutions, modes of production, and so on. Now, whereas social *philosophical* ontology is concerned with identifying the common properties of such entities, which it summarizes in concepts such as social structure and social totality, social *scientific* ontology is concerned with identifying and elaborating the nature of such entities – that is, their ways of working, what particular powers and liabilities each possesses, and so on (Lawson, 2004: 3). Social scientific ontology, then, is more specific in its orientation than social philosophical ontology.[9] But, it is because we can identify specific objects as social and can use social philosophical ontology to help us in this respect that we can know what falls within the domain of social science and what does not. In short, the intellectual context of social science involves assumptions not only about the general nature of social reality but also about which objects constitute the social.

If social science presupposes a set of scientific ontological assumptions about what specific objects are social, the specialized social sciences, such as politics and economics, in turn presuppose scientific ontological assumptions about what specific objects are political and economic; and from there we can identify yet more specific assumptions that define distinct fields or specialties within politics and economics, that define distinct topics within specialties, and that define distinct questions or problems within topics. For example, if we accept for a moment Leftwich's argument that the study of politics, broadly understood, is concerned with '*power*, political power – and its effects' (2004a: 19), from this discipline-level scientific assumption we can identify a range of field- or specialty-level assumptions that qualify or refine the discipline-level assumption. Perhaps the object of inquiry is the distribution and exercise of power in developing countries, which is one of the concerns of the field of development studies. Within this specialty, we can identify specific assumptions distinguishing various topics such as democratization, governance, globalization, and so on; and within democratization we can identify specific assumptions distinguishing various problem areas such as political inclusion and exclusion, activism and authoritarianism. In short, we can distinguish scientific ontological assumptions by their degree of specificity. This means that scientific ontological assumptions pertaining to different domains of inquiry will be nested within each other, as Figure 3.2 shows, so that the division of labour in science may be highly differentiated.

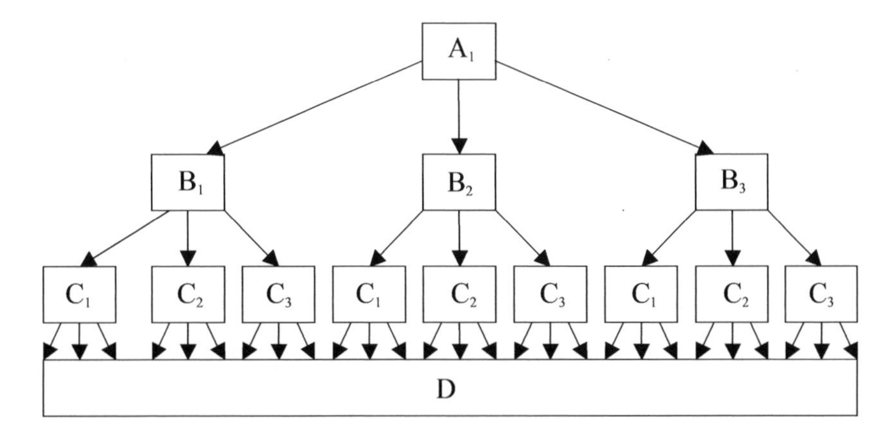


Level of scientific ontological assumption: A = discipline; B = field; C= topic; D = problem

*Figure 3.2* The scientific division of labour

Now, the representation of the scientific division of labour in Figure 3.2 is problematic, to the extent that it oversimplifies the intellectual divisions within scientific disciplines, for scientific fields or specialties frequently overlap. For example, although development studies is concerned with democratization, it may also cover globalization, a topic that is traditionally seen as falling within the domain of international political economy, while democratization may also fall within the remit of area studies. The distinctions between the fields of political science, then, are far from clear-cut. Indeed, there may even be overlap between the fields of different disciplines. For example, international political economy, to the extent that it examines relationships between states and markets, brings together two of the central concerns of the disciplines of politics and economics respectively. Nevertheless, although the scientific division of labour is complex and fluid, particularly in the social sciences (Dogan and Pahre, 1990), I do think that we can identify a core concern that distinguishes one discipline, specialty, topic or problem from another. Therefore, I suggest that we should think of the divisions in Figure 3.2 as referring to distinctive *focuses* or *emphases* of inquiry.

However, what complicates the preceding account of the scientific division of labour is the fact that the precise content of the scientific ontological assumption may vary according to the *philosophical* ontological assumption. We can understand the relationship between the philosophical and scientific ontological assumptions if we consider the nature of the political. There are two key questions we can ask about the nature of the political: what sort of object it is and what its scope or reach is. Leftwich argues that 'what *unites* political analysts is a concern with the provenance, forms, distribution, use, control, consequences and analysis of political power'. Yet, he also argues that political analysts are divided according to 'their focus and the levels and frameworks of analysis' (2004a: 20). What this means, in other words, is that political analysts will understand the nature of power in different ways. For example, it is not hard to discern the positivist assumptions informing the behaviouralist conception of power developed by Dahl (1957) and Bachrach and Baratz (1962, 1963, 1970). It is clear from Hay's critical discussion of this approach that it treats power as something that inheres in individuals and can therefore be easily measured as the outcome of individuals' decision making (2002: 172–4). By contrast, Hay's own conception of power as 'context-shaping' and 'conduct-shaping' (which critically develops the work of Lukes [1974]) presupposes a rather different philosophical position, one in which unobservable social structures and causal mechanisms constitute the context for human agency and thereby modify the capacity for individuals to act back on, and so transform, this context (Hay, 2002: 18–87).

Given such differences in the understanding of the nature of power, it is not surprising that we also find differences in the scope or range of possibilities for the investigation of power. Again, Hay's critical discussion of this issue provides an appropriate entry point to my own argument. Hay distinguishes between a 'restrictive' and an 'inclusive' conception of the scope of the political: the former limits the study of politics to the 'public' sphere, to the 'state' and to 'government', whereas the latter extends the study of politics to include the 'private' sphere, 'extra-governmental' institutions, and 'society' (2002: 67–9). Of more significance for our purposes, though, is Hay's identification of a 'characteristic affinity between a restrictive view of the political and a positivistic view of scientific method' (ibid: 68). Hay argues that this association is certainly 'not based on logical correspondence' (ibid.) because different epistemological positions may be consistent with both the restrictive and the inclusive conception of the scope of political inquiry so that one could investigate either the 'public' or 'private' spheres of politics using either positivistic or non-positivistic methods;[10] rather, Hay suggests that the association most likely reflects the need to secure a strong professional identity for the study of politics, which a restrictive conception of the scope of the political and a positivist conception of science provide. In this respect, we can agree with Hay. Clearly, if one adopts an inclusive conception and allows political science to embrace, say, the market and the family, as well as the institutions of government, one will find it difficult to distinguish clearly between the discipline of political science and the disciplines of economics and sociology, which have traditionally laid claims to the study of the market and the family respectively. We can also agree that, if one adopts a *positivist* conception of science, one can claim *professional* status. (Why certain political scientists draw on the rhetoric of positivism is a question I consider in the third section and in Chapter 5.)

What I want to suggest, though, is that the reason for the 'characteristic affinity' identified by Hay also has to do with the nature of positivist philosophy itself. Recall that positivist knowledge can only be knowledge generated through sensory experience; that is why, ontologically speaking, it is an *empirical* realism. If that is so, how is one to differentiate the mass of events and states of affairs that may be observed? What is to count as a political event and what is to count as a non-political event? Positivists do not have a satisfactory answer to these questions because they cannot supply any grounds for treating one event as political and another as, say, economic. Consequently, they are forced to rely on *conventionalist* understandings of which events are political, which are economic, and so on; I suggest that it is the restrictive conception of the political that positivists take as the conventional understanding of the political because, in treating politicians and other elected governing representatives as objects of inquiry, positivists can claim that political events are simply the effects of what politicians and other elected governing representatives 'do'. In this way, positivist-inspired political inquiry trades on what one might call an everyday, commonsense understanding of politics (an understanding perhaps unintentionally secreted by the news media in their focus on Westminster politics) as what politicians do.

By contrast, transcendental realists do not have to rely on conventional understandings of what politics is (or, for that matter, what economics is) because they can argue, firstly, that observed events and states of affairs are the empirical grounds for scientific laws, which describe the operation of unobservable social structures and mechanisms generative of the observed events and states of affairs; and, secondly, that the differentiation of social structure – which is where the terms political, economic, cultural, and so on come into play – is justified by the practical success of social scientific theories informed by this sort of philosophy. How well social scientists explain empirical facts, then, will depend on how they differentiate social objects and understand their interconnections and dynamics.[11]

In short, I am arguing that it is in virtue of philosophical ontological differences that there are differences in political scientists' understanding of the nature and scope of the political. Political scientists may claim that their basic object of study is the distribution and exercise of power but they may disagree about what power is and where it is located. In identifying a particular specialty or field as distinctive, then, we are presupposing that political scientists working in that field have a basic level of scientific agreement that allows them to locate their work within that field but that a deeper level of philosophical disagreement underpins the different understandings of the nature and scope of the objects of that field. Alternatively, we may say that, given the existence of distinctive philosophical approaches to scientific inquiry, different groups of political scientists may share distinctive philosophical assumptions but that different scientific assumptions within each philosophical grouping underpin different research interests and so fields of inquiry. This is why Marsh and Stoker (2002a, 2010) can differentiate political science primarily by philosophical approach,[12] whereas Goodin and Klingemann (1996) can differentiate it primarily by scientific specialty or field.

We can represent the intellectual context of knowledge production graphically, as in Figure 3.3. Now, there are at least three points to make about Figure 3.3, given the nature of the previous discussion. The first concerns the precise relationship between the various elements. The arrows in the diagram denote relations of logical consistency. So, for example, a particular type of scientific theory logically presupposes a particular methodological position, which presupposes

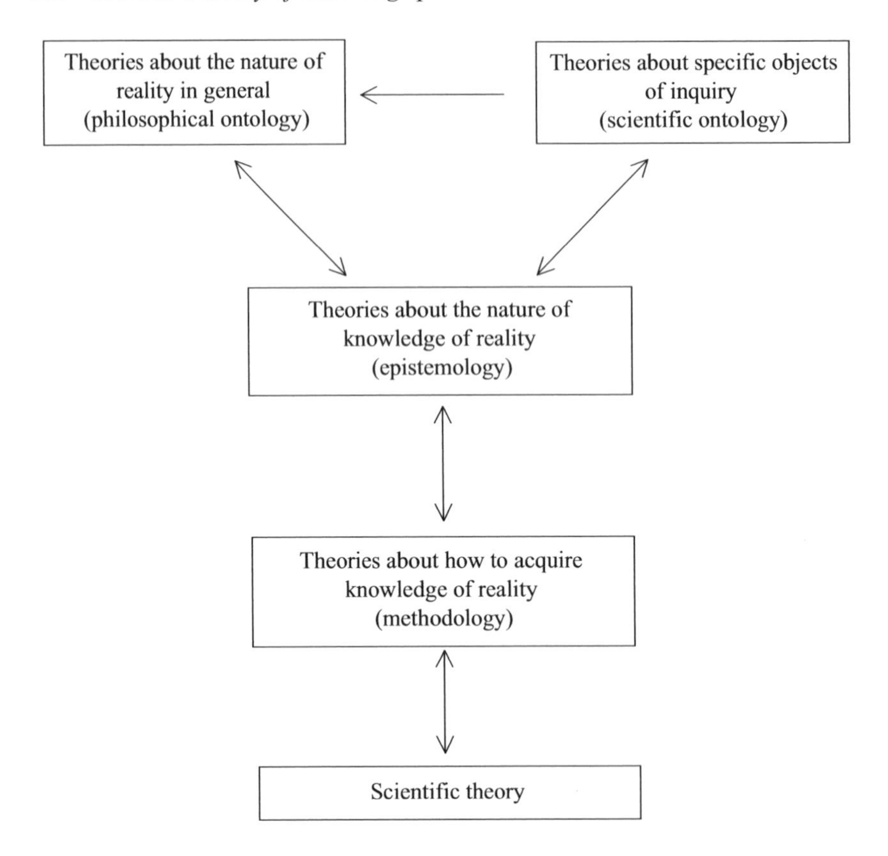


*Figure 3.3* Elements of the intellectual context of knowledge production

both a scientific and philosophical ontological position. (Note that, by virtue of the specific focus of scientific ontology and the general focus of philosophical ontology, the former presupposes the latter.) Equally, moving in the opposite direction, we can say that a particular philosophical ontological position – such as empirical realism – logically entails an empiricist epistemological position, which, in turn, logically entails an inductivist methodological position, which entails a conception of scientific theory as essentially an empirical regularity.

The second point to note, which also follows from the discussion earlier on, is that the extent to which each element of the intellectual context is implicit in the understanding of the scientist in question will differ. Indeed, it seems reasonable to suppose that the further removed is a particular element from the level of scientific theory, the more implicit it will be in scientists' thinking. So, a particular methodological position may be much more explicitly understood than the particular ontological position it presupposes.

The third point to note is that it is quite possible that a given scientific theory will presuppose more than one philosophy of science. Indeed, philosophical confusion and inconsistency will often be manifest as weaknesses or anomalies in the scientific theory in question. For example, Fleetwood has argued that heterodox economic theorists, despite being intuitively uncomfortable – indeed critical – of the assumptions of orthodox economic theory, have failed to break completely from these assumptions to the extent that their theories of the labour market presuppose both empirical realist and transcendental realist ontological positions – manifest in what Fleetwood calls 'watered down' versions of orthodox accounts of the labour market (2006: 67). However, if it is possible for the same scientific theory to presuppose different, competing philosophical assumptions, it is also possible for the same philosophy to sponsor different, competing scientific theories so that the production of new knowledge by the transformation of old knowledge need not imply a change of philosophical approach. That said, repeated explanatory and predictive failures relating to a particular form of scientific theorizing may lead to a general questioning of the largely taken-for-granted, philosophical context of that form of science and thence to a transformation not only in the form of scientific theorizing but also the philosophical assumptions underpinning it. Such an intellectual transformation is the hope of many critics of orthodox economic theorizing, such as Lawson (1997, 2003). Even so, if intentional human action always has unintentional consequences, we should expect that intellectual change may lead to theoretical incoherence, as when vestigial elements of the old philosophy continue to exist in tension and contradiction with elements of the new. In other words, intellectual change may be not so much a case of the simple replacement of one philosophical paradigm by another, as Kuhn assumes, as the complex and partial displacement of one or more paradigms by another. (I return to this issue in Chapter 4.)

### *The relationship between the social and intellectual conditions of knowledge production*

Let me summarize the argument so far. I have argued that the intellectual conditions of knowledge production consist of different sorts of ideas, logically related to each other – some of which are more fundamental than others, some of which are more implicitly understood than others and some of which contradict others. I have also argued that the social conditions of knowledge production consist of different types of social structure, some of which are internally related to each other (both symmetrically and asymmetrically) and others of which are externally related in the sense that they are either counteracting or reinforcing forces. Moreover, given the concept-dependence of social structures, we should expect that some of the social structures constituting the social conditions of knowledge production are more implicitly understood than others.

How, though, are the two sets of conditions related? I suggest that we should see the intellectual conditions as the basis for the division of labour in science; in other words, we should see the social norms of science as being dependent on pre-existing scientific and philosophical ideas. It is in virtue of the existence of these ideas that scientists can locate their work within a particular field of inquiry and it is by virtue of the division of labour in science and its connections to the structures of recognition and reward, academic employment, research, education and funding that failure to draw on the ideas that define the division of labour may lead to material penalties such as a lack of career progression. Equally, the ideas that define scientific fields of inquiry would not continue to exist unless there were scientists who had the material resources with which to transform existing ideas into new knowledge. Hence, the intellectual conditions of knowledge production depend, ultimately, on the social conditions – the materially embodied structures that make possible the practice of scientific inquiry. Moreover, in light of the argument that I presented earlier about the nature of the relationship between social structure and human agency, we must also recognize that social structures and ideas are irreducible to the practices they govern.

We can represent the (internal) relations between the social and intellectual conditions of knowledge production and scientific inquiry as shown in Figure 3.4 below.

Note that the same sort of relationship between social structure and ideas may apply to practices other than scientific inquiry. For example, we could just as easily have taken, say, teaching as the premise of our argument and reproduced the social and intellectual conditions for this practice. If we did this, we would find, I am sure, a particular set of social norms or rules existing in an interdependent relationship with a particular set of intellectual norms. Note also that this argument applies whether the ideas are lay or scientific. If we go back to the practice of scientific inquiry, for example, we may find that the intellectual materials with which scientists work may in part be lay ideas acquired through everyday practices, which are then transformed into knowledge. Moreover, if social scientific inquiry can give us knowledge of the social organization of social (and natural) science, social science will be internally related to itself.

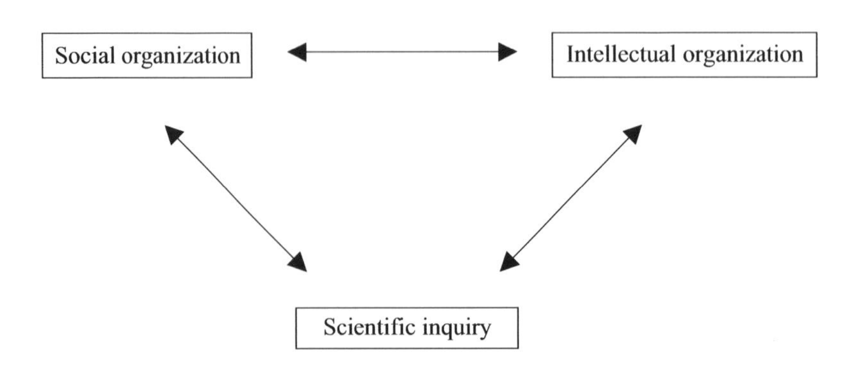


*Figure 3.4* The socio-intellectual conditions of scientific inquiry

Finally, note that an important implication of the relationship between the social and intellectual conditions of knowledge production is that scientific ideas do not exist independently of the wider sociocultural context. What this means, as I argue below, is that social science depends on society (for material resources), just as natural science does, whereas the justification of a particular form of society depends on a particular form of social science but not on natural science. Moreover, society may affect what sort of social and natural science is carried out precisely because both social and natural scientists rely on society to provide the material resources for scientific inquiry, while the results of both natural and social scientific inquiry may affect society in the sense of changing people's understanding of themselves and the world around them. In short, social science and society are causally interdependent in a way that natural science and society are not (Bhaskar, 1998: 47).

## Further development and illustration of the argument: the case of economics

Having elaborated upon the nature of the social and intellectual conditions of knowledge production, I am now in a position to return to the question considered at the end of the first section of this chapter – that is, why economics has become dominated by arithmetical reasoning. Whitley has argued that the structural division and status differential between formal modelling and empirical work in economics insulates and so protects the former from the latter. But, I suggest that, if we want to understand why formal modelling in economics has survived and has become hegemonic, we need also to consider the relationship between the nature of economics – in particular, the philosophical assumptions of orthodox economics – and the nature of society.

Let me start by reconsidering the philosophical basis of 'mathematical-deductivist modelling', to use Lawson's terminology (2003: 3). Now deductivism, as a particular methodological position, presupposes a positivist epistemology – that is, the theory that knowledge of reality is limited to the observation and experience of given facts or naturally occurring atomistic events and states of affairs.[13] Clearly, if knowledge of reality is to take this form, reality itself must be of a particular form. It follows that the epistemological position of positivism presupposes the ontological position of atomism – the doctrine that reality consists of nothing but atomistic events and states of affairs. It also follows that social reality must consist of nothing but autonomous people and their effects because only people and the events and states of affairs to which they give rise can be the observable constituents of the social realm. Hence, sociological individualism also entails methodological individualism, the doctrine that social phenomena are to be explained solely by recourse to the given preferences of individuals (Lawson, 1997: 15–20, 36–42, 91–107).

If, however, social reality consists of nothing but autonomous individuals and their effects, positivist social science must be the product of individual scientists passively recording constant conjunctions of events and states of affairs (the only form that scientific laws can take according to this philosophy) and, once these have been accurately recorded, scientific inquiry can simply stop. In other words, positivist knowledge of social reality is knowledge that is incorrigible, complete and so final. However, if scientific development is marked by change as well as continuity, by conflict as well as consensus, and if the practical application of scientific theories leads to failure as well as success, positivism is thoroughly misleading. By presenting knowledge as final, positivism undercuts arguments for social change because, if scientific theories are final and so unchangeable, so is the reality they purport to describe; and, by denying the reality of unobservable sociocultural objects positivism further undercuts arguments for social change because, given the nature of positivist scientific laws, it is unclear what the basis for social change is (Bhaskar, 1989: 22–3).

Positivist knowledge of social reality, then, tacitly justifies the current organization of society and, as such, is inherently conservative in its ideological implications. In this way, the current organization of society comes to depend on positivism. Moreover, if certain social sciences, such as economics, are dominated by positivism, and if economics graduates absorb positivist assumptions, positivist philosophy may become an increasingly influential set of ideas throughout society as economics graduates take up positions as bankers, journalists, accountants, civil servants, and so on. Furthermore, because social (and natural) science depends on society for material and cultural support, it is possible that society may impose conditions on the sort of knowledge social (and natural) scientists produce. For example, if it is the case that elite groups in society are the funders of science and that these groups share a positivist mindset so that they believe that 'proper' science is positivist science, it is not difficult to see how non-positivist science – particularly transcendental realist science – may be a discredited form of science in the eyes of social and intellectual elites, especially if non-positivist science presents a potential ideological challenge to the vested interests of elite groups. This is why, I suggest, certain sciences take on a positivist professional identity because it is only through this identity that they can obtain public respect and esteem. In this way, dominant sociocultural forms, as the preconditions for social scientific inquiry, may be said to influence the nature of social science so that we have a two-way process of causal interaction (as well as of causal interdependence) between social science and society.[14]

If positivist social science is a source of mystification in presenting a distorted image of society, it follows that it presents a distorted image of its own socio-intellectual conditions of production. Hence, positivist-inspired research on science may well be seriously misleading as to the real nature of the underlying socio-intellectual conditions of scientific inquiry. Now, this sort of argument, which, strictly speaking, falls within the domain of the sociology of knowledge, can explain why positivist forms of knowledge continue to dominate non-positivist forms in a particular scientific field. But, I suggest that, to reach a deeper explanation of the dominance of positivism – particularly within the field of economics – we need to incorporate the argument developed in the second section of this chapter, which concerns the relationship between the mode of knowledge production internal to science and the nature of the knowledge produced (an argument that falls within the domain of the sociology of science). In other words, to explain the present state of economics we need to combine 'cognitive, internal, and external factors' – as Blume recommends (1977: 12). Let us return, then, to the theory of knowledge production developed in the previous section and consider in more detail how the academic employment structure works in the case of economics, before examining the relationship between economics and broader social forces.

Now, I think it is not contentious to state that, in the UK, in most instances the academic employment structure comprises a hierarchy of positions from, say, research assistant at the bottom to professor at the top, so that career progression from a lower to a higher position implies an increase in responsibility, status, resources and power.[15] Now, if this is the case, it follows that those at the top of the hierarchy – the intellectual elite – will have more control over the direction of scientific development than those at the bottom. Typically, it will be members of the intellectual elite who define what is to be taught in the field and who are asked to edit leading journals and assess research proposals in the field because, clearly, one cannot be a credible educator and peer reviewer unless one has already acquired a public reputation within the scientific community of which one is a member. This means that those at the bottom of the academic hierarchy will have to abide by the intellectual norms and rules set by those at the top. They will have to pass the examinations set and examined by the elite, if they are to qualify as members of the scientific field and if they are to be considered for academic employment; and they will have to publish work in journals that the elite considers to be of such a quality that publications therein constitute valid contributions to the field of knowledge, if they are to establish a public reputation and gain academic promotion.

Scientists are disciplined, then, by their peers, primarily through the mechanisms of education and training, which help novitiates to acquire the requisite disciplinary mindset and associated skills and expertise, and through the mechanism of peer review, which defines what is to be a valid contribution to knowledge in the field. Indeed, the latter implies that the editors of scientific journals are the 'gatekeepers of science' (Crane, 1967) because they can control what sort of knowledge enters the public domain, just as reviewers of research council grant applications can influence which research proposals are funded and which are not, and just as the judgments that Research Excellence Framework subject panels make about research quality may affect what sort of research profile university departments present – at least if these judgments inform decisions about how much government funding universities will receive for research. Of course, it may be that the scientific elite considers some journals to be more prestigious than others, in the sense that it regards work published in the former to be of a higher quality and so more valuable than work published in the latter. If it restricts the content of such journals to a particular form of research, it is easy to see how a particular school of thought within the field can become dominant because, if one's career progression depends on the quality of one's publication record, one will try to publish in the most prestigious journals as much as possible. In short, through a policy of 'divide and rule' the scientific elite can define the research priorities within the field and allocate resources accordingly.

We can apply this argument to the case of economics. Interpretations of the development of economics suggest, for example, that it was the neoclassical school of thought within economics, led by Alfred Marshall, that captured the elite positions in the academic hierarchy at the time when professional self-consciousness in the discipline was just emerging, and that the concentration of scientific research and teaching in a small number of elite universities in the UK made it possible for the neoclassical school to dominate other schools of thought within economics. The hierarchically organized system of higher education in the UK meant that it was a small university elite – particularly Oxford, Cambridge and London – that set the benchmark for academic competence so that, when these universities introduced the sciences into the curriculum, they set the benchmark for scientific competence throughout the higher education system. So it was that, when economics was establishing itself as a separate field of inquiry, the highly prestigious Cambridge economics tripos (launched in 1903) was the model for a university education in economics (although it had a competitor in the recently founded London School of Economics) and it was the highly prestigious Cambridge economics graduate who typically filled the chairs of economics at the provincial universities. Of course, neoclassical economics was not without its critics – particularly the economic historians Cunningham and Ashley at Oxford – so that the dominance of neoclassical economics was always a *tendency*.

The divisions within the field of economics between the historians on the one hand and the orthodox theorists on the other set the stage for the subsequent emergence in economics of a particular division of labour that Whitley has called a 'partitioned bureaucracy' (1986: 190) and that is defined and reinforced by the peer review mechanism acting through a ranking of economics journals. Whitley argues that the field of economics is divided between a 'core' of formal, theoretical modellers and a 'periphery' of applied economists and that this division is sustained through the status differential between the two types of scientific work. The theoretical 'core' is characterized by a higher degree of 'mutual dependence', which is defined as 'the extent to which scientists are dependent upon each other to complete solutions to problems and obtain high reputations from particular groups of colleagues/competitors' and a lower degree of 'task uncertainty', which is defined as 'the degree to which the outcomes of research activities are predictable, visible, replicable, and stable', than the peripheral, applied subfields because the analytical results of mathematical models are much more stable and easier to control and are therefore easier to integrate than the results of empirical analyses, which are more difficult to interpret and therefore more difficult to integrate. Hence, if there is always the possibility that the unstable outcomes of the empirical testing of mathematical models may call into question the credibility of these models, the public reputations of theoretical economists must not depend on the results of the application of economic theory. Therefore, the most prestigious journals in economics – those in which economists must publish to secure public recognition for their work and rapid career promotion – are journals publishing theoretical work and the least prestigious are those publishing applied work. In this way, the theoretical 'core' is insulated from potential empirical challenges emanating from the applied 'periphery' (Whitley, 1986: 190–6).

However, research on the relationship between the structure of economics and the Research Assessment Exercise (RAE) indicates that there is an equally significant division of labour within economics, that between the 'mainstream' and 'non-mainstream'.[16] Harley and Lee (1997), for example, argue that this division of labour is reflected in, and reinforced by, the status rankings of economics journals. The most prestigious economics journals, as defined by various published lists,[17] are those tending to publish predominantly mainstream or orthodox research, whether theoretical or applied, whereas the least prestigious are those tending to publish predominantly non-mainstream or heterodox research, again whether theoretical or applied.

Harley and Lee argue that journal ratings lists were used unofficially by RAE economics panels when deciding what research rating to award a department, and that mainstream dominance of the constitution of such panels has led to a bias in the assessment process in favour of mainstream and against non-mainstream research. Moreover, because the ratings that the RAE economics panel gave to economics departments determined how much research funding universities received directly from the Higher Education Funding Councils, the members of the economics panel were in a position to influence the nature of the research done in economics. Harley and Lee show that there is a clear correlation between rating received and research profile in the sense that non-mainstream-oriented economics departments tended to receive a lower rating than mainstream-oriented ones. They also provide empirical evidence to suggest that many economics departments responded to this pattern of research rating by changing their recruitment and management practices so that mainstream rather than non-mainstream candidates are now preferred in appointments to academic posts and existing non-mainstream economists are being steered away from non-mainstream research interests (1997: 1436–53).

In short, by carefully controlling the selection process for appointments to the RAE economics panel, the mainstream economics elite has ensured that it continues to dominate the field of economics. Given the crucial connections I have traced in this chapter between academic career progression, peer review and the division of labour in science, it is not surprising that the advent of the RAE has increased the degree of differentiation within the economics profession and, given the status differential between mainstream and non-mainstream work that pre-existed the RAE, it is not surprising that it is the non-mainstream that appears to have lost out in the RAE. In a context of limited public funding for social science and growing criticism of, and philosophical challenges to, the mainstream project (Bell and Kristol, 1981; Wiles and Routh, 1984; Ormerod, 1994; Lawson, 1997, 2003; Shapiro, 2005; Fullbrook, 2003, 2004, 2007; Keen, 2011) it is important that the economics mainstream wins the competition for funding and receives the largest prize if it is to survive.[18]

The continuing dominance of positivist-inspired research within economics also has to be understood from an external perspective; that is, we need to examine the relationship between the nature of economics as a particular form of knowledge and the nature of society – particularly the prevailing ideological currents within it. In Chapter 5, I consider the fate of those American economists who openly advocated quasi-socialist public policies in the late nineteenth century and whose academic careers suffered as a result. Such open advocacy was clearly dangerous for the survival of the academic sector and, hence, for the American economics profession because it conflicted ideologically with the vested interests of elite social groups in American society, many of which were major funders of university research. But, if socialist-inspired economists were to be silenced, economists of *all* ideological dispositions would have to disengage from open sectarianism. Positivist ideas afforded them the opportunity to do this because in proclaiming that economics was objective and value-free American economists could claim the authority of impartial experts. In this way, a positivist professional identity could insulate American economists – as it could other American social scientists – from external sectarian attack and from the charge that they were engaging in political propaganda.

British economists, it seems, faced similar external social pressures. For example, Coats reports that after 14 economics professors wrote to *The Times* in 1903 arguing against the proposed policy of tariff reform, Balfour, the then Prime Minister and vice-president of the Royal Economic Society, warned British economists against engaging in sectarian policy disputes, if they wanted to retain their scientific authority (Coats, 1967: 724). Coats also reports that the founders of the British Economic Association (which later became the Royal Economic Society) kept the membership policy of the Association and the editorial policy of the *Economic Journal* as open as possible in order to avoid creating the impression that the Association was sectarian, and avoided holding public meetings in case any intellectual disagreements that arose damaged the reputation of the profession (Coats, 1968: 359–62). Moreover, Sidney Webb had similar concerns when launching the London School of Economics in 1895. On the one hand, Webb was clearly under pressure from the Fabians to ensure that the new school would help to propagate Fabian ideas – that, after all, was one of the conditions attached to the initial endowment. On the other hand, Webb knew that, if the school were seen to be sectarian, it would lose credibility and scientific authority and put in jeopardy alternative possible sources of funding (Coats, 1967: 717–18).

I want to suggest that the external social pressures attending the emergence of a professional consciousness amongst economists in America and Britain in the late nineteenth century attest to a dominant belief in both countries that only positivist science is legitimate science. Whether or not the non-scientists and scientists alike who held this belief understood fully the conservative ideological implications of positivist science is unclear and is a question for further research. But, if we assume for the moment that the ideological implications of positivism were not understood, the unintended consequence of the growth of positivist-inspired social science was to support indirectly the interests of American and

British social elites, who had most to lose from a programme of socialist-inspired public policy reform. Moreover, if it is the case that a given organization of society is legitimized by positivism and that the dominant form of knowledge within social science is positivist, in producing knowledge of this sort social scientists strengthen – again, unintentionally – the hold of positivist ideas outside of science. For example, as economics graduates have taken up positions as professionals, economic theories have become increasingly influential throughout British society, not least in government and the civil service (Colvin, 1985; Cairncross, 1986).

The relationship between science and society, therefore, is one of causal interaction: society affects social science by setting limits to what sort of knowledge of society is legitimate, while social science affects society by influencing how people understand the nature of society. However, the relationship is also one of causal interdependence, at least if we consider the particular form of society and the particular form of social science. On the one hand, social scientists depend on material resources provided by society – especially the state; this puts them in a relatively weak position because to criticize those on whom they rely for support is to put in jeopardy that source of support. Hence, if society is dominated by positivist ideas, it is perhaps not surprising that social science to a certain extent falls in line with the positivist creed. On the other hand, the particular organization of society and the ideology that justifies it may come to depend on the sort of knowledge social scientists produce. As I argued above, positivism undercuts arguments for social change by obscuring the underlying basis of experience. But, at the same time, the social ontological position of positivism – sociological individualism – acts as an intellectual buttress to the ideology of economic liberalism, which, as Marx famously argued, obscures the existence of, and so sustains, capitalist relations of production.

In short, the upshot of my argument is that the dominance of positivism in social science both reflects and reinforces the dominance of positivism in society. Note that the recent flourishing of interpretivist philosophy in the social sciences reinforces the dominance of positivism in the social sciences and in society. Why is this? Recall that, although interpretivism acknowledges the social ontological significance of ideas and discourse, its critique of naturalistic positivism is only partial because it too presupposes an empirical realist ontology and thereby denies that reality has depth. It follows that interpretivist-inspired social science is also implicitly conservative. Even the postmodernist and poststructuralist creeds end up in this ideological position. Despite acknowledging the voices of the oppressed and marginalized, postmodernists and poststructuralists undercut arguments for social change and thus the emancipation of the oppressed and marginalized by mounting an assault on truth and progress (Hay, 2002: 216–50); for, if there is no truth to the reality of social oppression and marginalization, how can we possibly change this state of affairs?

However, I do not want to suggest that the strength of positivist ideas is the same across all societies. It is striking, for example, that, despite the mounting criticisms of orthodox economics coming from within the social science community referred to above, the criticisms coming from outside academic social science – in the UK at least – have been until recently rather sporadic and muted.[19] By contrast, in France, a recent revolt by university economics students generated national media interest and prompted the French government to launch an inquiry into the state of economics teaching in French universities (Fullbrook, 2003). But, the so-called post-autistic economics movement that developed out of the French revolt and that inspired similar protests in other Western countries has aroused very little public debate in the UK,[20] suggesting perhaps that a positivist consciousness is much stronger in the UK than in France – at least among the governing elite.

What has triggered public debate in the UK is the decline in the numbers of students choosing to study economics at doctoral level. Machin and Oswald's research for the ESRC and the Royal Economic Society shows that, in the 1990s, there was a sharp fall in the number of UK graduate students enrolling on doctoral programmes in economics in leading UK universities and that this was reflected in a similar drop in the applications for ESRC postgraduate research studentships in economics. Machin and Oswald attribute the decline to changes in relative salary levels, estimating that 'Over ten years, academic pay has fallen behind the remuneration packages of economists working in the private sector by approximately 20–30%' (2000: F340). They focus on relative pay levels because 'this was the single most commonly mentioned factor in our interview work, and in the questionnaire sent to Heads of economics departments' (ibid: F346). However, the problem with this argument is that, if relatively low academic salary levels are deterring economics graduates from pursuing an academic career, why are the numbers of graduates from other social sciences applying for ESRC studentships so much higher? In a footnote, Machin and Oswald state that:

> In 1997 only 84 people applied for research studentships in economics (41 offers were made, of which 33 were taken up). This compares to 207 (40 offers, 38 taken up) in politics and international relations, 180 (41, 40) in psychology and 152 (36, 34) in sociology. The numbers applying for economics PhD studentships has (sic) fallen further to 66 and 67 in 1998 and 1999 respectively.
>
> (Machin and Oswald, 2000: F335, fn. 2)

If higher pay in the private sector is such an important factor in influencing graduates' career choices, we would expect to find a decline in PhD enrolment levels across the social sciences.[21] After all, although many private-sector occupations – such as economics consultant and research economist – do require a prior training in economics, financial institutions may employ graduates from a range of disciplines to fill a variety of positions.[22]

I suggest, therefore, that we should consider the possibility that economics students are deserting the subject not only in light of the financial implications but also out of lack of intellectual interest. The decline in student numbers taking economics at undergraduate and at 'A' level is at least consistent with this interpretation. For example, in their study of student subject choice at secondary and tertiary level Ashworth and Evans report that:

> Since 1989, student numbers in 'A' level economics have fallen by over 50 percent, which is all the more dramatic because participation in A-level education has been rising over this period... In addition, the number of students applying to study economics as a (major) discipline at university has also been falling.
>
> (Ashworth and Evans, 2001: 312)

Ashworth and Evans find that, the higher a student's interest in economics relative to arts and other social science subjects at 'A' level, the more likely the student will continue to study the subject at degree level. Yet, they say no more about this result, particularly when they discuss appropriate policy responses in the conclusion to their study. They warn that the economics profession should not 'underestimate the importance of the evidence that student underachievement in economics discourages student pursuit of the subject' (ibid: 319); yet, they do not recognize the possibility that underachievement in economics may well be linked to lack of interest in the subject.

We may ask, then, why lack of interest was not the most commonly cited reason for not studying economics at doctoral level in Machin and Oswald's study. In addition to surveys of economics departments and economics postgraduates, Machin and Oswald carried out face-to-face interviews 'with 21 well-informed individuals of different sorts', a selection of whose comments on the problem of recruiting economics PhDs they report (Machin and Oswald, 1999: 4). We are told in Appendix A that the 'well-informed individuals' were mainly heads of department, students, administration staff and consultants (ibid: 49); yet, we are not told how many from each category were interviewed and why the views of heads of economics departments were sought. It is highly unlikely that lack of interest in economics will be cited as a reason by someone who has made a career out of research in the subject and has risen to the top of the profession. If Machin and Oswald had interviewed a wider range of final-year undergraduate economics students, for example, the range of survey responses might have been different. Moreover, it is telling that in their survey of economics postgraduates only 17 per cent of Master's students said that they were studying economics out of intellectual curiosity, whereas 66 per cent said they were studying it to enhance their career prospects (ibid: 37, Table 14). This is hardly evidence of a high level of intellectual satisfaction with economics, yet Machin and Oswald ignore this result. Only Freeman dared to suggest that money might not be 'the only thing that matters' and that the 'intrinsic rewards of the discipline – the intellectual excitement it generates – also count heavily' (2000: F356).[23]

I suggest that the recent fall in the number of economics students at all levels of education constitutes an indirect challenge to the dominance of mainstream economics because the discipline will find it increasingly difficult to reproduce itself, if this trend continues. Whether or not the economics elite will recognize that it may be the nature of the subject that is discouraging students and will open up the discipline to non-mainstream approaches is a difficult question to answer. It may be that the profession will continue to recruit academic economists and postgraduates from abroad as seems to be happening at the moment. Machin and Oswald hope that UK vice chancellors will increase the salary levels of academic economists as a way of counteracting the supply deficit (2000: F348–9). If this were to happen, mainstream dominance may continue.[24] What is clear, though, is that the economics elite has not accepted that alternative ways of studying economics are legitimate forms of social science and that these alternatives might be more interesting than the mathematical modelling that currently dominates the economics curriculum.

## Conclusion

To conclude this chapter, I want to draw out the implications of my argument for the possibility of integrating knowledge through interdisciplinary research. Given that the theory of knowledge production that I have developed in this chapter makes an analytical distinction between social and intellectual conditions, we may ask what must be the social and intellectual conditions for the integration of knowledge from different disciplines. The intellectual condition must be that the integrating theoretical components from the different disciplines presuppose the same set of philosophical assumptions. Social scientists need to be keenly aware of this condition given the wide variety of philosophical approaches to social inquiry.[25] Indeed, in interdisciplinary team research in the social sciences it is particularly important that there is philosophical consistency across the different disciplines represented. Clearly, it would be difficult for two social scientists to work together if their understandings of what constituted valid knowledge were incompatible. It is difficult to envisage, for example, how a positivist economist and a postmodernist sociologist could work together so as to produce a philosophically coherent research output unless the two researchers were willing to break free of their traditional philosophical worldviews. If they were not willing to do so, they might end up simply talking past each other. Managers of interdisciplinary team research projects will therefore have to consider not only which disciplinary experts they require but also what sort of philosophical approach they require.

However, it may still be possible for social scientists from different disciplines to overcome their philosophical differences through a period of education. They would have to be open to new philosophical perspectives and would have to be willing to accept intellectual change. But, the question is how willing social scientists will be to change established ways of thinking if this means challenging the prevailing intellectual norms of the discipline in which they have been educated – which takes us back to the social context of science. I suggest that the extent to which scientific integration will be possible will depend on how scientists are disciplined. It may be that scientists are disciplined such that intellectual integration across scientific fields is the norm and is rewarded through peer review and employment structures. But, as I argued in Chapter 1, specialization is currently the dominant form of scientific inquiry, whether it is on the basis of a specific domain of inquiry – as seems to be the case in political science, for example – or on the basis of a specific philosophical approach – as seems to be the case in economics. Of course, it may be claimed that the advent of 'economics imperialism' (Fine, 2003), which I discussed briefly in Chapter 1, shows that interdisciplinary research is flourishing – at least in economics. However, if this sort of interdisciplinarity presupposes a positivist philosophy and if positivism is unable to provide coherent grounds for differentiating social reality, as I argued in Chapter 2, 'economics imperialism' will be an incoherent form of scientific integration.

What, though, of fields of social scientific inquiry such as sociology and political science, commonly regarded as being more intellectually pluralistic than economics? To the extent that these fields of inquiry offer a more secure philosophical grounding for scientific integration – one that recognizes the depth of reality – the possibility that practitioners in these fields will at least consider working with scientists from different disciplines ought to be greater. But, the degree to which they will be able to realize any interdisciplinary ambitions will depend, I suspect, on how rigidly the domain assumptions of these fields are enforced through the education system and through peer review. There may be ways around this problem so that integrative interdisciplinarity can still survive, even in a prevailing context of specialization. Ultimately, the question we must ask is whether the intellectual compromises involved would actually help to sustain the current trend towards specialization and diminish the underlying philosophical argument for scientific integration. It is appropriate, then, that we should now turn to examining the thinking and strategies of those who have actually engaged in integrative, interdisciplinary research so as to gain a clearer idea of the constraints on, and possibilities for, scientific integration.

# 4 The intellectual context of knowledge production

In the previous chapter, I presented a theory of knowledge production that distinguishes between a social and an intellectual context of knowledge production. I argued that the nature of these two contexts is similar to the extent that they represent a reality beyond what we can experience directly yet different to the extent that they comprise different sorts of entity related in different ways.

In this chapter, I apply part of this theory to three cases of (collaborative) interdisciplinary research (full details of which are presented in the Appendix) in an attempt to explain why scientists make particular choices about how to produce knowledge; in doing so, I focus on the second of the two decisions deriving from the problem of integrating knowledge from different disciplines that I set out at the end of Chapter 1. There, I argued that researchers faced a decision about what sort of knowledge to produce – either specialized, disciplinary research or integrative, interdisciplinary research – and a decision about how to produce the chosen type of knowledge (or what sort of methodological approach to adopt). I argued further that these two decisions imply that the problem under investigation presupposes both a social and an intellectual dimension. In this chapter, I focus on the second decision – about how to produce the chosen type of knowledge – and examine the influence that the intellectual context of knowledge production has on how scientists make this decision.

At the same time as relating my theory of knowledge production to empirical evidence generated through case studies of (collaborative) interdisciplinary research, I also develop it. For example, through analyzing the empirical evidence generated through the case studies, I explore in greater depth the tacit philosophical and scientific assumptions that researchers work with and show how contradictions between these assumptions may occur not only externally – that is, between the intellectual frameworks drawn upon by two or more scientists from different fields of inquiry – but also internally – that is, between the intellectual frameworks drawn upon by the same scientist. Indeed, I argue that the latter instance of intellectual contradiction reflects a distinction that we may make between professional and lay knowledge and reveals the influence of conscious and subconscious levels of thought. I conclude the chapter by considering what difficulties and opportunities the complexity of the intellectual context of knowledge production poses for the integration of knowledge from different disciplines.

## External intellectual contradictions

Let me start, then, by comparing the philosophical frameworks of the researchers from case study B with those of the researchers from case study A. Case study B is a research project in the comparative political economy of development, led by an economist on one side who, in conjunction with a research assistant, was responsible for the construction and estimation of a large-scale econometric model, and by two political scientists on the other side, who, in conjunction with another research assistant, were responsible for organizing most of the qualitative case studies of selected developing-world countries. One of the chief difficulties the researchers faced in this project was working out how the results of the econometric investigation would relate to the results of the qualitative case studies. What is interesting is that this difficulty was clearly more apparent to the political scientists than to the economist, especially since there was a delay in generating results from the quantitative study. For example, one of the political scientists, when thinking about all the problems she had faced so far in the project, had this to say:

> some of the problems result... from established methodologies of work, which we've just put into place in the absence of any major input from the economics side, because what happens when something doesn't come along with this data-set for you, then you fall back... on your own ways of working. So while we have a massive amount now of qualitative data it won't be easy to go back and make it fit... anything that will come out from the economics side.

The same political scientist expanded upon the notion of 'established methodologies of work' and the difficulties, as she saw it, these had caused for the economist, who was also carrying out some of the qualitative work for the case studies:

> on my side there was a certain view that, because I have no problems working with different people, people who perhaps think differently, that I wouldn't encounter problems with [ ], that I would be able to manage an economist, and I don't think I quite grasped how hard I would find it to... how inflexible I would find *his* frames, given that I'd always thought of my own as flexible. But obviously *they're* not as flexible as I thought either! And at the same time I hadn't also grasped... [ ] *genuinely* and *honestly* wants to break out of macroeconomics. He has a belief in qualitative work... he has a commitment to... field research in a way that a lot of economists don't have; and what he can't do... what I didn't realize he couldn't do, was think about what qualitative and field research, kind of deep field research, observation and all of that kind of stuff, *does*... and so [ ] can't match those two things: he can't match his macroeconomic skill with his desire to do qualitative field work because he doesn't know what to do with it when he gets it!

We can understand the nature of this methodological conflict more clearly if we consider in more detail the nature of the contending scientific and philosophical frameworks. Now, the economist from case study B described himself not only as an 'interdisciplinary development economist' concerned with understanding primarily the problem of developing-world poverty and its implications for policymaking but also as a 'positive economist who tries to explain things which are... measurable and the relationships between things that are measurable'. What is interesting, though, is that this 'positive economist' did not seem to recognize any radical incompatibility between his own approach to social inquiry and the approaches that his political science colleagues took. For example, when asked about how his conception of the political aspect of social life differed from the way a political scientist might conceptualize the political, the economist had this to say:

> I don't think it does. I think that what I do is... indeed political science in the sense of an attempt to explain policies maybe with more formal modelling than a lot of political scientists do, although... there are these days very many numerate political scientists so that's not by any means the disparity... It's simply to say that my approach is *definitely* at the quantitative end of that aspect.

And later on, when asked directly how he thought the quantitative modelling in the project would relate to the findings from the interviews carried out by the political scientists, the economist recognized the methodological differences involved but did not see the issue of their compatibility as problematic in the way that the political scientist (quoted above) did:

> *So you used the formal modelling approach. So... how is that going to relate to the sort of methods that the others are using in their case studies?*
> I guess that it formalizes a set of relationships which are the ones which all of us are trying to understand, namely, the relationships between political structures, economic policymaking, political violence, and... poverty reduction. All of us are concerned with that chain of causation. But I'm modelling it formally; they are not modelling it formally but describing the relationships in prose, and I suspect... that they're much, much more concerned with issues of process, and political structures, and the influence of those on the other variables I've talked about than I am.

What the economist has not realized is that, if the political scientists are concerned with 'issues of process' and 'political structures', the sort of relationships they are dealing with may be very different from the sort of relationships implied by the use of formal modelling.

Why, though, does the political scientist recognize, if only implicitly, a conflict between the two methodologies yet the economist does not? It is not the use of different methods of inquiry *per se* that is the source of the conflict but how the findings from the use of the different types of method are to be interpreted. The economist's methodological reflections presuppose an empiricist theory of causation, according to which causal relationships are simply regularities between observed events and states of affairs, which the use of statistical regression techniques is designed to uncover. It follows from this theory that to explain a phenomenon is to show how it is an instance of a well-defined, regular relationship between a set of dependent and independent variables (given a set of initial conditions and triggering actions). Now, although the economist does not articulate the covering-law model of explanation completely, it is nevertheless *implicit* in the passage quoted above and in the passage quoted below, in which the economist talks about the relationship between theory and empirical evidence:

> *when it comes to, say, constructing the argument in relation to this problem... how are you going to do that?... what sort of inferences would you be making between, say, theory and evidence?*
> Well... we estimate a model in which there are five dependent variables or five... phenomena, which we try to explain, and these are the trends in... poverty and violence... and then there are various policy instruments including aid, public expenditure and investment... So we're trying to explain those things, and how they interrelate, and how policy can intervene.

The economist's (implicit) commitment to an empiricist theory of causation is also consistent with the economist's published research outputs. For example, in a case study on a developing country in South America, the economist again presents a formal model, which he has estimated using statistical regression techniques and the results of which he interprets as evidence for the existence of causal relationships between the dependent and independent variables. Indeed, what this piece of work demonstrates quite clearly is the assumption that the political aspect of social life is something that can be observed directly and so treated as just another 'variable' to be inserted into an equation.

The economist from case study B, therefore, works implicitly with a positivist-inspired approach to scientific inquiry, which drives a distinctive social scientific ontological position, according to which the 'political' and the 'economic' are simply variables to be modelled formally and their coefficients estimated empirically. But, the political scientist from case study B, who reflected on the problem of methodological conflict discussed above, worked with a different approach to scientific inquiry and a different set of assumptions about the nature of the political domain. Professing a commitment to a 'problem-oriented approach' and emphasizing that she was very much '*question* driven rather than perspective driven', the political scientist refused to identify with any of the approaches defined by Marsh and Stoker (2002a, 2010) as characterizing the discipline of politics because what sort of approach she adopted would depend on the nature of the question asked:

> *people have talked about different schools of thought in politics... To what extent do you identify with any of those labels? I'm thinking of the Marsh and Stoker book.*
> Yes, I know the Marsh and Stoker book. No, I don't. I don't at all... I can see institutionalism, for example... has a great *utility* in terms of particular research questions... But I don't identify in any sense with any of those labels. They seem to me labels that can... methodologies, perspectives that can be useful for particular research questions.

However, the sorts of topics she was interested in and the sorts of issues she had addressed over the course of her academic career – such as thinking about 'embedded patterns of behaviour' and explaining 'decision making', 'patterns of social inclusion and political inclusion' and 'mentalities of behaviour' – did betray the influence of a distinctive *philosophical* approach to social inquiry. The nature of this underlying philosophical position can be discerned more clearly in the following extract, which is the political scientist's response to a question about the nature of social phenomena:

> if I want to explain social inclusion... given the nature of my methods, given my view about the importance of local knowledge of... if you like, opening up the historical construction of that process of social exclusion, I've got no choice really but to think about what you might want to see as invisible structures or about the importance of... those social relationships, those mind-sets, those embedded state patterns, which have led to that process of visible social exclusion... So... it's clear to *me* that it's not enough to identify or to think about something that is only visible.

Now, what is explicit in the foregoing extract is the idea that social reality has depth – that there is an unobservable but nevertheless real context underlying the phenomena we observe directly. But, what is more implicit is the idea that this underlying context – of 'social relationships' and 'mind-sets' – is somehow the cause of what we observe and experience directly and that it is the task of social science to understand how this context works. Indeed, these remarks are highly consistent with the philosophical approach implicit in the political scientist's other published research outputs, which are broadly concerned with the roles that different actors – such as aid donors, local social movements and governments at different levels – play in different contexts, and the nature of their interrelationships. We might summarize her approach to social inquiry in these works as comparative–historical and structural–agential in their method of explanation and qualitative-led in their method of inquiry (since they rely predominantly on the use of documentary and interview evidence to infer the existence of social structures and causal mechanisms underlying the course of events).

Moreover, although she does not articulate it explicitly, in both her oral account and published research outputs the political scientist presents a distinctive conception of the nature of political phenomena. The political is not a conventionally defined event or state of affairs, such as a riot or some other type of violence; rather, it refers to the differential exercise of power in society and thus describes an 'aspect' of social reality that lies beyond direct experience.

In short, the intellectual position that can be discerned in the foregoing extract and in the written work of one of the political scientists from case study B is consistent with (although by no means completely defining of) the philosophy of transcendental realism that I elaborated in Chapter 2 because it presupposes that there is a reality beyond what we can experience directly; and it stands in contrast to the intellectual position of the economist she is working with, which, as we have seen, is consistent with (although, again, not defining of) a positivist philosophy in presupposing that reality can be reduced to what we can observe and measure directly. Hence, both intellectual frameworks entail different political scientific ontological assumptions – that is, assumptions about the meaning of the political – and social philosophical assumptions – that is, assumptions about the nature of social objects in general and how they can be known.

Now, 'positivist' is a label that the political scientist previously discussed explicitly rejected. The other political scientist with whom she was working also rejected the use of the term positivist to describe his intellectual position. Because science meant *positivist* science, he was 'anxious' about describing what he did as political science; rather, he was someone who wanted to engage in politics by trying to construct forms of understanding of the political that might be 'useful', an approach to inquiry he described as 'narrative-conceptual'. The following extracts give an indication of this way of thinking:

> *so you described your sort of approach as narrative-conceptual*
> As I guess in contrast to model building, data testing . . . in general I'm . . . not a great believer that there are general laws of social behaviour. I think I . . . actually that's the other way I quite like to describe it – I think of it more 'doing politics stuff' . . . I get a bit anxious about 'political science'.
>
> so there are . . . there are patterns . . . there are useful ways of thinking about stuff that you learn and that you acquire . . . I'm not really looking for general laws; I'm looking for sort of familiar ways of thinking about stuff that are useful.

Now, the foregoing methodological reflections are suggestive of an intellectual position that is a mixture of pragmatism and hermeneutics. The political scientist himself was actually rather reluctant to describe himself as a constructivist. However, the sorts of questions he was interested in asking – 'discursive–normative kind of questions about . . . the way the IMF talks about stuff, the kinds of language that can be used' – the explicit concern with trying to understand the subjective viewpoint – 'empathy kind of stuff' – and the scepticism about 'seeking truth' are all broadly consistent with a philosophy of strong or 'thick' social constructivism (Hay, 2002: 208), according to which social objects are the product of the mind and of discourse and thus do not exist independently of the human subject. This philosophical position was also implicit in an answer the political scientist gave to a question about the ontological status of social structure:

> I would say that people perceive structures, and that it makes sense to think in terms of structures because... they very nearly exist. But in the end I think I'm an individualist. So... I think it makes sense to *talk* about classes... from the point of view of me... engaging in either democratic debate or something, it makes sense for me to think of a class... or a group of economists or something like that. But I think in the end you need to have... some kind of story about how individuals make up that class... I get nervy about... very sort of solid, social entities.

Moreover, this political scientist also recognized the methodological difficulties involved in working with a positivist-inclined economist, the result of which was that what was at the start one project had splintered into two radically different projects:

> I think the reason it's turned into two different projects is *partly* different interests, but I think it's partly very radically different ways of presenting *fairly* similar questions... in other words I think disciplines aren't just defined by subject matter – they're also defined by methodological preferences... and it's the methodological preferences that are a real problem... so... it's where subject matter might want to cross and methodologies clash that you have problems.

Indeed, given his background in both economics and politics, the political scientist saw himself as occupying a 'kind of middle position' in the project from which he would try to 'bridge the gap' between the two methodologies. However, he subsequently realized that he could not be 'the neutral arbitrator between the two' because he had not realized just how inflexible was the economist's methodological frame of reference. As he saw it – and as we have seen above – the economist's conception of doing 'some nice politics' was 'using economic methodology on political phenomena' – a conception that he (the political scientist) explicitly rejected (although the economist did not seem to realize this because the fact that the political scientist could understand economic theory gave the impression that he was more of a positivist than he actually was).

In case study B, then, we have a clear example of methodological conflict, in which three different intellectual frameworks, working against each other, generate a tendency towards intellectual specialization, despite the general consensus at the start of the project, expressed by all three researchers in the interviews, that it would not be possible to understand the politics of the problem they were addressing without at the same time understanding the economics of it and *vice versa*. That said, since most of the research outputs from this project have yet to be produced (at the time of writing), it is difficult to say what the nature of the final outcome will be – an integrated set of results or separate disciplinary analyses (although with two separate books planned – representing more or less the two sides of the project – it seems that the latter – intellectual separation – will be the final outcome).

It may help at this point to contrast case study B with case study A, also a project in political economy but one that addressed a different problem and, because it is completed, one from which research outputs have been published. The project can be neatly divided into two stages (corresponding to different blocks of funding): a first stage, involving a political scientist, lawyer and economist, assisted by a research officer whose intellectual background straddled all three disciplines, and a second stage involving political scientists, a lawyer and a sociologist. Now, an important question to ask is why the economist dropped out of the second stage of the project. Certainly, the research questions posed at the first stage were slightly different from those posed at the first stage and demanded the incorporation of an additional political scientist and sociologist into the research team. But, the fact that both stages of the project were concerned with the same subject matter – political economy – and the fact that the research questions posed at both stages concerned the nature of the firm – one of the economist's areas of expertise – suggests that there was a problem at a methodological level.

Let us examine the nature of this problem in more detail. As in case study B, the general consensus amongst the research team in case study A was that different disciplines were required to address different aspects of the research problem. However, the bid leader for the project – an experienced political scientist – explicitly recognized that a mainstream economist would not have been intellectually compatible with a research team whose theoretical inclination was broadly historical and institutional and in which political science and law were the 'controlling discourses'. The bid leader, then, sought the assistance of an institutional economist because – in his words – a mainstream economist 'would not have agreed with the results'.

Despite all the members of the research team being 'exposed to the way different disciplines conceptualized the company' – particularly law and economics, which both had well-developed literatures on the nature of the firm – any intellectual integration that did occur involved only the disciplines of political science and law – as the jointly authored journal articles arising from the project clearly demonstrate. The economist's research output was limited to one single-authored journal article and his work was not included in the book that was subsequently published. Moreover, when asked why he did not participate in the second stage of the project, the economist revealed that one of the main reasons for this had been intellectual conflict:

> *because I was going to ask you why you didn't participate in the second stage...*
> ...partly because I think [the bid leader] didn't like some of the things I was saying, because it is historical and I actually made this stupid statement where 'History needn't always be relevant'...but now I think that is wrong.

In essence, the intellectual problem was that the economist, despite being an institutional economist who had 'always been interdisciplinary', was at that point in his academic career much closer to the orthodox neoclassical paradigm, which is fundamentally *a*historical in its assumptions, than the bid leader had realized. Indeed, the bid leader had told him explicitly that a historical approach was required but the economist had 'backed off this'.

## Internal intellectual contradictions

Let me now consider the nature of the nature of the intellectual framework drawn on by the economist from case study A in more depth – and, in particular, how it has changed – because up to this point I have been assuming that the intellectual context of knowledge production that individual scientists draw on is completely coherent. However, if the sorts of philosophical contradictions that I have argued exist *between* the intellectual frameworks drawn on by *different* scientists also exist *between* the intellectual frameworks drawn on by the *same* scientist, we cannot simply assume that the intellectual context of knowledge production drawn on by an individual scientist is philosophically coherent.

The intellectual difficulty facing the economist from case study A was that, at the time of the project, he had not found a way to reconcile the transaction cost approach to the firm, which assumes economic equilibrium, with the non-equilibrium assumption that the production base of the firm may change through time. (He had by that point in his career developed a critique of transaction cost economics, which, he had argued, assumed that the production base of the firm was unchanging.) In other words, he had wanted to show how 'both transaction costs and the actual production base of the economy become *relevant* in terms of explaining institutions' but, because he was unable to work out the precise 'mixture' of the two, he felt unable intellectually to follow an historical approach to economic inquiry.

However, since the end of his participation in the collaborative, interdisciplinary research project in political economy, the economist's intellectual position had changed, which is why he thought that his earlier comment about the irrelevance of history was mistaken. What had made him change his mind was his discovery of evolutionary theory, which had allowed him to understand how to combine a static with a dynamic approach to the theory of the firm. As he put it, he had developed 'a particular take on evolutionary theory' in which 'static theory' featured as 'a special case'. In other words, he was not concerned with developing an alternative to equilibrium economics – the path that some of his colleagues in institutional economics had taken – but with trying to incorporate equilibrium economics into evolutionary economics. Crucially, in his view this approach implies that 'the ontology of the firm' is 'inevitably interdisciplinary' in the sense that different disciplinary perspectives become 'relevant' at different stages in the evolution of the firm. The following extract from the economist's oral account describes the basic contours of this line of thought:

> when you're talking about the fundamental restructuring, the early restructuring of institutional arrangements, then you do that from a pre-given set of... institutional arrangements; and that is basically often the insight and the world that sociologists exist in... But then, once you actually get the initial shock within a given world order, then you get this enormous political problem about how can *dominant* agents or the leading agents then guide the evolution of existing institutions... And then, after that, then I think the... traditional economic approaches become relevant.

In other words, the primary and secondary stages in the evolution of the firm – the pre-equilibrium stages – have to be studied from the perspectives of sociology and political science, whereas the third and final stage, the equilibrium stage, which may never be reached because it is simply a point of attraction to which the economy converges, has to be studied from the perspective of orthodox economics. The upshot of this line of thought is that the study of the firm, as a quintessentially interdisciplinary object, requires – in the words of the economist – 'multiple methodologies', which are 'relevant in different contexts' and which, in his view, the 'imperialistic' application of orthodox economic approaches across the social sciences is 'wrong' to deny.

However, the economist in case study A also professed, without realizing, an alternative conception of the firm, according to which the different disciplinary perspectives previously identified as being 'relevant' are somehow ontologically inseparable:

> The firm *is* an interdisciplinary unit... and so to have a peculiar view that you can actually isolate the economic factors in that, separate from the non-economic factors, whether it's psychology, sociology, politics – I'm particularly interested in sociology and politics – but you have to have a really *peculiar* view of how the firm operates, that somehow its psychological, political and sociological context or whatever is somehow *separate* from its economic context.

Now, implicit in the foregoing extract is a philosophical theory about the nature of social objects, which is that, in virtue of the ontological interdependence of their different aspects, social objects, such as the firm, are complex. (We met this theory in Chapters 1 and 2.) This theory also emerged in the economist's response to a question about the nature of the economic:

> economics is basically everything because anything that involves the exchange of any good or service – it doesn't have to be a monetary exchange, it could be a gift relationship, it could be intra-family transfers, it could be transfers within the firm – *anything* that involves a transfer of goods and services of any resource, then, is up for grabs as an economic issue... So it becomes *everything* in a way, everything in a social *science* context... But equally, everything is equally sociological, and psychological, and political. It's just that economists often ignore them!

However, there is an obvious contradiction between claiming, on the one hand, that different aspects of social reality are interdependent and must be understood as such and, on the other hand, claiming that different aspects of social reality exist somehow in juxtaposition to each other, which is the implication of the economist's attempt to incorporate a static analysis of the firm into an evolutionary framework. To put it in a different way, we cannot assume that the different aspects of a social object are ontologically inseparable and then try to explain the nature of this object in a way that presupposes that its different aspects are *not* inseparable without contradicting ourselves.

We can relate this contradiction to the theories of intellectual integration considered in Chapter 1 and, more broadly, to the philosophies of science discussed in Chapter 2. For example, the idea that different disciplinary perspectives become relevant at different times, which we may call 'ontological independence', resonates with the concept of multidisciplinarity, according to which separate disciplinary analyses of a common problem are juxtaposed rather than synthesized. Moreover, the teleological take on social evolution, with which the concept of ontological independence is combined, resonates with the closed systems ontology of positivism, according to which historical change is simply a process of adjustment from a state of disequilibrium back to a state of equilibrium. By contrast, the concept of ontological *inter*dependence is consistent with the concept of integrative interdisciplinarity, according to which connections are formed between different disciplinary analyses of the same phenomenon. But, it is also consistent with the closely related concepts of emergence and stratification, which, as we saw in Chapter 2, are the crucial building blocks of a transcendental realist ontology – an ontology of open systems (and hence contingent evolution), in which historical change and continuity exist in symbiosis and (in the social sphere) as (largely) unintentional transformation and reproduction. Once again, then, we can see in the oral account of the economist from case study A that contradictory social *scientific* ontological assumptions about the interdisciplinary nature of the firm derive from contradictory social *philosophical* ontological assumptions about the nature of social objects in general.

We can detect similar sorts of contradiction in the oral account of the development economist from case study B. As we saw above, some elements of the economist's professed account of science are consistent with a positivist way of thinking – in particular, the implicit regularity theory of causation, which is associated with an empiricist epistemology. However, other elements in his thinking are clearly consistent with a structural theory of causation (according to which manifest events and states of affairs are the outcomes of the contingent and complex exercise of the casual powers and liabilities of underlying entities) and thus imply a transcendental realist philosophy of science. For example, in response to a question about why he preferred interdisciplinary research the economist had this to say:

> I think it's because of my approach, which... is rather arts side; in other words it's an approach which tries to understand the story and the plot which

> underlies processes in which I'm interested, like...creation of poverty or unemployment. So I'm very, very impatient with... models which don't have any explanatory power in the sense of explaining what are the forces at work but have lots of explanatory power in the sense of having high correlation coefficients. I really can't stand that kind of...research, that kind of estimation process, and maybe it could be said that my approach is a little bit sort of detective story or arts side, rather than the approach which is trying to establish formal models. I mean, I do...design models. On the other hand I...insist that they be models which tell a story, and I insist that the... story be *validated* by the qualitative evidence of people who are actually telling stories about their own experience.

The same sort of contradiction can be detected in the economist's published research output. For example, if we examine the country-specific case study that the economist prepared as a pilot study for the main project, we find an extensive historical narrative, which implicitly assumes a structural theory of causation, juxtaposed with a formal model – a system of simultaneous equations – which has been estimated using techniques of statistical regression. Yet, it is ambiguous how the formal model relates to the historical narrative. The impression given is that the two sorts of analysis are telling the same sort of explanatory story; but it is far from clear if the explanation is to be found at a purely empirical level of reality, which is what the interpretation of the results of the model (the coefficients of the independent variables) suggests, or if it is to be found at a deeper level of reality, which would imply that the dependent and independent variables in the formal model are indicators of the effects of the operation of underlying social structures and causal mechanisms. I suggest that we can only make sense of this ambiguity if we are prepared to accept that there may be a contradiction within the philosophical part of the intellectual context that the development economist implicitly draws on.

### *Professional and lay knowledge: under-theorization*

We can think about the philosophical contradictions previously identified as reflections of two different types of persona: the professional and the lay. The professional persona embodies the knowledge that a person has acquired through a period of education and training by means of which that person gains entry to a professional occupation. For example, doctors, lawyers, priests and, in our case, scientists all adopt a particular professional persona in accordance with the particular role they play in society – a role that society recognizes as, and so grants the status of, professional. The professional persona of scientist, therefore, embodies the knowledge a person has acquired through a systematic programme of education and training that qualifies that person to practise as a scientist and thus to produce knowledge of particular objects of reality. By contrast, lay personas – for example, that of parent or guardian – embody the knowledge a person has acquired through carrying out a range of non-scientific, sociocultural practices.

This sort of knowledge reflects the awareness we develop of the way in which our lives are regulated. It is practical knowledge, just as scientific knowledge is, because it is generated through practical engagement with the world and hence through experience of practical success and failure; but, it is practical knowledge of a different sort because it is acquired non-systematically. Lay practical knowledge is distinguished from scientifically produced practical knowledge, therefore, according to the degree to which it represents an incomplete and false understanding of the world. So, as lay actors we may tend to think of the wage form as equal to the value of what we produce, whereas as professional social scientists we may understand it as equal to the value of human labour power.

However, the property that both lay and scientific knowledge have in common is that both may be *under-theorized*. By this I mean that, as forms of practical knowledge, both lay and scientific knowledge presuppose philosophical assumptions – about the nature of knowledge and the nature of reality. But, because these assumptions are typically *implicitly* understood, they tend to be under-theorized; that is, both lay actor and scientist may be able to explain only some of these assumptions. For example, I have already discussed the case of an economist whose professed understanding of social science revealed only some of the components of a positivist theory of science; that is, the economist was unable to articulate the full set of methodological, epistemological and ontological principles characteristic of positivism.

Not only do lay and scientific practical knowledge have in common the property that they may be under-theorized, they also have in common the property that they may presuppose *contradictory* philosophical assumptions. For example, the knowledge we acquire through our everyday experiences of living in society and of the successes and failures that go with this, may presuppose that there is a reality beyond what is directly accessible by sensory experience but one that we can still know about through inference from direct experience. Yet, the knowledge we produce as professionals through scientific inquiry may presuppose a contradictory set of philosophical assumptions. Thus, as scientists, we may understand our use of certain methods in a way that implicitly assumes that what we can know is limited to what we can observe and measure, so that, whereas our professional persona may reflect a positivist or empirical realist ontology, our lay persona may reflect a transcendental realist one. Alternatively, our professional persona may reflect the influence of an implicit transcendental realist ontology, whereas our lay persona may reflect the influence of an implicit empirical realist ontology. For example, in our spontaneous way of thinking and in our everyday interventions in the natural world – perhaps through primitive scientific experimentation – we may come to expect that when one thing regularly follows another, the latter is the cause and the former the effect. Indeed, this sort of 'everyday empiricism of common sense' (Mills, 1959: 123) may be very much an unintended consequence of social practices. Thus, we may read newspaper reports of scientific studies that present the results of such studies in a way that encourages us to form simple associations between things, such as eating certain foods and developing certain diseases. (Of course, this sort of regularity determinism may be implicit in the interpretation offered by the scientific studies themselves.)

### *Conscious and subconscious thinking: cross-theorization*

In the previous section, I have argued that the lay and scientific forms of practical knowledge may be philosophically contradictory. However, such contradictions may exist not only between lay actors and professional scientists, where these roles are occupied by different people, but also within the same person occupying both types of role. Now, if we are to explain why we often find inconsistencies between what scientists profess about science (their theorization of science) and how they actually practise scientific inquiry, we need to refer to conscious and subconscious levels of thought. What is happening, I suggest, is that when a person takes on the role of social scientist, the professional persona dominates the lay persona, in the sense that it is professional knowledge that emerges at the conscious level of the person and it is lay knowledge that remains at the subconscious level. This pattern is only a tendency because there may be situations (such as an interview) in which the influence of the subconscious form of thought is triggered (perhaps by a particular interview question) so that what emerges at the conscious level is a contradiction in what is said. By contrast, when the person acts in a lay capacity, the reverse occurs; that is, it is the lay persona that dominates the professional persona and it is the person's exercise of subconsciously held professional knowledge that may affect his or her conscious performance in the role of lay actor. It is this process, I suggest, of slipping back and forth between consciously held and subconsciously held forms of thought that explains the appearance of contradictions and ambiguities in both the oral account and the published research outputs of the economist in case study B. However, to reinforce a point I made earlier, because the philosophical presuppositions of scientific knowledge are (largely) implicitly understood, the economist did not realize that what he was professing in the interview and doing in practice was often contradictory and ambiguous. (Indeed, the fact that social research may still make sense in some way or other, and may have relative practical success, may also tend to obscure from view the contradictions and ambiguities embedded within it.)

Therefore, it is important to emphasize that the terms 'implicit' and 'explicit' should not be confused with the terms 'subconscious' and 'conscious'. Given an appropriate education, the scientist may be able to articulate the philosophical assumptions of his or her thinking so that both the scientific and philosophical elements are rendered explicit to his or her audience. He or she may also be able to articulate explicitly the philosophical assumptions inherent in his or her lay persona. Even so, the latter will tend to remain at a subconscious level of thought when the professional persona of scientist is assumed. Furthermore, it is also important to emphasize that it is the social context that provides the contingent conditions for the exercise of lay and professional forms of thought. Hence, when I say that the professional persona is dominant, I mean to say that the social context is such that it grants the professional persona greater causal effect than the lay persona and *vice versa*. In short, what we have are two different sorts of intellectual structure, whose causal powers are being triggered to different extents in different social conditions. The result is that not only are many of the claims scientists make about the nature of science *under-theorized* but they are also *cross-theorized* in virtue of the way in which the stratification of the mind mediates the causal effect of pre-existing (contradictory) ideas.[1]

## The complexity of the intellectual context of science

I now want to draw out the implications of the preceding argument for the possibility of integrating knowledge from different disciplines in a philosophically coherent way. Let me do this by using the distinction between the professional and lay persona to compare the intellectual position of the economist in case study B with that of one of the political scientists from the same project. Now, the major *difference* between these two scientists lies at the professional level because one is implicitly committed to a positivist approach to social inquiry, whereas the other is (less) implicitly committed to an interpretivist approach. But, the major *similarity* between them lies at a lay level because both seem to draw on an implicit 'everyday depth-realism' in the historical narratives they produce. Certainly, the emphasis in the political scientist's publications is on how actors understand and discursively construct their roles in society; indeed, in one particular published research paper the political scientist offers an interpretation of a particular set of events and state of affairs that draws on two different ways of thinking and talking about civil society. But, much of the historical narrative, which refers to the patterns of economic and political development of specific countries, trades on an ontological and epistemological materialism, which is implicit in the author's discussion of political challenge and social conflict and which contradicts the political scientist's professed commitment to a position of (strong) social constructivism.

We may easily conclude, then, that the political scientist's intellectual position turns on a contradiction between interpretivism–pragmatism, characteristic of the professional persona, and depth–realism, characteristic of the lay persona. But, that would be to ignore the fact that the political scientist's professional persona has emerged through a critical engagement with positivist philosophy. This critical engagement, as the extracts from the political scientist's oral account above suggest, has taken the political scientist towards interpretivism and pragmatism rather than transcendental realism. The result is that the political scientist's professed understanding of *natural* science is explicitly positivist, whereas his professed understanding of *social* science is implicitly interpretivist. Hence, not only is there a philosophical contradiction between the political scientist's professional and lay persona but there is also a philosophical contradiction *within* the political scientist's professional persona. This is why, despite claiming to be an interpretivist – albeit implicitly – the political scientist thinks of 'general laws of social behaviour' in a positivist sense yet fails to realize that in his publications he implicitly trades on a transcendental realist conception of social scientific laws as descriptions of ways of working of underlying social structures.

The research officer from case study A, whose intellectual background was in economics and law, had also engaged critically with positivism; however, that critical engagement had taken him towards transcendental realism rather than interpretivism. As a student of orthodox economics the research officer had found the 'theoretical rigour' of deductivist methodology intellectually appealing but, at the same time, he had 'always been questioning of fairly conventional economics and felt that it was missing something'. This 'questioning' had led to an increasing interest in the 'political, historical, institutional and legal side of things', as the following extract reveals:

> I think what I got interested in was... believing that there was an intellectual merit to the sort of structure of first-principles-based thought... knowing that there was something in the critique of those assumptions, which then made you question the whole edifice; and then from that... saying, 'What happens when you start to question the assumptions but keep assumptions?' So it was... playing around... with public choice theory... I suppose that was the sort of space... which seemed to sort of try and take some of the critique but not throw the whole approach out – that... was basically where I was coming from. I think I probably ended up... still interested in that but also thinking... that without just the sort of deeper, richer, historical knowledge of a particular subject area... that that sort of approach – even refined – can only take you so far. So I ended up getting very into the sort of historical–institutionalist type literature.

So, despite having engaged critically with 'first-principles-based thought' and despite having moved towards an 'historical–institutionalist' approach, the research officer still found the deductivist methodology of orthodox economics intellectually attractive. In other words, the process of critical engagement led to, not intellectual replacement of, but intellectual *dis*placement within, the professional persona of one form of thought by another. But, once again, the result was that the research officer's professional persona on its own now embodied a philosophical contradiction. This can be discerned clearly in his PhD thesis on regional finance, where, on the one hand, he draws on historical institutionalism to explain the development of the financial system in three different countries and, on the other hand, he draws on the 'new informational economics' to explain how different types of financial system allocate credit. Yet, these two analytical approaches presuppose contradictory conceptions of human agency. The imperfect information models of credit markets may well be more realistic in the sense that they relax many of the assumptions made in orthodox economics models – most obviously in this case the assumption of perfect information – but they are still formal, equilibrium-based models in which agents are assumed to be utility maximizers, amongst other things. In assuming that agents everywhere make optimal decisions we are once again back in a world of regularity determinism and positivist-style scientific laws. By contrast, in explaining the institutional diversity of financial systems the research officer presupposes a much broader and, ultimately, more intelligible conception of human agency, which implicitly recognizes people's powers of consciousness – for example, reflexivity and intentionality – properties that presuppose that social life is characterized as much by indeterminacy as determinacy – a conception of human agency that is consistent with a transcendental realist conception of causation as complex and contingent.

Therefore, the empirical evidence I have just discussed suggests that intellectual change amounts to something much more subtle and gradual than a 'gestalt switch' (Kuhn, 1970c: 204) – that it involves a complex process of philosophical displacement and incorporation rather than a simple process of philosophical replacement. Scientific paradigms cannot be closed, philosophically consistent and autonomous wholes, as Kuhn assumes, but must be open and so characterized by variations in philosophical consistency and inconsistency and dependence and interdependence of their elements. If a paradigm is open in this sense, it will be a contingent matter in which direction it develops when one or more of its elements is subjected to critique. We have seen, for example, that a critique of positivist empiricism has taken one social scientist in the direction of interpretivism, while a critique of positivist deductivism has taken another in the direction of transcendental realism.[2] But, the fact that, in the latter case, residues of the displaced philosophy still remain influential means that the intellectual context in that case is characterized by philosophical inconsistency (although determining to what degree would require further investigation);[3] and the fact that in the former case the displacing philosophical theory – that is, interpretivism – depends on the displaced philosophical theory – that is, positivism – means that the intellectual context in that case comprises interconnected philosophical theories. In short, the possibility of intellectual change, from which multiple, contradictory philosophical theories may emerge, means that the intellectual context a person (implicitly) draws on, whether in the guise of professional scientist or layperson, may be highly *complex*.

However, I want to suggest that the very complexity of the intellectual context of knowledge production, although clearly problematic if it generates methodological conflict between scientists (as we have seen), may, at the same time, provide an opportunity for the emergence of philosophical consensus between scientists. For example, I suggest that it is by virtue of the complexity of their intellectual positions that the two researchers I have just discussed may be able to find a way of reconciling their methodological differences. Consider the following sets of extracts. The first set comes from the oral account of the political scientist from case study B, who was asked to reflect upon how the two different methodologies in the project might be brought together so as to generate a coherent outcome:

> I would say that my way of doing social science is more philosophically sophisticated...and I recognize a variety of different ways of answering a

> political question...And so when I use, for example, a nice econometric thing, probably I think it says less than the person who wrote it thinks it says; so I'm probably more critical about what's been proved...and so I'll use it as part of a tool for understanding the social world.

> I would argue that...what you've got is a correlation...and what's key about that is when somebody does find a strong correlation there's something that needs to be explained if the correlation doesn't fit with your causal theory. But likewise...once you've got the correlation you need to have some theoretical account of causation that produces the correlation...and if you haven't got that, then I'm not happy.

The second set of extracts comes from the oral account of the research officer from case study A, who was asked to reflect upon the meaning of 'rigour' in social science:

> I don't believe that economics has got a monopoly on rigour...at all...It was just...it was *a form* of rigour, which I thought had something to offer...and that...there are other forms of rigour.

> the thing that I remember feeling quite sceptical about...and thinking...'I don't want to do that', I just read quite a few PhDs, or just academic articles...all they did was describe lots of historical trends...and you never felt that you got to the roots of what was the underlying causation...but for me, I wanted my PhD to be political causation, and trying to have a theoretical understanding of...what might be explaining causation as well as an empirical understanding of what...actually happened...I guess that was what I was after in terms of rigour...and if you just describe patterns of historical events without really understanding what caused them...then you didn't really understand all the causes and...I suppose I wanted to understand all the causes, best I could, of why we saw certain economic phenomena in one place and not in another place.

In both cases, the researchers understand that empirical regularities are something to be explained at a deeper level of reality. Yet, it is interesting to observe that, whereas depth realism is implicit to the political scientist's lay persona, it is implicit to the research officer's professional persona. We may wonder, then, why the development economist in case study B, who was working with the same political scientist and whose lay persona also embodied an implicit depth realism, cannot understand the relationship between the results of the econometric modelling and the results of the qualitative case studies in the same way. The answer, I suggest, lies in the difference between the structures of economics and political science in the United Kingdom. As I argued in the previous chapter and as I discuss in the next, positivist philosophy of science continues to dominate the field of economics in a way that tends to discourage methodological reflection and critique. Of course, this is not to deny that there are voices within economics critical of the dominant orthodoxy. For example, the institutional economist in case study A is clearly someone who has engaged critically with the neoclassical core of economics. Yet, this critical engagement did not take him as far away from orthodox thinking as it took the research officer from case study A and the political scientist from case study B. Indeed, this suggests that there is much greater acceptance of methodological pluralism within the UK politics profession than within UK economics. (As I show in the next chapter, all the political scientists interviewed agreed that political scientists in Britain were generally more eclectic in their greater tolerance of methodological diversity than political scientists in the United States.)

Finally, it is also interesting to observe that when asked to think about the possibility of reconciling the two sides of the project in case study B, the political scientist seemed to slip back from a professional persona, which presupposed an interpretivist approach, to a lay persona, which embodied a transcendental realist approach. (This should not come as a surprise because, as we have seen in Chapter 2, transcendental realism has developed dialectically by way of reconciliation of pre-existing philosophical dichotomies.) Now, given that the intellectual frameworks of the economist and the political scientist from case study B both embody the philosophy of transcendental realism, at least in a lay sense, I suggest that the two researchers have the *potential* to produce a philosophically coherent integrative outcome when working together. However, if intellectual positions are typically under-theorized as well as cross-theorized, as I argued earlier, both researchers would need to recognize the philosophical and scientific commonalities and differences in their intellectual positions – all of which would require a period of re-education for the researchers concerned. However, in the absence of that re-education and in the presence of unrecognized intellectual contradictions, successful intellectual integration through interdisciplinary research will be difficult to achieve, whether the integration is to be carried out by a single researcher or by a team of disciplinary specialists.

## Conclusion

The objective of this chapter was to examine the relationship between the intellectual context of knowledge production and the decisions scientists make about how to produce knowledge in light of evidence from three case studies of (collaborative) interdisciplinary research projects. In focusing in this chapter on the relationship between the intellectual context of knowledge production and scientific practice, I am of course taking out of consideration temporarily – that is, abstracting from – the effect of the social context of knowledge production. This abstraction is justified once it is understood that the social context of knowledge production reveals its effect through the decisions scientists make about what sort of knowledge to produce, which, in the case of scientists interested in integrating knowledge, is a decision about whether to produce disciplinary or interdisciplinary research (and, if the latter, whether to do so individually or collaboratively). Focusing on the effect of the intellectual context, therefore – which, to recall the argument of Chapter 3, must be conceived as the pre-existing (largely unacknowledged) condition for, and so the (largely unintended) outcome of, (intentional) scientific practice – allows us to understand how human agents – in this case scientists – mediate the effect of underlying philosophical ideas and, to a lesser extent, how the development of scientists' thinking mediates the transformation of such ideas. Of course, philosophical ideas are not the only pre-existing conditions for scientific activity, for scientists will draw first and foremost on the products (that is, scientific theories) of other scientists' work and will transform these through the logic of scientific discovery.[4] But, in doing so they will be reproducing (typically unintentionally) a more fundamental set or framework of philosophical ideas, which their scientific products presuppose. It is the nature of this framework that is our chief concern because we cannot begin to explain the difficulties scientists get into when attempting to produce integrative, interdisciplinary research without understanding the effect it has on scientists' thinking.

How, then, is the effect of underlying philosophical ideas mediated by scientists? The essence of my argument is that this effect is mediated by the structure of the mind – through the conscious and subconscious – and that the evidence for this comes in the form of inconsistencies in the philosophical ideas that scientists' discursive reflections and actual practices presuppose. These inconsistencies, I suggest, are the result of scientists' developing contradictory forms of knowledge when occupying different roles in society – those of scientist (the professional persona) and non-scientist (the lay persona). When the professional persona of scientist is assumed, it is scientific knowledge that dominates the conscious thinking of the actor but this is only a tendency, by virtue of the possibility of the social context triggering the effect of subconsciously held lay knowledge, which may be philosophically contradictory. Likewise, when the lay persona is assumed, it is lay knowledge that dominates the conscious thinking of the actor. Again, this is only tendency, by virtue of the possibility of the social context triggering the effect of subconsciously held scientific knowledge, which may be philosophically contradictory. Hence, we may find philosophical contradictions: (a) within scientists' discursive reflections on the nature of scientific inquiry – a situation of theory–theory inconsistency (a type of formal-logical contradiction); (b) within scientists' actual research products – a situation of practice–practice inconsistency (a type of axiological contradiction); and (c) between scientists' discursive reflections and actual research products – a situation of theory–practice inconsistency (a type of quasi-logical contradiction).

Moreover, I also argued that philosophical contradictions may be evident *within* the professional persona of the scientist as a result of the scientist's intellectual development. What this process suggests, though, is that scientists are capable of becoming aware of the contradictions in their thinking and of attempting to resolve them through critical reflection. However, typically, this process leads to the displacement rather than replacement of one form of thought by another within the conscious thinking of the scientist so that vestiges of the displaced form continue to exert an effect via the triggering of subconscious thoughts.

The susceptibility of pre-existing intellectual frameworks to change, though, takes us to questions about their constitution. What can we say about the nature of these frameworks? I suggest that we should think of particular frameworks or forms of thought as partial totalities comprising logical relations of necessity between theories and/or concepts. For example, we can think of the philosophy of transcendental realism as a totality in virtue of the logical relations of entailment and presupposition between its various elements – the ideas contained within the categories of ontology, epistemology and methodology. Thus, to recall the discussion of the first section of Chapter 2, the ontological concepts of intransitivity, stratification and transfactuality entail the epistemological concepts of relativism, fallibilism and judgemental rationality and *vice versa* – relativism, fallibilism and judgemental rationality presuppose intransitivity, stratification and transfactuality. In turn, any epistemological position entails a methodological position; hence, relativism, fallibilism and judgemental rationality entail methodological unity-in-diversity or critical methodological pluralism and *vice versa* – methodological unity-in-diversity or critical methodological pluralism, presupposes relativism, fallibilism and judgemental rationality. So, we can understand how these sets of concepts 'emerge' – in the sense of derive – from each other so as to form a lattice-work of logically connected ideas. Yet, the susceptibility of philosophical systems to change, by virtue of the *aporiai* within them, indicates that they must be understood as incomplete and so open. Again, the development of critical realism through successive stages is a clear example of intellectual change, whereby conceptual absences at each stage are remedied through 'totalising depth praxis' (Bhaskar, 1993: 179). Hence, the openness of totalities of ideas to further expansion establishes them as partial.

However, the existence of philosophical inconsistencies in the products of scientific inquiry and in scientists' discursive reflections suggests that the intellectual context of knowledge production as a whole not only comprises partial totalities but is also shot through with, or punctuated by, '*sub-totalities*' (ibid: 126), which may be seen as various instances of the 'irrealist ensemble' (ibid: 383) – such as positivism. The contradictions entrained by irrealist forms of thought become blocks on the production of integrative forms of knowledge in the sense that (residual) irrealist forms of thought come into conflict with realist forms of thought via the stratification of the mind, so that scientists find it difficult to understand the possibility of scientific differentiation and integration. If scientists are to develop an understanding of the possibility of integration, therefore, they will have to become aware of the blocks in their thinking and overcome them in a way that resolves (rather than simply glosses over) the identified contradiction(s). But, whether or not scientists will be able or willing to develop such an understanding depends on the nature of the social context of knowledge production, which I consider in the following chapter.

# 5 The social context of knowledge production

In the previous chapter, I examined in some detail the relationship between the intellectual context of knowledge production and the decisions that scientists take about how to produce knowledge in abstraction from the social context of knowledge production. I now want to examine the relationship between the social context of knowledge production and the decisions that scientists take about what sort of knowledge to produce – whether specialized, disciplinary or integrative, interdisciplinary research – but in abstraction from the intellectual context of knowledge production. My objective is to shed further light both on the nature of the social context of knowledge production – that is, the types of social entity of which it is comprised – and on how its causal effect is mediated by the agency of scientists. The underlying assumption is that we can understand both the nature and effect of this context through comparison of the challenges, choices and dilemmas facing scientists from different disciplines and the strategies they adopt in response – from which we can then draw conclusions about the degree to which the production of integrative forms of knowledge varies across disciplines.

However, although I focus in the first section of the chapter on the nature and effect of the social context of knowledge production – in particular, the connections between the structures of peer review, academic employment and the division of labour in (social) science, their effect on choice of publication strategy and thus how intellectual boundaries between disciplines are maintained – I bring the intellectual context back in to the argument explicitly in the second section, where I consider the relationship between social science and society, because, as I argued in Chapter 3, the social and intellectual contexts of knowledge production are interdependent.

## The social scientific division of labour, peer review and the academic career ladder

### *The Research Assessment Exercise and publication strategy*

Let me start the discussion by comparing the way in which social considerations weigh in the minds of the economist in case study A and the economist in case study B. Now, despite their obvious substantive differences – the former professing a commitment to institutionalist economics, the latter to development economics – both economists described their work as interdisciplinary. However, we saw in the previous chapter that the research outputs and oral accounts of both researchers presuppose radically different conceptions of interdisciplinarity. On the one hand, the economist in case study A is working with a 'heterodox' conception of scientific integration, according to which different social science disciplines study distinct, yet interdependent, aspects of a social object – a conception consistent with a transcendental realist philosophy of science. On the other hand, the economist in case study B is working with an 'orthodox' conception of scientific integration, according to which the subject matter of different social science disciplines becomes a set of different variables to be modelled formally and estimated empirically – a conception consistent with a positivist philosophy of science.

Now, the problem facing the economist from case study A was that heterodox interdisciplinary work was not 'Research Assessment Exercise (RAE) submittable'; that is, such work would not help a research-led economics department to achieve a relatively high score in the RAE. Producing such work in such a department, therefore, could have adverse material consequences:

> RAE submittable means that you've got good – but good defined in terms of economic criteria – refereed articles... A lot of my work is actually considered not up to the mark to be honest. But... I tend to ignore it!
>
> I was held back from promotion, to be honest. I know that because I don't publish. I've been told by my head of department that if I can publish three economically respectable papers they'll get me a chair... But to be honest I'm quite happy where I'm working. If those three economically respectable papers emerge, then I wouldn't say 'No'.

It is not that heterodox interdisciplinary work cannot be submitted to an RAE review panel, then; rather it is that, given the structure of economics, which, as I argued in Chapter 3, is such that a highly restrictive orthodox core dominates a more open heterodox periphery, submitting heterodox interdisciplinary work to an RAE panel that reflected this structural dominance may be counterproductive because the danger is that a majority of panel members will regard heterodox work published in 'one-star' journals as having less value than orthodox work published in 'three-star' journals. In short, the problem facing the economist in case study A is that it is orthodox economics that defines the criteria for professional competence in the discipline.

Now, the fact that the disciplinary elite in economics considered heterodox interdisciplinary work to be substandard posed a 'challenge' for heterodox theorists. On the one hand, the economist did not want to move out of economics and into management (the department in which he had worked originally before economics separated from it) and, on the other hand, the economist did not want to become a full-blown orthodox theorist because both strategies would have been an intellectual sacrifice too far. The economist responded to this dilemma, therefore, by compromising with the departmental agenda. The informal understanding that emerged was that the department would let him pursue his interests in heterodox political economy and, in return, he would try to inject an orthodox approach into his work so as to produce more 'acceptable' research outputs for the department. He described this strategy as 'schizophrenic':

> I actually am a bit schizophrenic here... for RAE purposes... you can't run away from the RAE... I've actually tried to do some heavyweight empirical econometric work. But I'm trying to do it in a way which recognizes my wider interests... and that makes it *really* hard. And so, for example, at the moment I'm doing some work using what's called neural networks... But... because they're mathematically quite heavyweight and econometrically quite heavyweight, they're actually instantly more acceptable – they're deemed more scientific by the economics community... But I don't see that as any different from my more political economy interests... which don't have any mathematics in at all.

> I'm actually *quite* explicit that I *have* to play the game to some extent; I have a responsibility to play the game, as long as they let me. I've been invited to a Galbraith Memorial session at the International Studies Association conference next year... as long as the department lets me do things like that... I'm also happy to spend a bit of my time doing things like neural networks... But they're more respectable because they're mathematical... So I *have* to play the game to some extent

By understanding that he had to 'play the game', the economist in case study A dealt with the pressures of the RAE pragmatically. By contrast, RAE pressures had a different set of consequences for the economist from case study B. For this researcher, there was no need to think about finding a compromise between orthodox and heterodox work because the sort of work he produced, even though it was interdisciplinary, was acceptable to the disciplinary elite, in the sense that it conformed to orthodox methodological criteria. Accordingly, this economist did not have difficulty publishing work in 'good' economics journals and had not been held back from promotion. What did concern him, though, was how 'good' his work was and whether or not he could improve it enough for it to be published in top-of-the-range journals:

> *moving on to the Research Assessment Exercise... I was wondering how this... if it has indeed at all... affected the sort of research you choose to do?* ... it has made me feel out of patriotism for my department I ought to try and get into the highest-level journals that I can... it doesn't worry me too much because... in the end one can always get published, it's a question of where, and I don't mind having sort of slightly more goes at the five-star journals... even if it means that I'm going to get knocked off my perch even

> more often . . . than usual . . . it's actually been quite good for me; for example, it's forced me to improve my econometrics . . . at a much, much greater rate than I otherwise would have done.

So far, I have compared how RAE pressures influenced the decisions that two different types of economist made about what to research and where to publish that research. We can also compare how RAE pressures are manifest in economics with how they are manifest in politics. The first interesting contrast relates to the status of different types of publication medium. In economics, we have seen that there is a general obsession with producing journal articles – particularly single-authored journal articles – and publishing them in high-ranking journals; research monographs and book chapters appear to hold much lower status within the discipline. In politics, by contrast, both journal articles and monographs are equally well-regarded publication media for RAE purposes. However, as one of the political scientists in case study B who was at the beginning of his academic career put it, the rules of the game, even in politics, were such that single-authored outputs generally carried more weight in the RAE than joint-authored ones:

> I grew up in the generation where you had to keep your eye on the RAE; and the rules of the RAE say – it really is like this! – single-authored monographs are good . . . journal articles are better regarded than book chapters, so you try to save your best stuff for journal articles . . . single-authored is less complicated than joint-authored, so on the whole that's preferable.

The second interesting contrast between politics and economics is that, because the former discipline is less obsessed with journal article publication than the latter, the ranking of journals in the former tends to be much less formal than it is in the latter. We have already seen in Chapter 3 that there have been several attempts to formalize the rankings of economics journals typically using data obtained from the Social Science Citation Index® (SSCI) (Liebowitz and Palmer, 1984; Diamond, 1989; Laband and Piette, 1994; Burton and Phimister, 1995). By contrast, according to one highly respected professor of politics, who was the bid leader for the project in case study A, the politics profession – in particular, the politics review panel for the 2001 RAE – has resisted attempts – for example, by Hix (2004) – to formalize the rankings of political science journals.

However, what became clear in the interviews with the political scientists involved in all three case studies was that there was still an *informal* sense of journal status within the discipline of politics. For example, respondents typically cited *Political Studies*, the *British Journal of Politics and International Relations*, *Government and Opposition* and the *Review of International Studies* as examples of leading British journals and the *American Political Science Review* and *International Organization* as leading North American journals. As in economics, the informal sense of journal prestige seemed to relate closely to the perceived opinion of the political science elite. But, this did not mean that *all* political scientists accepted the view that articles published in leading British and American journals necessarily represented work of international excellence and impact. As one of the political scientists from case study B put it:

> Well, I think some people would think that... *Political Studies*, for example, which is supposed to show close to whole of British work done in British politics departments... has got some kind of leading edge. But I'm not convinced about that... I'm not convinced that's really in terms of academics' perceptions of it. I think there may, beyond the publishing, politics might have a little core of people whom they claim beyond others to politics... but I'm not... I'm not sure really if that's particularly important actually.

Indeed, the same political scientist, who worked in the field of development studies, made a clear distinction between what the disciplinary elite perceives as 'good' journals for the purposes of an RAE submission and what her colleagues in development studies would regard as 'good' journals to publish in:

> *So what is the status of development studies journals... how would they fit into the whole politics?*
> Well, I suppose it depends whether you're talking about... whether my colleagues would regard them as good journals to publish in or whether we would be confident in the RAE assessment... and there may be a different answer there because it's quite clear that my colleagues are, would be, very respectful, and there's a good number of people in this department who... in one loose way or another could fit into the development camp, and I don't think anybody would ever suggest that where they publish is not... not good, if they're good journals!
>
> *So what would the alternative answer be for the RAE, then?*
> Well the RAE... depends entirely on the construction of the panel. So... until you know the panel, and until you're absolutely sure about the panel, and you can never be sure who's going to read your work on that panel, then you must be certain you don't get... you don't want somebody picking this up and saying 'Development and Change. What sort of a journal's that?'... and it may be that they won't know it so... you might want to be cautious and make sure that something's published as well in... Political Studies or whatever.

Just as in economics, then, journal publication in politics is used as an indicator of research quality – at least it is for RAE purposes – but more flexibly in the former than in the latter discipline – by which I mean that there is much more variation within the politics profession than within the economics profession in what is chosen as an indicator of research quality. This fact brings us to the third interesting contrast between the two disciplines, which is that the more flexible or informal use of journal publication as an indicator of research quality suggests that politics is the more open of the two disciplines; that is, it is more tolerant of different philosophical approaches to social inquiry. As the political scientist working in development studies put it:

> Well, it seems to me that ... politics departments are more ... broad church than they're often given credit for. So my experience here, for example, is that although I'm far from being a mainstream politics or IR person, that's not really been an issue. It's not been an issue in apparently mainstream politics and IR journals ... So ... there is a breadth here which is often not ... tapped in these debates about perspectives.

Certainly, the current editorial policies of the two elite journals of the British Political Studies Association suggest that politics in the UK is more of a 'broad church' than economics. For example, in 2006 the incoming editors of *Political Studies* professed a commitment:

> to publishing work of high quality whatever its theory, methodology or empirical substance. The way in which we study politics in the UK has never been dominated by a single method or theory and the richness of political science is its pluralism. As editors, we would like to endorse the notion that there is more than one way to do good social science.
>
> (*PS* Editors, 2006: 1)

The particular attention paid to epistemology and methodology is also evident in the introductory editorial for the 1999 launch issue of the *British Journal of Politics and International Relations*. For example, the editors of this journal state that:

> The third aim of the journal is to encourage students of British politics to take epistemological questions more seriously; we strongly advocate epistemological and methodological pluralism in contributions to this journal ... we argue for authors explicitly to acknowledge their positions and for more diversity of epistemological approaches.
>
> (*BJPIR* Editors, 1999: 2)

But, although there may be greater methodological pluralism in politics than in economics, when it comes to defining and defending the boundaries of the domain of the political a different picture emerges. The political scientists interviewed generally felt that it was important to publish not only in leading-edge journals but also in journals that reflected the mainstream or core of politics. Of course, leading-edge journals tended to be mainstream politics journals but the main point was that it was considered dangerous – again, especially for RAE purposes – to limit one's publications to non-mainstream – perhaps interdisciplinary – journals. For example, the political scientist from case study B who worked in the field of development could publish in area studies journals and development studies journals. But, given the interdisciplinary nature of these two fields, she felt she needed to publish in mainstream journals to satisfy the requirements for the RAE:

> we all have to do this, we also have to make sure we touch all the right buttons for the RAE, and we have to make sure we publish in some very mainstream journals. So I would publish in the *European Journal of International Relations*... I would publish in *Government and Opposition*... but equally I would publish in *Global Governance, Third World Quarterly*... *Journal of Latin American Studies*... *Journal of Common Market Studies*.

The political scientist from case study B who worked in the field of international political economy made a similar point:

> I have a feeling that, again, strategically from a professional point of view I probably ought to concentrate on international relations journals... at the moment I have a couple of things that I'm trying to find time to work on which are quite strategically directed at mainstream IR journals... because I think that's a good thing to have on my CV if I'm looking for jobs somewhere else one day. In other words... you need to prove that you can publish in stuff that's at the very core of the discipline... and then if you've done that a bit, it's fine to publish quite a lot elsewhere in something that actually suits what you do better.

It seems, therefore, that, although there is more tolerance of interdisciplinary work in politics than there is in economics – at least if by interdisciplinary we mean the sort of heterodox work defined in the previous chapter – there is clearly a limit to that tolerance if one wants to remain part of the politics discipline. One could, of course, try to publish interdisciplinary work in mainstream politics journals but, for it to be accepted, one would have to frame such work in a way that ensured that it was still relevant to a particular disciplinary audience. As one of the political scientists from case study B, who was an editor of the *Review of International Studies*, explained:

> we're very explicitly open to interdisciplinary work... but I think, having said that... it needs to be framed in a way that clearly addresses our kind of core interests in stuff that's international and political. So we publish things on migration for instance. But it... needs to be saying... it can't just be about the social life of migrant workers in Indonesia; it needs to be how that relates to international politics in some way... and I guess if you stray too far you end up talking a kind of weird language... somebody needs to have gone and read a bit of IR literature as well.

And the department of international relations for which the same researcher worked took a similar attitude to interdisciplinary research:

> it's not that it's actively supportive but it's also not discouraging... it's just that it may not count for very much... unless it's interdisciplinary in a way which feeds so neatly into the IR discipline that there's no question anyway... and... again I kind of get away with that in the sense that there's economics in my stuff... so long as I frame it in a way that looks interesting to IR scholars, it's not a problem.

Indeed, it is interesting to observe the editors of the *British Journal of Politics and International Relations* sounding the same note of caution about interdisciplinarity and the problem it poses for defining and defending disciplinary boundaries. On the one hand, the editors make the point that disciplinary boundaries in the social sciences are far from clear and that political scientists can learn from fellow social scientists in other disciplines; on the other hand, they accept implicitly that boundaries between disciplines do exist and that they should be defended:

> Much is made of the need for interdisciplinary research. Whilst we must be wary of trends which lead to the actual dissolution of social science disciplines (including political science and international relations), the boundaries which separate such disciplines are ill-defined and porous. It is our view that political science and international relations has much to learn from (as well as contribute to) the study of other social sciences. Indeed, some of the best work on British politics is informed by questions and methods found in other disciplines, such as sociology, political economy and geography. We will encourage articles exploring the theoretical utility of such interdisciplinary research.
>
> (*BJPIR* Editors, 1999: 4)

In short, part of the UK politics profession appears to take the view that interdisciplinary research is valuable – at least to the extent that it helps political scientists to understand more clearly how the political fits into, or is embedded within, a wider social context. According to this view, interdisciplinarity helps to enrich political science but the focus of research in politics must still be an essentially political problem or question. As the professor of politics in case study A put it, through interdisciplinary research, political scientists 'accommodate the insights of other disciplines' so that one is left with 'a more informed and sensitive disciplinary account'.

It is also interesting to extend the comparison to other disciplines. One of the researchers from case study A was a sociologist who was working in a department of management, having previously worked in an interdisciplinary social science institute in Germany. Now, the fact that a sociologist was working in a department of management might suggest that management is more open to interdisciplinary scholarship than either politics or economics. Certainly, the sociologist described it as a 'heterogeneous discipline', in the sense that it is a mixture of disciplinary perspectives all concerned with the same research area. However, RAE pressures mean that, just as in politics and economics, practitioners of management studies have to think carefully about where to publish so that even if they are working from a particular disciplinary base, such as sociology, they must still produce work that is relevant to the field of management:

> you know there's more jobs in management departments because there's a higher demand for teaching... but with that comes some demand to publish in different journals so, although... sociology journals are... acceptable... Academy of Management publications... nonplus... ultra!... So... there's some different demands attached with that... I suppose in terms of... where you should publish...

> in the sense that management... doesn't have such a strong theoretical core – it's a kind of heterogeneous discipline – it doesn't... stop me from... working with the political scientists as long as I can publish it in a management journal. It does make me think twice... if I were to write something to publish in a politics journal... well... for me, why not... that could be good; but that's not going to... improve my... RAE preparedness. So... let's say I talk to my colleague, 'Oh, let's publish it in the *Journal of International Business Studies* rather than, say, *Politics and Society*...' They're both journals and they can be both... equally good in different fields but... you would feel... 'Oh, I'm not sure I can really use... that publication for my return, if I'm being assessed in a particular field'.

To the extent, then, that practitioners of management studies interested in interdisciplinary research must steer their work in a particular disciplinary direction, the structure of management studies is similar to that of politics; that is, there is a particular domain of inquiry to be defined and defended through academic peer review. However, the structure of management studies also bears similarities to the structure of economics to the extent that journal articles count much more than research monographs, which, in turn, count much more than book chapters – at least when it comes to putting together an RAE submission:

> journal articles are absolutely much, much more important for career purposes... I think... I mean I've done enough of them that... my... career's in good shape.

> I suppose in... sociology *per se*... I would not say edited books are not so important but... if you write a whole book on... a sociological topic, that has a certain sway... in management you could never write a book and no-one would care at all... journal articles would be... just fine.

> had I gone to work in a sociology department I would... revisit my thesis and make an effort to turn it into a good book... I might do that but it's not so much... incentive to do that... because... it's much more important to get two or three... big hits... in a mainstream... and it could even be in a...

> sociology journal...*American Journal of Sociology*, *American Sociological Review*...those would be considered...very good...top journals as well.

The fact that the discipline of management studies is obsessed with journal article publication could be taken as evidence for the superior status of economics within the discipline. However, formalistic modelling has not yet become the common currency of management studies, so that there is still a greater amount of space than there is in economics for different approaches to scientific inquiry, even in the leading management journals:

> Well...I think...in empirical economics and in...business management journals...there is a...bias or preference for quantitative...research... But...I think also that...I think you can publish case studies and things in these very top...journals as well.

> I suppose...what's a contribution in economics is...much more tightly defined by...existing bodies of theory, whereas in management or sociology...more sort of general level about approaches and...there's more scope for sort of case-driven...

We can also compare the disciplines of economics and politics with that of biology, the sole natural science discipline that was one of the two contributing perspectives to the project in case study C. I noted in the previous chapter that there is a basic division within orthodox economics between theoretical and applied work and a further, broader division between economic orthodoxy and heterodoxy. The structure of biology, it seems, is similar to that of economics to the extent that there is a status differential between theoretical and applied journals, as the following extracts from the biologist's oral account reveal:

> when I go abroad to conferences...the work that I do is very well received and a lot of people come up to you and say 'I really liked that paper you've given, that's really good and that work's made a lot of difference to our work' whereas...you get the feeling that...applied work isn't valued that...highly in the United Kingdom...I think that's a shame...because it shouldn't be a split between fundamental work and applied work; it's whether it's good work or bad work.

What is also interesting is that the division between theoretical and applied work became much more apparent when the funding base of the organization for which the biologist worked changed. Up until 2004, the biologist had been working in a government-funded and government-evaluated research institute. After 2004, the research institute joined the academic system, which meant that its funding base now depended on its performance in the RAE:

> Well, when we merged into the University in 2004, beforehand we were evaluated... by Defra [Department for Environment, Food and Rural Affairs ] to see how we were performing because they were... our main funders; and we were evaluated by the BBSRC [Biotechnology and Biological Sciences Research Council]... The actual demands for those two sets of review were quite different because they were funding different kinds of work. Then, once we merged with the University, we had to get the Research Assessment Exercise and... that's all about high-impact-factor publications, which makes it extremely difficult for someone like me, to actually even be put into the RAE assessment because my funders aren't interested in publication... In fact in our organization there's a real split at the moment. The... internal politics has gone through the roof since we've merged with the University. It's a split between people who do fundamental work and... those doing applied work; and the people doing the fundamental work see themselves as... being more important than the others because they're going to be put into the RAE.

The problem facing the biologist, then, was that, because he was interested in interdisciplinary research, which was applied work, the disciplinary elite in biology considered his work to be less valuable than fundamental work. This status differential had two consequences. The first was that, given the high level of competition for research council funding, interdisciplinary projects were unlikely to be funded if they were not deemed 'fashionable':

> the research funding base is limited, and it's extremely competitive... and... the consequences of that are that the people who hand out the research money, sit on the research committees, have huge amounts of power, and... there'll be an obvious bias towards what they deem to be fashionable... and so research is going to get focused more and more narrow into areas that people believe they can actually get funding for... and... there will be huge gaps which you just won't get funding for; and that's a problem with... having limited resources for funding.

Indeed, the fact that his research interests were *not* narrow – in virtue of their interdisciplinary nature – had a second consequence – a career penalty:

> having a narrow focus is actually quite good for your career because it means you just concentrate on one thing... I know that my broad focus is detrimental to my career; it's stopped me being promoted. I've been told that I have too broad a range of interests and I'm not known for any one thing and therefore... I've been passed for promotion twice now because... I've been told: 'You're too broad'.

The preceding comparison between the disciplines of economics, politics, management and biology suggests that producing interdisciplinary work from a disciplinary base demands intellectual compromises but that the nature of the intellectual compromise varies across disciplines. The comparison between economics and politics offers the most striking contrast perhaps. We have seen that, in politics, researchers who wish to produce interdisciplinary work face a difficult choice between, on the one hand, meeting the disciplinary requirements of the RAE and treating interdisciplinary work as a side interest and, on the other hand, making interdisciplinary work their main interest but having to adjust it to meet the demands of a disciplinary audience. Choosing the former strategy means that less time can be spent on interdisciplinary work because mainstream disciplinary work has to take priority. If interdisciplinary work is published, but only in relatively low-ranking journals, it is unlikely to be accorded the same respect and have the same value as mainstream disciplinary work published in relatively high-ranking journals. Choosing the latter strategy increases the chance of publishing interdisciplinary work in mainstream journals but the possibility of such work being genuinely holistic, in which equal emphasis is given to all the contributing scientific perspectives, has to be sacrificed for a disciplinary attuned emphasis. In both cases, therefore, interdisciplinarity, and thus the goal of scientific integration, is short-changed.

In economics, the compromise involved in producing interdisciplinary work is slightly different. Whereas the politics profession is more concerned with defending a set of boundary assumptions about the nature of the political, the economics profession is more concerned with defending a particular conception of social scientific inquiry. For example, we find that disciplinary self-reflection in economics almost exclusively turns on a debate about the appropriateness of orthodox methodology (Lawson, 1997, 2003), whereas disciplinary self-reflection in politics – although not ignoring epistemological and methodological differences (as we saw above in the two editorials) – focuses on clarifying the scope and limits of the political domain of inquiry (Hay, 2002; Leftwich, 2004b). The implication of this is that it is possible to publish interdisciplinary work in leading economics journals as long as it conforms to the scientific criteria of orthodox economics. However, the question we must then ask is to what extent this sort of interdisciplinary work represents a coherent integration of disciplinary insights. We saw in Chapter 2 that orthodox interdisciplinarity is not a coherent form of integration. If this argument is accepted, it in turn implies that there is even less intellectual space for heterodox interdisciplinarity in economics than there is in politics. In economics, heterodox interdisciplinary work can only be a side interest because it is highly unlikely that such work will be accepted for publication in a 'good' economics journal and, if it cannot be published in such a journal, any research-led economics department is highly unlikely to consider such work as valuable for an RAE submission.

### *Social scientific specialization and peer review*

Now, the preceding discussion gives rise to further questions about the structural characteristics of disciplines:

- Why is journal article publication so much more important in some disciplines than in others?
- Why do some disciplines rely on formal journal rankings whereas others make do with informal journal rankings?
- Why are some disciplines more tolerant of differences in approach to scientific inquiry and are more concerned with defending scientific ontological boundaries, whereas others are more tolerant of transgressions of scientific ontological boundaries and are more concerned with defending a particular approach to scientific inquiry?

I want to suggest that the contrasts contained within these questions have much to do with developments in the intellectual context of knowledge production and with the relationship between academic science and the nature of the society in which it is embedded. In Chapter 3, I argued that the scientific part of the intellectual context of knowledge production is characterized by a continuing re-division of labour, which is manifest as specialization by discipline, field, topic and problem. I also observed that the intellectual contours of science turn not only on the way that objects are divided up for investigation but also on how scientific investigation should proceed so that the scientific part of the intellectual context presupposes a philosophical part. Indeed, we have seen in the previous chapter examples of the variety of approaches to social inquiry: positivist, interpretivist and transcendental realist. So, not only do we find specialization according to *what* specific objects are studied – whether it be power in politics or wealth in economics – which is a matter of (social) scientific ontology – but we also find specialization according to *how* objects are studied – which is a matter of philosophical ontology, epistemology and methodology.[1]

Now, given that specialization in science proceeds along two different routes, it is easy to see how, when these routes meet, the result will be severe complexity in the intellectual division of labour. Two or more researchers may be working on the same topic in the same field in the same discipline yet, by virtue of their philosophical differences, they may understand that topic in radically different ways and so ask radically different questions about it. The problem facing the scientific community, then, is how to deal with this complexity, given that resources for research are finite. If the allocation of resources is to be decided by competition, how are social scientists to judge the work of their peers if they cannot agree on the 'right' approach to social inquiry and if they cannot agree on which objects are worthy of investigation? I suggest that social scientists have solved this problem in different ways. One way is for scientific elites to impose a particular approach to social inquiry across disciplinary research fields so that it becomes dominant; another way is for scientific elites to define and defend a set of scientific ontological boundaries – that is, to stake a disciplinary claim to particular objects of inquiry. Thus, in economics, the disciplinary elite has adopted the former strategy so that professional competence in economics is defined by adherence to positivist orthodoxy rather than by adherence to the investigation of a specific set of objects. By contrast, in politics, professional competence is defined by adherence to questions about the exercise and distribution of power in society rather than by adherence to a particular approach to scientific inquiry.

This difference, in turn, explains why the single-authored journal article is the preferred publication medium in economics, whereas both single-authored journal articles and monographs are acceptable publication media in politics. Journals work, I suggest, as signalling devices, in the sense that the journal in which an article is published is treated as a rough-and-ready indication of its quality – just as a researcher's education background is treated as a rough-and-ready indication of his or her academic capability and research potential. Journals work in this way because, given the complexity of the landscape of knowledge and the enduring fact of specialization, it is difficult for any one scientist to acquire the requisite knowledge and expertise to be able to judge the quality of work done in every field of a given discipline. Hence, even if an RAE panel reviewer does not have the expertise to assess the work done in a particular area, he or she will most likely have a general sense of the rankings of disciplinary journals and may well use these as rough-and-ready indicators of the quality of the work done in that area. Journal editors can signal publication criteria and the standards they require relatively easily through editorial policy statements and can enforce and so standardize publication through a rigorous process of peer review. Thus, particular journals become 'known' for publishing a particular type of research, so that comparing journals is relatively easy. By contrast, research monographs are much less effective as indicators of quality because their high degree of variegation makes them difficult to compare. Although research monographs are peer reviewed before publication, the potential size of the market for the publication weighs just as heavily in the minds of publishers as the quality of the research.

Now, if it is the case that what counts as 'good' research in politics is less tightly defined than what counts as 'good' research in economics, it follows that research monographs, whose quality is difficult to assess, will be acceptable in the former discipline but not in the latter. It also follows that there will be greater resistance to the formalization of journal rankings in politics than in economics, if distinctions in the quality of research in politics are not as clear-cut as they are in economics. Remember that it becomes difficult to understand what 'power' means in politics if, say, one political scientist approaches it from a rational choice perspective and another approaches it from a Marxist perspective. By contrast, it is easier to understand what a contribution to economics is, if economics is simply the study of rational behaviour. Therefore, to return to the argument and evidence presented in Chapter 3, what we find in economics is that the leading journals are 'closed' in the sense that they place tight restrictions on what is an acceptable approach to scientific inquiry but are 'open' in the sense that they allow a broad range of objects to be investigated; whereas, in politics, we find that the leading journals are closed in the sense that they place restrictions on which objects can be investigated – but restrictions that are less tightly defined than those that apply in economics – but are open in the sense that they permit a broad range of approaches to social scientific inquiry.

However, it is important to realize that, although the boundary assumptions of economics are more open than those of politics, this does not mean that economists can make a contribution to knowledge by publishing interdisciplinary work in the journals of another discipline – whether or not this work is orthodox or heterodox. If the quality of economics research is to be assessed easily, that research must still be published in journals that the economics profession recognizes and has ranked. This is why interdisciplinary journals in economics, such as the *Journal of Law and Economics* and *Public Choice*, are recognized as economics journals rather than as law and politics journals, respectively. For example, the development economist in case study B often published interdisciplinary work in political science journals, such as *New Political Economy*, as well as in orthodox development journals. But publishing in the former could have detrimental career consequences:

> if too much of... what you produce is published in the journals of another discipline, then that's actually regarded as a negative, a liability rather than an asset. Certainly as an economist I feel that it's doing me no good in my current employment that about a third of what I produce has been published in political science journals.

In short, peer review has a crucial role to play in reflecting as well as reinforcing scientific structures and, given that the allocation of a significant proportion of government funding for academic research is dependent on the results of the RAE (now the Research Excellence Framework), we can also see how peer review – and, by implication, disciplinary identities – has attained an even higher level of importance and influence in the academic system of knowledge production.

## The social scientific division of labour and society

If we are to make sense of the differences in the way the social sciences of economics and politics are structured, we also need to take account of the wider sociocultural forces impinging on academic science. We can understand the significance of these forces most clearly if we compare the structure of political science in the United States with the structure of political science in the United Kingdom. I have argued that political science is more open than economics when it comes to defining a particular approach to scientific inquiry but less open when it comes to defining a particular domain of objects of inquiry. However, this sort of structure appears to be characteristic of political science only in the United Kingdom; a different sort of structure, one that is similar to the core–periphery model of economics discussed in Chapter 3, appears to be characteristic of political science in the United States. For example, Crewe and Norris (1991) compared British and American political scientists' subjective evaluations of, and familiarity with, political science journals. They found that, although there was 'a strong and significant correlation... between British and American evaluations of journal quality', the exceptions to this trend suggested that journals publishing 'formal, mathematical and quantitative approaches' tended to be more highly regarded by American political scientists, whereas journals publishing 'qualitative, reflective and theoretical work' tended to be more highly regarded by British political scientists (ibid: 525). Moreover, when it came to comparing journal familiarity, the relationship between British and American political scientists was much weaker, which also suggests that British and American political science represent somewhat distinct intellectual traditions (ibid: 525–6).

We can compare these subjective rankings of journal quality with the results of Clara Riba's comparison of the mathematical content of a representative sample of American and British political science journals for the period from 1988 to 1992. She found significant differences in the mathematical content of political science journals across different regions of America and Europe:

> generally speaking, publications from the United States contain more mathematics than their Anglo-German European counterparts; that Anglo-German European publications contain more mathematics than their Southern European counterparts; and lastly, that Southern European publications contain only a slightly higher percentage of mathematics than their Latin American counterparts.
>
> (Riba, 1996: 493)

Riba also found that the *American Political Science Review* and the *American Journal of Political Science* contained the highest proportions of mathematics of both an 'empirical–inductive' and 'analytical–deductive' type, while the *Journal of Politics* contained the highest proportion of only the 'empirical–inductive' type of mathematics. These three North American journals occupy third, fifth and sixth places, respectively, in American political scientists' rankings of journal quality reported in Crewe and Norris's study (1991: 525). By contrast, *Political Studies*, which failed to make the top 20 journals evaluated by American political scientists in the same study, was 'below the average' in the proportions of both types of mathematics that it contained (Riba, 1996: 496–8).[2]

The surveys of political science journals performed by Bennett *et al.* (2003) and Marsh and Savigny (2004) provide further evidence to suggest that a greater variety of approaches to social scientific inquiry is tolerated within the European tradition of political inquiry than within the North American tradition. Bennett *et al.*'s analysis of the methods content of the *American Political Science Review*, for example, shows that, in the latter half of the 1960s, there was a sharp increase in the proportion of articles using statistical methods, matched by a sharp decrease in the proportion using case studies and, in the early 1980s, there was another sharp increase – this time in the proportion of articles using formal modelling – compensated for by a decrease in the proportion using statistical methods and a further decrease in the proportion using case studies. By the mid-1990s, the majority of work published in the *American Political Science Review* and other leading journals, such as the *American Journal of Political Science* and the *Journal of Politics*, was dominated by the use of formal modelling and statistical methods.

Marsh and Savigny attempt to quantify journal content according to approach to inquiry rather than method of inquiry. Nevertheless, their findings corroborate those of Bennett *et al.* They find that rational choice and behaviouralist approaches dominated the content of articles published in the *American Journal of Political Science* and the *American Political Science Review* between 1975 and 1979. For the period from 1997 to 2002, the mixture of rational choice and behaviouralism changed in both journals in the sense that the proportion of articles using rational choice increased slightly while the proportion adopting a behaviouralist approach decreased. However, the dominance of these two positivist approaches continued. Marsh and Savigny also quantified the content of two leading British journals, the *British Journal of Political Science* and *Political Studies*. They found that the majority of articles published in the former journal reflected a positivist approach across both time periods but that there was a greater mixture of positivist and non-positivist approaches in the latter, at least for the period from 1997 to 2002 when rational choice accounted for six per cent of articles published, behaviouralism 38 per cent, normative theory 31 per cent and other, non-positivist approaches 25 per cent.[3]

However, although it seems that leading North American political science journals are more restrictive when it comes to philosophical approach than their British counterparts, it seems that positivist-inspired formal modelling and statistical work is not (yet) as dominant in North American political science as it is in North American economics. For example, Bennett *et al.* (2003) found that *Comparative Politics* and *World Politics* published a relatively high proportion of case-study work in the mid-1990s – two journals that were ranked ninth and first, respectively, for journal quality by American political scientists in Crewe and Norris's study. Indeed, if we return to Bennett *et al.*'s time-series analysis of the methods content of the *American Political Science Review*, we find that, since 1983, the use of formal modelling has followed a slight downward trend, while the use of case studies and statistics has fluctuated such that a rise in the use of one method is matched by a fall in the use of the other. Bennett *et al.* find similar falls in the use of formal modelling since the mid-1980s in the *American Journal of Political Science* and *International Studies Quarterly*, both of which also made the top 20 journals ranked for quality by American political scientists in Crewe and Norris's study.

Considered as a whole, then, the evidence on journal content suggests that the structure of North American political science may be distinguished from the structure of UK political science according to the degree to which one particular approach to scientific inquiry is dominant. What, though, explains this difference? McKay (1991) has argued that North American and European political science have become separate intellectual traditions reproduced through separate markets in labour and ideas, not because the European tradition is 'inferior' to the North American tradition but simply because it is 'different' (ibid: 463). He attributes the intellectual difference to a difference in the ideological foundations of North American and European society:

> in no European country is the business of politics infused with the liberal individualism so intimately associated with the USA. Instead, European democracies are a complex melange of liberalism, corporatism, consociationalism, elitism, populism, statism and socialism. European political science reflects this in just the same way as American political science – which is primarily concerned with the study of the USA – reflects the individualism of American politics. The fact that many contrasting – and usually conflicting – approaches are sometimes represented in just one department may demonstrate how 'unprofessionalized' is European political science. But it also shows a degree of intellectual eclecticism which is almost wholly absent from American departments.
>
> (McKay, 1991: 464)

Now, the idea to which McKay is alluding – that the nature of social science reflects the nature of the society in which it is embedded – is borne out in historical studies of the emergence of professionalized social science in America at the end of the nineteenth century. For example, both Furner (1975) and Haskell (1977) document the battle between the historical and neoclassical schools of economics in America, which was played out in the context of the professionalization of economics. Members of the historical school, such as Ely and Ross, openly advocated social reform, greater state intervention and more support for trades unions. By contrast, orthodox economists argued that 'objectivity' – by which they meant a clear separation of facts from values – was the true measure of scientific worth and thereby implied that the historical school's public, moral stance on policy issues was unscientific. But, given the reliance of American universities on funding from philanthropists and private foundations, it was always likely that the historical economists would have to back down and adopt the mantle of 'objectivity' because, if the economics profession was to survive, it could not be seen to be disunited – otherwise its claim to expert status would have sounded hollow and, most of all, because it could not be seen to be challenging the very interests that supported university research and thus the careers of social scientists. So it was that the historical economists lost control of the American Economics Association, an organization they had founded in 1885 as a means of counteracting the emerging influence of neoclassical economics.

Similarly, as Gunnell (2006) argues, it was a positivist conception of science that implicitly informed the thinking of the founders of the American Political Science Association, who had observed the fate of the American Economics Association and who had realized that as social scientists they could no longer afford to be public advocates of particular moral positions relating to questions of public policy. But, positivism represented a direct challenge to the tradition of political philosophy that had characterized the study of politics in the pre-professional era. Political philosophers took ideas as their subject matter and addressed questions of normative and practical significance. Positivist political science challenged this sort of inquiry because it assumed that facts about politics related to the observable world of government, not to an unobservable world of ideas about how best to organize society, and that questions about facts and values, and thus theory and practice, could and should be clearly separated. As Gunnell points out, only through a positivist professional identity and under increasingly ideologically diverse social conditions did American political scientists think that their work would remain relevant to, and so influential upon, the world of practical politics, even if they were unsure exactly how it would be. However, if McKay is right to claim that American society is heavily imbued with the ideology of classical liberalism, then Gunnell's argument perhaps overlooks the point that positivist social science represents a form of knowledge that *resonates*[4] with the dominant ideological tradition within American society. In taking the individual as the unit of analysis – because only individuals and their actions were the observable components of society – positivist social science, whether expressed in the form of rationalism, as in neoclassical economics, or behaviouralism, as in political science, helps to justify the doctrine of liberal individualism. More than that, though, positivist social science, in reifying and eternalizing the scientific 'fact', undercuts the possibility of arguing for social change and so is politically conservative – a point that was not lost on the critics of the behavioural 'revolution' in the 1960s. In attacking this ideological position, as certain American economists had done by publicly advocating social reform, American social scientists threatened to destroy the support of those whose interests lay clearly in preserving a society organized in tune with classical liberalist ideology.

Positivism was attractive to American social scientists, then, because the sort of objective, value-free social science that it justified offered a way of insulating social scientists from the problem of ideological diversity that Weber (1904) had identified as increasingly characteristic of Western society and thereby of protecting the cognitive authority of science. It was also attractive – perhaps at a subconscious level – because it chimed with the ideological disposition of those who provided the material resources for the mass production of knowledge. Moreover, if positivist social science fitted with the pre-existing ideological worldview of the generation of political scientists who initiated the professionalization of political science, it is easy to see how it must have seemed the obvious choice of professional identity. Indeed, if American political scientists did not understand the full ideological implications of positivism, they had only to find the promise of a predictive science of the political appealing for the adoption of a positivist professional image to have unintended ideological consequences. If the disciplinary elite did understand these consequences, it could sell the positivist identity as the discipline's best hope of survival – even if the way in which political science would influence practice, which was still a strong hope within the discipline, remained unclear.

But, if American society has been characterized by an aggressive form of libertarianism, the ideological foundations of European societies are rather different. If all societies are characterized by a 'dialectic' of liberalism and collectivism (Greenleaf, 1993: 28), what sets them apart is the relative strength of these two ideologies. If, for example, collectivism has posed a much stronger challenge to liberalism in Britain than it has in America, it is reasonable to suppose that the study of politics in these two countries reflects this difference. Certainly, Hayward's (1999) account of British approaches to the study of politics suggests that there has been greater resistance in Britain than in America to scientism and rationalism – a resistance reflected most famously in the work of Crick (1959). Indeed, it is by virtue of this anti-positivist strand of thinking, I suggest, that British scholars have recognized the possibility of social change – and even publicly advocated it, as in the work of G. D. H. Cole and Harold Laski. But, if we are to make sense of the incorporation of behaviouralist and rational choice approaches into the discipline of politics in the UK in the 1960s and 1970s, we also have to recognize the positivist strand of thinking implicit in the traditional study of British political institutions; for it is the empiricist tendency latent in this line of work, I suggest, that underpins a historicist view of British politics and tacitly justifies the Westminster model of parliamentary government – the so-called 'Whig' interpretation of British history. In other words, if we accept the possibility of philosophical contradiction – to return to the theme of the previous chapter – we can start to understand how British political scholarship implicitly supported both social change and continuity and thus both reflected and reinforced the tension between liberal–conservative and socialist pressures throughout society.

All this is not to suggest that contradictory philosophical currents are not also evident in the work of American political scientists; rather, it is to suggest that the positivist impulse appears to be much stronger within the American than the British discipline. Just because positivism is dominant in American political science does not mean that there is a complete consensus about the 'right' approach to scientific inquiry, as the recent *Perestroika* rebellion indicates (Monroe, 2005). Indeed, the fact that there is not total agreement leaves the disciplinary elite in American political science in a difficult position, because if it attempts to extend the dominance of positivism too far, it may provoke a philosophical reaction and so undermine the image of professional unity it wishes to present to the American public. This contradiction is clearly evident in the thinking of the incoming editor of the *American Political Science Review* in March 2002. Having noted the 'overriding intellectual diversity' that existed within American political science, the editor, Lee Siegelman, was concerned that:

> in many ways we have become less of a discipline over the years . . . These days it is harder than ever to find a center of intellectual gravity in our discipline. More and more we are a confederation of narrowly defined and loosely connected, or even disconnected, specializations. Our heightened specialization is further fragmenting our already disjointed discipline, to the extent that most of us have little knowledge, understanding, or appreciation of what our colleagues in other subfields are doing.
>
> (Siegelman, 2002: viii)

Nevertheless, unable to avoid the criticisms made by the leaders of the *Perestroika* movement that the *Review* was unrepresentative of the breadth of American political science, the editor signalled – by modifying the review procedures and composition of the editorial board – an important change of direction for the journal. Now, whether these changes have significantly altered the content of the *American Political Science Review* over the last few years or whether the inclusion of a greater variety of approaches is merely a token gesture designed to accommodate and so neutralize dissenting voices within the discipline is a question for further research. What is interesting for our purposes is that the editor claimed that the lack of theoretical diversity within the content of the *American Political Science Review* was the result of a 'vicious circle' driven by a perception that the journal was biased towards a particular type of political inquiry. This perception was false in Siegelman's view because the journal did 'a good job of publishing the best papers that are submitted to it' (ibid: ix). The blame, then, lay with the political science community, not with editorial policy but this simply brings us back to the problem that I have been emphasizing throughout this chapter; that is, how to present a public image of unity when social scientists cannot agree on what counts as the 'best' research. Because research quality is only meaningful in a wider context of ontological assumptions, both scientific and philosophical, it is easy to see how a journal can reject a research paper on purely technical grounds, when the apparent technical failure actually implies either a failure to adopt the 'right' approach to scientific inquiry or a failure to stay within the 'right' domain of inquiry. If researchers then perceive, correctly, that editorial policy is biased in a certain direction and so choose not to submit certain kinds of work, this is a perception the editorial board of the leading journal in the discipline need not discourage, if it is concerned with securing and protecting a particular professional identity.

Moreover, just as the meaning of science may be contested within a particular disciplinary community, so may the meaning of the subject matter to which scientific inquiry is addressed. In Britain, for example, recent disciplinary reflections on the state of political science have been just as concerned with competing conceptions of the scope and limits to the domain of the political as with competing conceptions of science (Marsh and Stoker, 2002b, 2002c; Leftwich, 2004a; Stoker and Marsh, 2010). Indeed, in his account of the founding of the Political Studies Association in the 1950s, Kenny draws attention to the fact that, although there was a debate about whether or not to use the term 'political science' rather than 'political studies', the question of which disciplinary practitioners should be admitted to the new profession was just as, if not more, important. Indeed, G. D. H. Cole, who was closely involved in these developments, had already addressed the question of disciplinary identity in a report on the teaching of politics in the United Kingdom. Although somewhat critical of the influence of the tradition of constitutional law, history and moral philosophy on the curriculum, Cole nevertheless advocated in Kenny's view not a discipline organized along American lines but 'an expanded, updated and more rigorous version' of the traditional British approach (Kenny, 2004: 568–71). Cole therefore helped to maintain the sense of 'scepticism' and 'eclecticism' that Dunleavy *et al.* argue is characteristic of British political science (2000: 6–8), while pointing British scholars towards a clearer professional identity focused on a particular object of inquiry.

However, just as American political scientists have challenged dominant intellectual norms, so British political scientists have shown that they do not necessarily agree with the mainstream conception of the political. For example, we saw above how one of the political scientists from case study B distinguished between the qualities of politics journals: what was considered to be a 'good' journal for RAE purposes was not necessarily what a particular subdisciplinary field considered to be a 'good' journal. We can get a clearer idea of this difference if we return to Crewe and Norris's (1991) study of British and American evaluations of politics journals. If we compare the British rankings of the top 20 politics journals by 'quality', we find many specialist journals such as *Soviet Studies*, the *Journal of Latin American Studies*, *Political Theory*, *China Quarterly* and *Slavic Review* ranked above generalist journals such as the *American Political Science Review* and *Political Studies* (Crewe and Norris, 1991: 525). However, when we look at the British rankings of the top 20 politics journals by 'impact', we find that the generalist journals are all either at or near the top of the table (ibid: 526–7).[5] If generalist journals have the highest impact ratings and if these journals are widely considered to be representative of mainstream scholarship, we can understand why political scientists treat these as 'good' journals for RAE purposes. But, for political scientists working in a particular field of the discipline, it makes sense to rank the quality of specialist journals above that of generalist journals because, in virtue of their specialized focus and expertise, they will be more able to assess the quality of specialist journals, which will be their chief intellectual resource, than the quality of generalist journals, which will contain articles from fields of which they may have little knowledge.

## Conclusion: the challenge of integrative interdisciplinary research

Let me conclude this chapter by drawing together the different strands of my argument in consideration of the objectives set out in the introduction to the chapter. My objective was to examine the relationship between the social context of knowledge production and the decisions scientists make about what sort of knowledge to produce in light of evidence from three cases studies of (collaborative) interdisciplinary research projects. This evidence, I suggest, supports the argument of Chapter 3: that the social context of knowledge production constitutes the (typically unacknowledged) conditions for the practices of scientific inquiry, through which it is reproduced and transformed (typically unintentionally) and that the decisions that scientists make about what sort of knowledge to produce (including where to publish it) reflect the holistic effect of a set of social structures – of peer review, the scientific division of labour and the academic career ladder. These three structures appear to be of particular significance for academics in the UK, so it may be helpful to clarify the internal relations between them. The discussion of the evidence reveals that:

- the division of labour in science and the structure of academic employment (the career ladder) are interdependent, because people need resources with which to practice as scientists, which they obtain through the academic employment relationship, while people could not be employed as academics unless there were a scientific field in which they could practise;

- the division of labour in science and the structure of peer review are interdependent, because the products of scientists' labour must be evaluated by the scientific community before they can be certified as knowledge to be included within the field, while people could not evaluate the products of scientific labour unless there were an existing body of knowledge against which to assess new work;
- the structure of academic employment and the structure of peer review are interdependent because entry to (and progression through) the career hierarchy depends on publication record, while the evaluation of new contributions to knowledge would not be possible unless the scientific community had the resources with which to review new work.

The internal relations between these structures indicate that we are dealing once again with a totality – not of ideas – but of materially based social structures. These are not the only social structures constitutive of the social context of knowledge production; as I argued in Chapter 3, we also have to understand connections with the structures of funding, research and education/training.[6] Indeed, if there are connections with other (hitherto unidentified) types of social structure, we must think of this totality as partial (and open to change). Moreover, we must also think of it as overlapping with the (partial and sub-) totalities of ideas that constitute the intellectual context of knowledge production because, if the social practices of scientific inquiry presuppose an intellectual context, the social context of knowledge production must be understood as permeated by the intellectual context.

What holds the social totality together is people's simultaneous occupancy of multiple positions within it. A person must occupy the positions of academic employee, scientist and peer reviewer at the same time if the system is to be reproduced. The decision that a person must make about what sort of knowledge to produce reflects the conjunctural impact of these structures, which is to encourage the production of specialized forms of knowledge at the expense of the production of integrative forms of knowledge. It is not that the production of integrative forms of knowledge is impossible; rather, it is that the system continually *restricts* the opportunities to do so. As we have seen in this chapter, the opportunities to produce integrative, interdisciplinary research are greater in politics than they are in economics so that we may say that the *tendency* among economists to produce core, mainstream – that is, specialized knowledge – is stronger than it is among political scientists. I am sure that, if we examined other fields of scientific inquiry, we would find similar tendencies towards specialization of varying strength. The key point to note, though, is that scientists who are interested in producing integrative forms of knowledge and who are thrown into this system face a continual dilemma: on the one hand, if they decide to spend the majority of their time on integrative, interdisciplinary research, they run the risk either of becoming unemployable or, if they are already in post, of stalling their career development; on the other hand, if they spend most of their time on specialized, disciplinary research to obtain and sustain academic employment, they are likely to become frustrated and may well become resigned to their situation, thinking that there is no alternative to the status quo.

By denying or at least continually restricting the opportunities for scientists to produce integrative, interdisciplinary research, the social context of knowledge production *alienates* scientists interested in this form of research. To put this another way: the social context of knowledge production tends to block the overt expression – the epistemological mediation – of an axiological necessity – that is, it tends to block the discovery of alethic truth, which in this case is the property that reality is interconnected (as well as differentiated). Let us look more closely at how this happens. I have argued that, in economics, the social context of knowledge production supports the dominance of a positivist approach to scientific inquiry – the standard in relation to which legitimate contributions to economics are defined and thus the boundaries of the field defended (even if this is done only implicitly). But, positivism – as I argued in Chapter 2 – cannot make sense of the interconnected nature of reality because it lacks a conception of vertical and horizontal depth. In this way, it denies what is necessary in practice, which is for scientists to understand a key property of reality (at least if they are committed to the discovery of alethic truth). But, that denial in theory of an axiological necessity – an inconsistency between theory and practice – sets in train a host of other theory–practice inconsistencies. For example, if positivism cannot make sense of the interconnection of reality, it cannot also make sense of the differentiation of reality (in virtue of their constitution as a duality). But, that brings into question the possibility of defining the economic as a distinct object of social scientific inquiry without resort to conventionalism and hence the legitimacy of economists calling what they do 'economics'. Ultimately, it is the influence of transcendental realist thinking, I suggest, that enables economists to operate with an implicit understanding of what the economic is. Yet, as I argued in Chapter 4, this influence is mediated by the structure of the mind so that what emerges is an inconsistency between economists' professed commitment to a positivist approach to scientific inquiry and practices which presuppose a transcendental realist philosophy – that is, a theory–practice inconsistency.

By contrast, in politics, the social context of knowledge production supports a conception of the 'political' as a distinctive aspect of social scientific inquiry (rather than as a distinctive approach to social scientific inquiry) and, in this way, defines the boundaries of the field. That this is possible, I suggest, is a result of the tolerance for philosophical diversity within the politics profession – the 'broad church' – which allows transcendental realist thinking to have a stronger effect within the field than it does within economics. We can understand, therefore, why the politics profession – at least in the United Kingdom – is more open to interdisciplinary thinking than the economics profession. Yet, there is still a limit to how much more open it is in this respect. For example, one strategy is for political scientists to produce integrative, interdisciplinary research as a side interest and publish it in non-mainstream journals – a strategy also available to heterodox economists. However, when such research becomes a side interest, it is unlikely to have the same impact as core, disciplinary research. An alternative strategy, which is not available to heterodox economists, is to produce interdisciplinary research but underemphasize its integrative character to make it publishable in core politics journals. So, although such research may be, and has the potential to be, integrative in nature, the extent to which its integrative nature has to be downplayed is a measure of the degree to which integrative research is undervalued and of the degree to which a greater understanding of how different disciplinary perspectives relate to each other is being blocked by the need to elevate one particular perspective – the political – to a higher level of importance.

Moreover, what supports this state of affairs is the very philosophical diversity of the politics profession because, if that diversity allows for transcendental realist thinking to have a stronger effect in politics than in economics, it also allows positivist thinking to survive – albeit in an attenuated form – and to continue to have an influence on political scientists' thinking – the result of which, I suggest, is to encourage the view that the political is not an ontologically interdependent aspect of social scientific inquiry but an ontologically *independent* one. The end result, in other words, is an implicit, *distorted* understanding of the stratification of social objects. Hence, political scientists, too, become trapped in a theory–practice inconsistency: between an implicit, transcendental-realist-inspired understanding of the nature of the political as a distinct yet interdependent aspect of social reality and a set of practices which presuppose that the political constitutes its own, independent domain of reality.

The comparison between the disciplines of politics and economics reveals that, in both cases, an axiological necessity (to produce integrative, interdisciplinary research) is denied at a philosophical and social level but in different ways. This denial sets in train further inconsistencies so that we have an example of a '*Tina formation*' (Bhaskar, 1993: 117) – an ensemble of internally related yet contradictory theories and/or practices, the overall effect of which is to sustain the denial in theory and/or practice of an axiological necessity.[7] What helps to sustain this particular Tina formation, I suggest, is the dominance of positivist thinking in British and American society, which, in turn, is reinforced by the dominance of positivist (and increasingly interpretivist) thinking within the social sciences, so that we have a process of causal interaction between society and social science. Given the dominance of such thinking in society, we can perhaps understand why higher education policymakers' attempts to encourage the production of integrative, interdisciplinary research simply by establishing interdisciplinary research centres and institutes have had little success. What motivates this policy is the implicit (or sometimes explicit) recognition of the differentiation and interconnection of reality and the axiological necessity to understand it as such; yet, implicit in the practical outcome is a positivist-inspired conception of academic disciplines as simply the products of what scientists do and thus a denial of the existence of an underlying social and intellectual context of knowledge production. So, we have once again a theory–practice inconsistency – one, moreover, that is compounded by the more recent policy of reorganizing previously separate disciplinary departments into new academic schools. Again, what appears to be motivating such a policy amongst university managers is an implicit understanding of the value of scientific integration and an expectation that bringing scientists together from different fields of inquiry under the umbrella of a single school will facilitate interaction among them, with integrative, interdisciplinary research as the synergetic by-product.[8] Yet, on closer inspection one finds that the original disciplinary identities and divisions are still in force, as reflected in disciplinary-based job descriptions for vacant posts. How we might change this state of affairs so as to achieve a greater degree of success in encouraging scientific integration is a question I take up in the final chapter.

# 6 Conclusion

In this book, I have attempted to explain what I have identified as the problem of integrating knowledge through interdisciplinary research. Broadly understood, this problem refers to the difficulties that researchers often experience when attempting to integrate knowledge from different disciplines, whether individually or collectively, despite higher education policymakers' attempts to encourage the production of such research through the establishment of interdisciplinary research institutes, centres and funding programmes. In this final chapter, I consider some of the policy implications of my explanation, because it is clear to me that current higher education policy presupposes that scientific integration can be facilitated simply by bringing together specialists from different disciplines. Yet, although it is important that researchers from different disciplines should have the opportunity to engage with each other in open discussion and debate, and should be provided with new spaces in which to do so, this sort of policy will be insufficient to encourage the integration of knowledge from different disciplines if it overlooks the effect of the underlying social and intellectual conditions of scientific inquiry. These conditions, I have argued, militate against the production of integrative, interdisciplinary research and in favour of the production of specialized, monodisciplinary research. If higher education policymakers are to encourage the production of integrative, interdisciplinary research, therefore, they will need to change the nature of the underlying context of knowledge production so as to give researchers a much greater incentive to integrate knowledge from different disciplines. But, before I suggest how policymakers should do this, let me summarize the main points of my argument.

## The nature of the argument

My objective in this project was to find answers to two key questions about integrative, interdisciplinary research, the rationale for which I set out in Chapter 1:

1. What justifies the production of integrative, interdisciplinary research?
2. To what extent is it possible to produce integrative, interdisciplinary research?

These two questions are closely related in the sense that question 2 constellationally embraces question 1 – that is, the production of knowledge presupposes an understanding of what there is to know, how we can come to know it and, fundamentally, what 'it' – that is, the nature of reality – is. I addressed the first question by means of a philosophical inquiry into the possibility of integrating (and differentiating) knowledge, the results of which I presented in Chapter 2. I addressed the second question by means of a social scientific inquiry into the conditions of knowledge production. Since there are intellectual conditions for scientific inquiry, in the sense that every scientific theory presupposes a particular philosophical position (and indeed may presuppose multiple, contradictory philosophical positions), I was able to incorporate the philosophical categories discussed in Chapter 2 into the construction of the theory of knowledge production discussed in Chapter 3.

Let me say a little more about the answer I have provided to the question of what justifies the production of integrative, interdisciplinary research. In Chapter 2, I argued that it is by virtue of the possibility of vertical and horizontal ontological depth that it is possible for scientists to produce both specialized and integrative forms of knowledge – by which I mean knowledge of different types of causal object – such as structures and systems (or totalities) – and of the different aspects of such objects, as well as knowledge of the different types of connection between them – connections that I analyzed using the concepts of causal dependence and interdependence (by virtue of the possibility of asymmetrical and symmetrical internal relations between entities) and causal influence and interaction (by virtue of the possibility of asymmetrical and symmetrical external relations between entities).

Moreover, I argued in the third section of Chapter 2 that it is because scientists have failed to sustain a conception of vertical and horizontal depth that they have often found it difficult to integrate knowledge coherently. I argued that, in the case of the classical political economists at least, this failure is the result of a retained, tacit commitment to an empiricist and rationalist epistemology, which is manifest in a host of inconsistencies: between the philosophical presuppositions of scientific practice (or practice–practice inconsistencies), between the philosophical presuppositions of scientists' discursive reflections on the nature of scientific inquiry (or theory–theory inconsistencies), and between the philosophical presuppositions of scientists' discursive reflections on the nature of scientific inquiry and the philosophical presuppositions of scientists' actual practices (or theory–practice inconsistencies).

I argued further that it is by virtue of the existence of anomalies and inconsistencies at both the level of scientific practice and philosophical theory that the intellectual context of knowledge production as a whole may be described as highly complex: as comprising (partial) totalities of (logically related) scientific and philosophical ideas subject to the internal constraints of their own incompleteness and the external constraints of contradictory, residual scientific and philosophical ideas or sub-totalities – the effects of which are mediated via the structuring of the mind and which become apparent in the contradictions between what scientists do, between what they claim they are doing, and between what they claim they are doing and what they are actually doing. I considered, in support of my argument, the situation in political science, where a transcendental-realist-inspired conception of the political (as concerned with the exercise and distribution of power in society) is contradicted, and so undercut, by the influence of positivist thinking, with the result that political scientists tend to treat the political as an ontologically independent domain of social scientific inquiry (rather than as an ontologically interdependent one, which is the implication of a transcendental realist social ontology). This situation, I suggested in Chapter 4, helps us to make sense of the widely observed phenomenon, which I noted in Chapter 1, of interdisciplinary research, which is intended to be a synthesis of different, disciplinary analyses ending up as multidisciplinary research or a juxtaposition of different, disciplinary analyses pertaining to a common problem – what I call *interdisciplinary-research-as-multidisciplinary-research*.

I also considered, in support of my argument, the situation in economics, where a positivist-inspired conception of economic inquiry (manifest in the practice of constructing formal models, amongst other things) is contradicted, and so undercut, by the influence of transcendental realist thinking, which, although of much weaker influence than positivist thinking, is what enables economists to sustain (if only implicitly) a coherent – that is, *non*-conventionalist – conception of the economic and thereby to define the boundaries of the field of economics. Yet, this weaker influence is contradicted by the stronger influence of positivist thinking and leads to the widely observed phenomenon, which I noted in Chapter 4, of economics imperialism, whereby the formalistic methods of economics are increasingly applied to non-economic fields of inquiry (such as politics and sociology). Orthodox economists may claim that this amounts to integrative, interdisciplinary research. Yet, as I argued in Chapter 3, positivism – as a type of irrealist thinking – cannot make sense of the multi-tiered stratification of reality and its differentiation. Hence, we should refer to the phenomenon of economics imperialism as *interdisciplinary-research-as-cross-disciplinary-unification*.

Finally, I also discussed in Chapter 2 another conception of interdisciplinary research – that inspired by postmodernist philosophy.[1] Again, postmodernists hold out the promise of scientific integration in the form of 'integrative praxes', which represent an attempt to question the assumptions of traditional, disciplinary-based scientific inquiry and bring into consideration the knowledge formations of the excluded and oppressed. The implication of this line of thinking is that interdisciplinary research amounts to the *de*construction and then *re*construction of ways of thinking and talking – or *interdisciplinary-research-as-deconstruction↔reconstruction*. Yet, once again, it is the implicit ontological position of postmodernism which is its undoing and which means that in the final analysis it too cannot make sense of the actual practices of scientific inquiry – of specialized, disciplinary-based scientific inquiry on the one hand and integrative, interdisciplinary scientific inquiry on the other; for it is the lack of a conception of vertical and horizontal ontological depth in postmodernism, which is established through the denial of existential intransitivity, that makes it impossible for the postmodernist to comprehend coherently – that is to say, without falling back on the crutch of conventionalism – both the differentiation and the interconnection of reality.

We can now see that, fundamentally, it is the (relatively) dominant influence of irrealist thinking, in the forms of positivism and postmodernism on the one hand, and the underdevelopment and so (relatively) weaker influence of (transcendental) realist thinking on the other that is the key intellectual limit to the production of *integrative*, interdisciplinary research. I emphasize the word 'integrative' because, as should be clear, both positivism and postmodernism may claim for themselves conceptions of interdisciplinary research but they cannot sustain a conception of interdisciplinary research as genuinely integrative research – that is, research that expresses the interconnected (and differentiated) nature of reality.

What about the *social* limits to the production of integrative, interdisciplinary research? What can we say about the causal influence of the social context of knowledge production? The upshot of my argument concerning the social context of knowledge production, which I set out in Chapter 5, is that it is more difficult for scientists to produce integrative, interdisciplinary research than specialized, monodisciplinary research – even if they have a coherent idea of what scientific integration is – because the former type of research tends to be undervalued as a form of knowledge. That is not to say that all scientists undervalue interdisciplinary research. We have seen through the case studies presented in this book that there are scientists who are willing to invest considerable time and effort on integrative, interdisciplinary research projects because they believe that such research is just as valuable as monodisciplinary research. However, such values run up against the monodisciplinary norms and conventions of the academic community – norms and conventions that are the dominant influence on scientists' thinking and that are the result of the interlocking structures of the social system of knowledge production that I analyzed in Chapters 3 and 5. Given the material rewards that accrue to those who produce specialized, monodisciplinary research, it is understandable that most (although not all) scientists will continue to accept the disciplinary mindset that they have acquired during their years of education and training and will follow pre-existing disciplinary-based career paths. Given these conditions, it is not surprising that the production of integrative, interdisciplinary research should be seen as a serious challenge to the boundaries of scientific fields, whether these are defined (explicitly) by a particular scientific ontology – as in political science – or a particular philosophical ontology – as in economics.

Of course, the fact that many scientific journals do publish interdisciplinary research may suggest that it is possible to build an academic career primarily as an interdisciplinary researcher. According to my argument this is indeed a possibility because, as I have argued above, one type of interdisciplinary research is not genuinely integrative research. This is the situation in economics where it would be possible for a researcher to publish interdisciplinary research in orthodox journals as long as the researcher produced the research in accordance with the principles of formalistic modelling. Another type of interdisciplinary research either is or at least has the potential to be, genuinely integrative research. This is the case in political science, where it would be possible for a researcher to publish interdisciplinary research in mainstream journals as long as the researcher demonstrated a clear focus on the political aspect of social reality and thereby underplayed the actually or potentially integrative character of the research. However, in both cases the production of integrative, interdisciplinary research is short-changed: on the one hand, the possibility of genuine integration is (implicitly) denied; on the other hand, the possibility of integration is (implicitly) accepted yet not fully realized. In short, in both cases it is the undervaluation of scientific integration that is the key social limit to the production of integrative, interdisciplinary research in the academy.

Given this understanding of both the social and intellectual limits to the production of integrative, interdisciplinary research, we can now understand why the production of such research is rarely considered, if at all, and if it is considered and attempted, why it runs into difficulties. Given the existence of multiple, contradictory conceptions of knowledge and of reality, it is understandable that attempts to integrate knowledge, whether through collaborative or individual research, often fail and end up as multidisciplinary research. A clear example of this situation is the research project in the political economy of development that was the basis for case study B. As we saw in Chapter 5, the political scientists and economist involved in this project recognized that the nature of the research questions they posed presupposed both a political and economic perspective, in virtue of the (implicit) influence of transcendental realism; yet, they found it difficult to integrate the findings of their analyses because, in practice, they understood the nature of the economic and political in contradictory ways; on the one hand, the economist understood the nature of the referents of these categories in a way that reflected the influence of positivist thinking; on the other hand, the political scientists understood the nature of the referents of these categories in a way that reflected the influence of transcendental realist thinking.

However, this is not to say that collaborative, integrative, interdisciplinary research projects will always fail to produce an integrated outcome. I argued in Chapter 4 that the intellectual context of scientific inquiry is highly complex in the sense that it is *cross-theorized* or characterized by philosophical contradiction; I suggested that it is by virtue of this characteristic that teams of scientists may be able to identify commonalities in their ways of thinking, as well as differences, and thereby find a way of working together. In this respect, critical realism should be an attractive underpinning philosophy for integrative, interdisciplinary researchers because, as I argued in Chapter 2, critical realism transcends the traditional philosophical contradictions emanating from the division between positivism and interpretivism and offers scientists a set of categories they can use to think about how reality is both differentiated and interconnected. However, if it is the case that the intellectual frameworks on which scientists draw are largely tacitly understood or *under-theorized* and if it is the case that scientists may vary psychologically in the extent to which they are able to embrace intellectual difference and change, it is far from clear that scientists engaging in collaborative, integrative, interdisciplinary research projects will be able to reach the sort of philosophical position that critical realist philosophers have developed. In case study B, for example, the economist seemed much less aware of the philosophical contradictions between members of the project team than the political scientists. Indeed, even if scientists are aware of the contradictions between their ways of thinking and are open to intellectual change, they may decide that the investment of time and effort required to change how they think about science and reality would bring few significant rewards, given the penalties they may incur for breaking disciplinary norms. In short, the incentive is for such scientists not to participate in collaborative, integrative, interdisciplinary research projects at all.

The obvious alternative to the production of integrative, interdisciplinary research through collaboration – as one of the political scientists in case study B suggested – is for interdisciplinary research to be an individual pursuit. However, the disadvantage of individual over collaborative integrative research is that the potential range of problems that can be addressed in the former is much more limited than the potential range that can be addressed in the latter. If the education and training system encourages researchers to specialize in one, or at most two, fields of inquiry, it is difficult to see how researchers will be able to cope with the demands of a project that requires knowledge of social science and natural science without having to undergo another extensive period of education that will certify them as qualified practitioners of the new discipline. Of course, many social scientists do acquire additional knowledge of cognate disciplinary fields but that is because the relationship between the social science disciplines is much closer than that between the various natural sciences and between the natural and social sciences considered as wholes. Again, in an academic environment in which disciplinary specialization is highly valued, it is unclear what would be the career rewards of investing time and effort on acquiring an additional body of knowledge.

However, even if the production of integrative, interdisciplinary research on an individual basis were to become a more feasible activity, that still leaves the problem of achieving a coherent outcome. We saw quite clearly in Chapter 2 that certain classical political economists, although implicitly committed to an integrative approach to social scientific inquiry, often failed to achieve this outcome because they had yet to break completely from the influence of positivist thinking. Indeed, if there is one philosophical form that has done more to obstruct the development of a coherent understanding of integrative, interdisciplinary research than any other, it is positivism. I suggest that, ultimately, the problem of integrating knowledge has to be understood within the wider context of dominant, irrealist forms of thought in science and society – of which positivism and postmodernism are but two examples. Indeed, their dominance is cemented through their dialectical relationship as overt antagonists and covert counterparts – reflecting their tacit complicity in (different types of) subject–object identity theory.[2] Positivist thinking, for example, obscures the reality of underlying social (and natural) structures by reducing reality to what can be detected through sensory experience. It thereby entails the reification of scientific ideas as naturally given facts. It is not surprising, therefore, that, if positivist thinking is dominant in society, policymakers should think of scientific disciplines, not as the underlying social and intellectual conditions of scientific inquiry but as simply sets of concepts, theories and laws which can be unproblematically combined. Interpretivist thinking merely reinforces this mode of thinking because, in reducing reality to language and/or thought, it, too, obscures the reality of social structure and thereby treats scientific facts as hypostatized ideas.[3] Through their joint influence, positivism and interpretivism undercut arguments for transforming the socio-intellectual conditions of knowledge production and thereby help to reinforce the dominance of disciplinary-based specialization. At the same time, the influence of irrealist thinking, both in science and society, prevents scientists and higher education policymakers from understanding the real basis for the differentiation and integration of knowledge. Irrealist thinking, in short, becomes a double bind. Yet, irrealist forms of thought are not completely dominant – as the varying degrees of influence of transcendental realist thinking within science indicate. Indeed, it is in virtue of their implicit knowledge of reality as structured, stratified and differentiated that scientists have understood that complex phenomena cannot be adequately addressed from the perspective of only one scientific discipline. (To claim that they can be understood as such would be to commit the error of reductionism.) It is also by virtue of the influence of transcendental realist thinking that scientists have developed an awareness of the social constraints on the production of integrative, interdisciplinary research. But, it is because the influence of transcendental realist thinking tends to be weaker than the influence of irrealist thinking that scientists' awareness of the social and intellectual conditions of knowledge production and their understanding of vertical and horizontal ontological depth are only *partial*. However, this *logical* contradiction – between irrealist and realist thinking – marks the site of a fundamental *dialectical* contradiction: between an underlying reality of structures possessing causal powers and liabilities and forms of thought that acknowledge only the surface features of reality. This relationship between irrealist thought and reality is a dialectical contradiction because irrealism is *distinct* from, although part of, the realty it purports to describe; is *opposed* to it, because it presupposes an incomplete account of reality; yet, is *internally related* to it because the surface features of reality that are the focus of irrealism are generated by deeper layers of causal objects. It is this dialectical contradiction, I suggest, that is propelling the calls for the production of integrative, interdisciplinary research that I discussed in Chapter 1: for the greater the development of scientific specialization (under the influence of irrealist thinking), the greater the limitations of the application of specialized knowledge become apparent (in the form of theory–practice inconsistencies).

## Policy recommendations

What, then, can higher education policymakers do to facilitate the production of integrative, interdisciplinary research? A salient starting point perhaps is to consider the relationship between the Research Assessment Exercise (RAE) and interdisciplinary research – a relationship that has been the subject of considerable debate. For example, the Roberts (2003) *Review of Research Assessment* stated:

> We are aware of a widespread concern that previous RAEs have disadvantaged multidisciplinary research. However, we are not persuaded that RAE panels have proved unable to assess the research submitted to them. Analysis of the results of the 1996 RAE failed to find that multidisciplinarity had any effect upon RAE decisions.
>
> (Roberts, 2003: 28)

Let us consider the reasons for Roberts' conclusion because the argument of this book has an important, critical bearing upon it. The conclusion relates to the results of a report, *Interdisciplinary Research and the Research Assessment Exercise* (Evaluation Associates, 1999). One of the key findings of this report, which the Roberts review quite clearly picked up on, was that the RAE was not biased against interdisciplinary research. The authors of the report state:

> Many researchers perceive the RAE as championing traditional disciplinary ways of working at the expense of their interdisciplinary approach . . . What is clear is that:
>
> - despite researchers' perceptions, there is no evidence that the RAE systematically discriminates against interdisciplinary research, though there are differences in how interdisciplinary research is treated at the panel level;
> - it is difficult to reconcile the strong opinions about the impact of the RAE and our findings that:
>     - interdisciplinary research is not discriminated against
>     - is pervasive in higher education research.
>
> (Evaluation Associates, 1999: 15)

The authors came to these conclusions because they found that there was no significant relationship between the amount of time researchers spent on interdisciplinary research and the rating their department received, and between the proportion of a department's projects that were interdisciplinary and the rating their department received (ibid: 28–9). However, the authors also found a lack of transparency in how panels in the 1996 RAE said they would deal with interdisciplinary research, and a lack of fit between panel membership, units of assessment and departmental research profiles. In light of all their conclusions the authors made five policy recommendations:

1. The Funding Bodies and panel chairs should take steps to ensure the representativeness of panels across all forms and areas of research, including interdisciplinary research.

2. Panel methodologies should specifically address assessment of interdisciplinary research.
3. New mechanisms for boundary critical submissions should be introduced based on a new proforma (5C).
4. The Funding Bodies should introduce monitoring mechanisms to ensure the effectiveness of cross-referral.
5. Feedback and reporting should embrace interdisciplinary research.

(Evaluation Associates, 1999: 36)

However, the report's conclusions invite two points of criticism. The first is that, while the authors of the report may implicitly understand interdisciplinary research as integrative research, in practice, they operated with a broad definition that encompassed both integrative and non-integrative forms of knowledge (such as multidisciplinary and cross-disciplinary research). Therefore, the authors' finding that interdisciplinary research is 'pervasive' in higher education does not necessarily imply that *integrative*, interdisciplinary research is pervasive in higher education. Indeed, if what is called interdisciplinary research is in reality only multidisciplinary (that is, non-integrative) research, it will be much easier to assess such research through disciplinary-based peer review panels because the individual disciplinary components can be assessed by the relevant panel. Hence, it is unsurprising that the authors found that there was no relationship between RAE panel ratings and the extent of interdisciplinarity; if they had operated with a narrower definition of interdisciplinary research that related to the issue of scientific integration, they might well have found a significant relationship.

The second, related point of criticism is that the policy recommendations proposed by the authors presuppose that interdisciplinary research is purely additive rather than integrative in nature. As we saw in Chapter 1, the nature of integrative, interdisciplinary research is such that it is more than the sum of a series of disciplinary-inspired analyses; it is an emergent outcome of the synthesis of different forms of knowledge. If that definition of interdisciplinary research is accepted, therefore, it is difficult to see how individual panels can assess such research adequately because inevitably they will assess it against their own disciplinary norms and criteria. Hence, the danger of cross-referral of integrative research outputs is that this will lead to a *distorted* understanding of their purpose and quality.

Therefore, the authors of the report may claim that the RAE does (or did) not discriminate against interdisciplinary research; yet, in practice the RAE may have ended up discriminating between integrative and non-integrative research – at least if the organizers of the RAE did not understand that the assessment structure of the RAE reflects the pre-existing structuring of scientific fields and the prevalence of scientific specialization. In other words, the dominance of disciplinary-based ways of thinking means that many scientists and policymakers will misunderstand the nature of integrative, interdisciplinary research and (erroneously) will believe that slight modifications to the existing organization of the RAE are all that is needed to deal with interdisciplinary submissions.

In fact, the organizers of the Research Excellence Framework (REF) 2014, the successor to the RAE, have made very few changes to the arrangements for handling interdisciplinary research outputs that were a feature of RAE 2008. For example, they have decided to continue to rely on the cross-referral mechanism and the appointment of specialist assessors and claim that the broadening of the content of panels will help to ensure that interdisciplinary research is 'reviewed fairly by people with appropriate expertise'.[4] Indeed, the organizers of REF 2014 state as one of their objectives to 'Support and encourage innovative and curiosity-driven research, including new approaches, new fields and interdisciplinary work'.[5]

Yet, it is interesting that responses to the second consultation on the proposals for assessing research in REF 2014 reveal a mixture of views on the question of whether or not the arrangements for handling interdisciplinary research outputs will ensure that they are assessed fairly. I quote in full the three (short) paragraphs summarizing these views:[6]

> 78. There was general recognition of the growing importance of interdisciplinary research. Views were mixed about whether our proposals would be sufficient to ensure that interdisciplinary research would be assessed on an equal footing.
> 79. Some felt that they would be sufficient, given the move to broader panels, the inclusion of support for collaborative and interdisciplinary research within the environment element, and measures for handling interdisciplinary submissions within and between people.
> 80. Some were concerned that more should be done, particularly to address perceptions about the treatment of interdisciplinary research and to ensure appropriate interdisciplinary expertise within panels. While some felt that the discipline-based panel structure posed challenges for the assessment of interdisciplinary research, they did not suggest alternative structures for the assessment.

What is interesting about these responses is that they seem to tie in closely with the arguments of this book. For example, the 'general recognition of the growing importance of interdisciplinary research' supports the observation I made in Chapter 1 that scientists are increasingly recognizing the limitations of traditional, specialized, monodisciplinary research in light of their (implicit) understanding of the complexity of reality. Moreover, the fact that there is a difference of opinion as to whether or not the proposals for handling interdisciplinary research in REF 2014 will be adequate also supports the observation I made in Chapter 1 that interdisciplinary research is understood in different ways. Although some scientists do define interdisciplinary research as the integration of knowledge from different disciplines, others define it as a much looser interaction between different disciplines, the end result of which is not an integrative form of knowledge. Many would regard the latter type of research as multidisciplinary. The point, though, is that it is much easier for the academic community to assess multidisciplinary research within a disciplinary-based panel system because the individual components of such research can be assessed separately by the relevant sub-panel. By contrast, it is not so easy to assess integrative, interdisciplinary research within a discipline-based panel system, for the reason I have given above – namely, that this is likely to lead to a distorted understanding of such research. It is this difficulty, I suggest, that explains the concern 'that more should be done . . . to ensure appropriate interdisciplinary expertise within panels'.

Finally, I suggest that the fact that those who responded to the issue of the handling of interdisciplinary research outputs in REF 2014 failed to 'suggest alternative structures for the assessment' of interdisciplinary research,[7] and the fact that policymakers seem not to have recognized the important difference between integrative and non-integrative forms of knowledge, also supports another key argument of this book, which is that the production of integrative, interdisciplinary research is hampered by the lack of understanding of the nature of, and justification for, such research. This lack of understanding is reflected in the expectation of the sub-panels constituting main panel C (which covers mainly the social sciences):[8]

> Each sub-panel expects to receive submissions whose primary research focus falls within the stated remit of its UOA. Submitting units are encouraged to submit their strongest work, including interdisciplinary work, in the UOA where it is most appropriate.

The problem with this expectation is that it is likely to discourage the submission of integrative, interdisciplinary research where the integrating elements have an equal weight or focus within the whole. The sub-panels of main panel C clearly expect 'research focus' to be a *disciplinary* focus rather than, say, a *research problem* focus, which would be more appropriate for integrative forms of knowledge. The implication of this expectation is that if integrative, interdisciplinary research were to be submitted to, say, sub-panel 21 (politics and international studies) or sub-panel 18 (economics and econometrics), it would have to give priority of understanding either to a particular aspect of reality (as in the case of politics) or to a particular conception of social scientific inquiry (as in the case of economics). However, as I have been at pains to point out throughout this book, forcing integrative, interdisciplinary researchers into this position is to undermine the rationale for integrating knowledge from different disciplines. The intended objective of REF 2014, therefore, may be to support the production of interdisciplinary research. Yet, if this objective includes the production of *integrative*, interdisciplinary research, it is likely to be (partially) contradicted by the effect of the structure of assessment, which reflects the disciplinary-based organization of knowledge – just as it was in RAE 2008.

Far from encouraging the production of integrative, interdisciplinary research, then, the REF is simply adding an extra layer of difficulty to an already difficult situation. For the fact is that the structure of assessment within the REF reflects (and reinforces through the link to allocation of research funding) the existing conditions of knowledge production. Hence, the fundamental problem facing higher education policymakers is not so much the logistics of the REF as the norms and values of the academic community. Any system of peer review, whether or not it is linked to national funding mechanisms, has to work with the grain of the academic community, so that simply abolishing peer review systems such as the RAE and REF will do nothing to change the fundamental forces encouraging disciplinary-based specialization in research. These are the forces that emerge from the complex linkages between academic employment structures, the peer review system, the structures of scientific fields and the structures of education and research. Certainly, in the absence of the REF there may be less pressure on researchers to publish in high-ranking, mainstream journals. But, because scientific fields are institutionalized as disciplines, students will still develop a disciplinary mindset and will go on to become the next generation of teachers and researchers in their fields, even in the absence of a peer review system such as the REF. Scientific fields, in short, become self-perpetuating. None of this is to deny that they are flexible and susceptible to change; rather, it is to claim that researchers develop enough of a (tacit) sense of disciplinary identity for disciplines to continue to be reproduced.

In fact, the difficulties associated with producing integrative, interdisciplinary research and teaching integrative, interdisciplinary courses, were recognized in the mid-1970s, at least a decade before the advent of the RAE. Gould, for example, reflecting on the experience of helping to organize the integrated studies modules for the BA degree in social science at the Polytechnic of Central London, writes:

> I think it is true to say that career prospects are at this point in time still predominantly discipline-based and that a member of staff is still first and foremost a member of a (discipline-based) teaching unit...
>
> It is clear that career prospects are at this point of time not enhanced by working in an Integrated Study any more than working in a discipline-based area, and even to the contrary, in the sense that publication outlets may be fewer and less prestigious than in the discipline specialisations. Within the Polytechnic sector it is still generally the case that promotion requires the applicant to prove first of all his expertise in his own discipline area, work in an Integrated Study being counted as secondary. One hopes this will change in the future.
>
> (Gould, 1975: 11–12)

Similarly, Milward and Kennedy, writing at about the same time, conclude that:

> The university teacher judges his expertise and receives his esteem and rewards for the most part within the framework of one subject. His courses and examinations belong to the traditions of that subject, his publications are judged by other teachers in that subject, he attends its annual conference and, if he is successful, he is promoted through a small and fairly familiar

> peer-group to a chair from which he continues to organize the teaching of the same subject. There are great penalties attached to breaking out of this cocoon into an insecure world of fewer peers, fewer conferences and fewer senior posts and the best and most confident of teachers is quite justified in looking very hard at what sort of prospects the system offers him if he at once casts aside his subject label.
>
> (cited in Squires *et al.*, 1975: 23)

How might higher education policymakers, research funders and university managers who have been persuaded of the value of producing integrative, interdisciplinary research facilitate the production of such research? How, in short, might they bring about change to the sort of knowledge that scientists produce? One possibility is for policymakers, managers and funders to establish distinct, interdisciplinary career trajectories running alongside traditional, disciplinary-based career trajectories. By this, I mean that policymakers could allow those scientists to obtain academic employment whose main interest is in the production of integrative, interdisciplinary research and the teaching of integrative, interdisciplinary courses. In this way, policymakers might enable new fields of inquiry to emerge, with the researchers working in them assessed perhaps against the degree to which the knowledge they produce leads to successful, practical interventions in the world. Such researchers could be located in the new interdisciplinary research institutes that many universities have set up. Indeed, it would be crucial for such centres to employ staff directly because, if staff were employed through traditional, disciplinary-based departments and then affiliated to interdisciplinary research centres, the danger is that disciplinary-based goals and priorities might take precedence over interdisciplinary goals and priorities.

However, the problem with a policy of bypassing traditional, disciplinary-based goals and priorities is that it does nothing to challenge the influence of irrealist thinking in science; for, the danger is that if integrative, interdisciplinary researchers work in isolation from those who work in established monodisciplinary fields of inquiry, a lack of understanding will emerge between the two groups. In other words, the danger is that scientists on one side will misunderstand those on the other side. Yet, as I argued in Chapter 2, scientific integration and differentiation constitute a duality so that one should not be seen as a replacement for the other – both are needed to make sense of the complexity of reality. Therefore, if all scientists are to understand the value of both scientific differentiation and integration, we will need radical changes to the philosophical basis of most research. But, that can only be achieved through education and persuasion amongst scientists. Where higher education policymakers, funders and managers can help is to make it possible for scientists to build careers as integrative researchers; that way the value of integrative, interdisciplinary research that is explicitly informed by the philosophy of transcendental realism will be difficult to ignore because it will no longer be research that is conducted on the side lines. Were the value of integrative, interdisciplinary research to be commonly recognized, it would then be possible for researchers to produce such research from any given base of inquiry without suffering career penalties. So, for example, it would be possible for a researcher working in a department of politics to integrate insights from the fields of politics and economics in a way that gave equal emphasis to both rather than producing integrative research biased towards the political. Hence, a transformation of the underlying conditions of knowledge production need not require abolishing existing academic departments; as I have argued throughout this book, the division of labour across academic departments does reflect – albeit fallibly – the differentiation of reality. Establishing new interdisciplinary research institutes and centres, therefore, is not an essential requirement for the production of integrative forms of knowledge. What is an essential requirement is that scientists be disciplined in a different way; disciplined not according to what they focus their inquiries on or how they approach their inquiry but according to the explanatory power and real-world impact of the knowledge they produce. Such criteria for assessing the value of research are broad enough to encompass the full spectrum of sciences – from abstract sciences at one end to concrete sciences at the other.

There may well be significant short-term problems to be overcome in transforming the underlying conditions of knowledge production – not least the lack of expertise in carrying out integrative research. At the moment it seems that the way round this problem is to send interdisciplinary project proposals to relevant disciplinary-based peer reviewers, as the ESRC does.[9] But, the problem with this strategy, as I mentioned above in relation to the RAE and REF, is that disciplinary specialists may not have an adequate understanding of the connections between scientific fields. Identifying scientists who have the expertise to review integrative research products, therefore, will be an important first step in establishing integrative, interdisciplinary research career trajectories. Moreover, research funders, such as the UK Funding Councils, can also help by specifying the production of integrative research as a condition for obtaining funding for interdisciplinary research projects.[10] Over time, scientists who have gained expertise in producing integrative research will be able to act as peer reviewers for subsequent interdisciplinary project bids and to become employees of newly established interdisciplinary research centres. They will also be able to run integrative, interdisciplinary courses at undergraduate and graduate levels.

I hope, therefore, that the argument of this book will help higher education policymakers, researchers, research funders and research managers to understand what justifies the differentiation and integration of knowledge, and that it will thereby play its part in helping to overcome the key intellectual obstacle to the production of integrative, interdisciplinary research, which is the *lack of understanding* of what justifies such research. I hope also that the argument will help higher education policymakers, researchers, research funders and research managers to develop a more sophisticated understanding of the *dominance of academic specialization* and to find ways of overcoming this key, social obstacle to the production of integrative, interdisciplinary research. That is why the title of this book treats the problem of integrating knowledge as both a problem of *theory* – that is, a problem relating to our understanding of the justification of particular forms of knowledge – and a problem of *practice* – that is, a problem of how to organize the production of particular forms of knowledge.

# Appendix
## Research design

In this appendix, I justify the specific research design that informed the social scientific investigation of the problem of interdisciplinarity. I argue that the individual elements of this design are logically consistent with each other and that the design, considered as a whole, is consistent with the philosophy of critical realism that I set out and defend in Chapter 2 of this book.

We can understand the term 'research design' in two different ways: on the one hand, we can think of research design in a general sense as the study of the different elements of the process of research and how they are related to each other; on the other hand, we can think of *a* research design as being an explanation of the content of each of the elements of a specific research project. It is customary to provide such an explanation at the end of the project – that is, after the researcher has produced the results. However, the actual explanation offered is typically the end product of a complex process of decision making; even though we may have made decisions about, say, which sources to consult and which methods to use at the start of the project, during the execution of the research plan we may find that the prior decisions we made must be altered in the light of unexpected problems. In other words, research design is something that usually evolves during the course of a project; it is a process of continual readjustment of the content of each of the elements of the design in the face of unexpected difficulties encountered and errors made, and with the aim of maintaining consistency between the different elements of the design. This is why so many social scientists talk about the complex, non-linear, iterative nature of the process of research. The research design that I now present, therefore, should be understood as the culmination of a process of decisionmaking that took place both before and during the generation and interpretation of empirical evidence.

The basic elements of the research design for this project follow the model devised by Blaikie (2000: 33) and are shown below in Figure A.1.

Let me explain how the specific instances of these elements cohere in this project. We can think of the research design specific to this investigation as an example of what Lawson calls 'contrast explanation' (2003: 92); that is, the overall aim of such research is to explain a set of surprising contrasts (which are observed as partial or demi-regularities) by identifying the underlying structures, mechanisms, powers, tendencies and so forth, responsible for generating them.

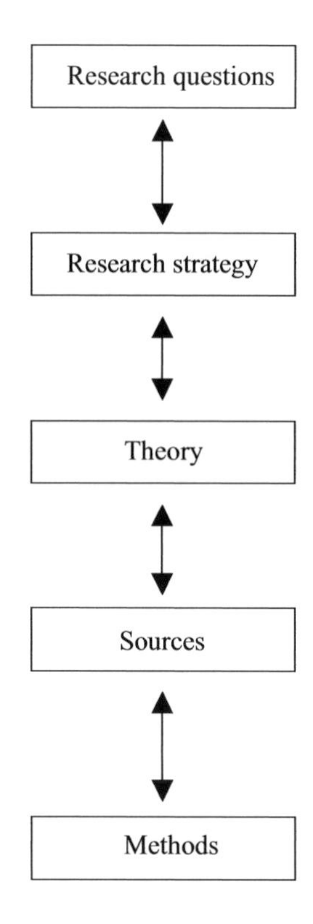


*Figure A.1* Elements of the research design

The particular contrasts that motivate this research project can be stated in the form of the following *research questions*:

1. Why is it that some researchers want to carry out integrative, interdisciplinary research whereas others want to carry out specialized, monodisciplinary research?
2. Why do there seem to be fewer integrative, interdisciplinary than specialized, monodisciplinary research products?
3 Why are some of those who carry out integrative, interdisciplinary research more successful in achieving the goal of integrating knowledge than others?

Now, I have already answered the first question, to a certain extent at least, in Chapter 1, where I examined critically the current debate about the possibility of, and justification for, integrative, interdisciplinary research. The reader will recall that I identified a particular set of beliefs that scientists held, deriving from a more general set of philosophical ideas about the nature of reality, which, in conjunction with the need expressed by policymakers for forms of knowledge that are more practically relevant to the complexities of contemporary society, explain the motivation for carrying out integrative, interdisciplinary research. Of course, in no way am I claiming that these are the only reasons for producing integrative, interdisciplinary research; there are likely to be additional motivating factors, the range and frequency of which could be ascertained through the application of a survey instrument. For example, it could be that researchers have a need to obtain research funding and that they believe that an interdisciplinary project proposal will be more likely to gain funding even if they know that the goal of integrating knowledge is something they neither want nor know how to achieve.

Why, though, are the contrasts contained within these questions surprising? What is it that is so interesting about them? Let us consider each question in turn. The contrast in question 1 is surprising because our expectation is that most, if not all, research is concerned with specialized forms of inquiry. In Chapter 1, we saw how complex is the contemporary division of labour in science, particularly in the social sciences. I suggest, therefore, that it is the tendency towards scientific fragmentation and differentiation that is the condition of our expectation that specialized, monodisciplinary research is the norm.

But, given our surprise that some researchers do want to produce integrative, interdisciplinary research, we now find that there are relatively few genuinely integrative research products; we are surprised by this, too, because, if there are so many examples of specialized, monodisciplinary research, we should expect there to be just as many examples of integrative, interdisciplinary research. So, the second contrast is grounded in the observation, also noted in Chapter 1, that there seems to be a gap between the extent to which researchers want to practise integrative, interdisciplinary research and the extent to which they actually do so.[1]

Finally, we observe that, of the relatively few researchers who do decide to carry out integrative, interdisciplinary research, some are more able to achieve the goal of integrating knowledge than others; that is, some interdisciplinary researchers are more able to produce a philosophically coherent, integrative form of knowledge than others. This is why, as I discussed in Chapter 1, commentators are noticing that much of what is claimed to be integrative, interdisciplinary research is in fact only multidisciplinary research – that is, a juxtaposition, rather than synthesis, of different disciplinary perspectives. Again, we are surprised by this because, if some interdisciplinary researchers are able to realize their research goals, we should expect that all interdisciplinary researchers will be able to do so too. And, I suggest that what seems to be the condition for this expectation is the idea that a scientific discipline is just a body of knowledge – or, more specifically, that it amounts to a set of objects of inquiry, methods, theories, etc; for, if this is the common way of conceptualizing a scientific discipline, it is but a short step to the idea, which I discussed in Chapter 1, that bringing together different subject specialists will result in the production of an integrative form of knowledge.

What we have, then, is a set of three research questions, grounded in three surprising contrasts, that are closely related (in the sense that question 3 presupposes question 2, which, in turn, presupposes question 1). Now, the next, and most obvious, step to consider is how to go about answering these questions systematically. Given that all three questions are explanatory, it makes sense to employ an intensive empirical procedure.[2] Such a procedure is clearly appropriate for the explanation of surprising contrasts because the richness of the evidence collected through in-depth empirical work will allow inferences to be made about the existence of social structures that may explain the observed contrasts. In other words, the explanation produced will involve a backwards movement from concrete phenomena of interest to the identification, by means of conceptual abstraction, of (unobservable) generative objects – a *research strategy* we may call 'retroductive' (Blaikie, 2000: 108–14).[3] However, perhaps an additional term we can use to characterize the research strategy of this investigation is 'retro*dictive*' because we are assuming that *existing* knowledge of the structures and causal mechanisms relating to the context of knowledge production can be used to explain the observed contrasts and to inform the generation of evidence. However, because the evidence we generate can also be used to *develop* existing knowledge of the context of knowledge production, we can also use the term 'retro*ductive*'. In other words, the nature of this investigation is such that it is an example of *theoretical and applied causal contrast explanation*; and I am arguing that the basis for the surprising contrasts observed is not that hitherto unknown causal mechanisms have emerged in the *contrast space*[4] (although, if social reality is an emergent, intrinsically dynamic and open realm, as critical realists claim it is, social change is clearly a possibility) but that our assumptions about the contrast space have been inadequate all along. Through causal explanation our aim will be to transform previously taken-for-granted understandings into more adequate understandings so that the contrast before us is no longer surprising.

If the observation of surprising contrasts is the starting point for explanatory inquiry, the question that confronts us next is how to direct this inquiry. Where should we look for an explanation? At first sight, this may seem a difficult task. Yet, if we examine carefully the specific nature of the surprising contrasts contained within the research questions, we may find clues about how to proceed. For example, the focus of the contrast in question 1 is a particular want or need: that is, to carry out integrative, interdisciplinary research. We may hypothesize, therefore, that a likely explanation for this particular need is a more fundamental need, held by scientists and policymakers alike, to solve the increasingly complex problems afflicting society and that it is the belief that integrative forms of knowledge will enable scientists and policymakers to solve such problems that is the additional motivating factor. So, our surprising contrast has pointed us towards a hierarchy of needs and beliefs, which together constitute what we may identify in an empirical inquiry as reasons for acting. (This was indeed the hypothesis that informed the answer to question 1 presented in Chapter 1.)

By contrast, the nature of the contrast in question 3, since it is concerned specifically with the issue of integrating *knowledge*, seems to point towards an explanation involving intellectual structures and causal mechanisms. This was the rationale for the argument of Chapter 2, where I argued that social scientists' failure to sustain a coherent philosophical justification for scientific integration and specialization has undermined their ability to produce integrative, interdisciplinary research.

Finally, the nature of the contrast in question 2 seems to point towards an explanation focusing on social structures and causal mechanisms because, if there is still an unmet need for more integrative, interdisciplinary research, as this contrast suggests, a social constraint or blockage may have something to do with it. In fact, critical realist ontology gives us reasons to suppose that social structures, as emergent properties, do have causal powers of this sort – that social structures constrain as well as enable human agency. Hence, the sociology of science should indicate which particular social structures have an important bearing on the contrast in question. I considered the issue of *theory* in Chapter 3, where I provided an evaluation and further development of existing theories of social and intellectual structures. I applied this theoretical framework in Chapters 4 and 5, where I attempted to explain the empirical findings of three case studies of collaborative, interdisciplinary research.

What is more, the use of different sorts of contrast allows us not only to give clear direction to our inquiry but also to discriminate between rival hypotheses. For example, if we come across an interdisciplinary research project in which the researchers involved are experiencing difficulties in achieving an integrated outcome, we may feel safer in concluding that philosophical conflicts explain these difficulties rather than social conflicts because, if social conflicts had been of prime importance, presumably the project would not have gone ahead in the first place. But, this means that evaluating the significance of social factors in decisions researchers take about whether or not to carry out integrative, interdisciplinary research will be a difficult task. If our hypothesis about social structures acting as constraints on interdisciplinary research is valid, we will have to find situations in which researchers have either rejected outright an opportunity to take part in an integrative, interdisciplinary project, even though their approaches to social inquiry were philosophically compatible, or have decided not to undertake integrative, interdisciplinary work on an individual basis. Clearly, we will need the help of a survey to try to identify relevant decision-making scenarios that can be followed up and investigated intensively. However, if it is the case that social factors make it difficult to carry out interdisciplinary research but do not rule it out altogether, we may expect to find scenarios where, say, a researcher has decided to carry out integrative, interdisciplinary research, either as part of a team or on an individual basis, despite either the possibility or actuality of the researcher suffering certain material penalties.

So far I have shown how a particular set of research questions embodying contrastive demi-regs, a retroductive research strategy, and theories about underlying structures and causal mechanisms are logically consistent parts of what I have called theoretical and applied causal contrast explanation. I turn now to the question of *sources*; that is, the question of from what we should construct evidence. I mentioned earlier that this research project employs an intensive empirical procedure. In line with the nature of such a procedure, therefore, and in line with the nature of the three contrasts to be explained, I decided to investigate three different interdisciplinary research projects in which the integration of knowledge from different disciplines was at least an implicit objective, so as to allow for comparison.[5]

The logic behind the selection of the three cases of interdisciplinary research is roughly analogous to that followed by a laboratory experimenter in the sense that the aim is to try to keep some conditions the same, while changing others, so as to demonstrate that the change in conditions is responsible for the change in outcome(s) observed. Case study A may be conveniently divided into two stages, which reflect different sources of funding and slightly different research questions (although the same research topic for both stages). In the first stage of case study A, neither the social nor intellectual condition for the integration of knowledge was met. Thus, there were significant philosophical differences between the heterodox economist and the political scientists involved in the first stage, while the social status of heterodox interdisciplinary work in the field of economics was lower than the social status of similar work in the field of political science. By contrast, in the second stage of case study A, both the social and intellectual conditions were met. Thus, the political scientists, lawyer and sociologist involved at the second stage adopted similar philosophical approaches to social inquiry and there was roughly the same degree of social tolerance for interdisciplinary work in their respective disciplines. The second stage of case study A may therefore be regarded as being very similar to an experimental control group.

In case study B, by contrast, the social condition for scientific integration was met but the intellectual condition for it was not. Thus, although the economist and political scientists were practising two different types of interdisciplinary research, it was by virtue of this difference that there was roughly the same degree of social tolerance for the sort of interdisciplinary work they were doing in their respective disciplines. However, it was also by virtue of this difference that there was a philosophical contradiction between the two sorts of scientist: between a positivist-inspired economist and two non-positivist-inspired political scientists.

In case study C, the social and intellectual conditions were the opposite of those of case study B; that is, the intellectual condition for the integration of knowledge was met but the social condition was not. Thus, although the political scientists and biologist involved in this project were committed to roughly the same philosophical approach to scientific inquiry (despite the obvious differences in the nature of their objects of inquiry), their research differed in social status. Thus, the biologist's interdisciplinary work, because it was widely regarded as applied work, held a lower status than theoretical work. By contrast, in political science applied, interdisciplinary work holds a higher status than it does in biology because the structure of the field – at least in the UK – is such that a fundamental division between theoretical and applied work is not in evidence.

What I have just explained is a sampling procedure that is theoretically driven. I have made an analogy with an experiment but it must always be remembered that the three research projects upon which the case studies are based took place in open conditions; in other words, in no way do the three cases represent the sort of closed conditions that may be found in a laboratory. Hence, we can talk about intellectual frameworks being only *roughly* similar because, as we have seen throughout this book, social scientists often imply contradictory philosophical theories both in what they say and in what they do; that is why I used the term 'positivist-inspired', rather than just 'positivist', above. Moreover, when we talk about the social status of interdisciplinary work being roughly the same between two or more disciplines, we must remember that different types of interdisciplinary work exist, that they are evaluated differently across disciplines and that the scientific division of labour may also differ between disciplines. In short, we must acknowledge the complexity of the social and intellectual processes involved in science but that does not mean we cannot still look for interesting cases where one particular process seems to 'stick out' over or dominate others. Essentially, that is what I am trying to identify in these three case studies. Of course, I need not have chosen three different projects: I could have investigated only case study A, where a philosophically coherent integration of disciplinary perspectives was achieved. However, attempting to explain *different* cases allowed me to draw stronger conclusions (via comparative analysis) about the operation of particular social and intellectual structures, and helped me to understand how they are related. The use of multiple case studies in a comparative framework, therefore, makes possible the 'analytic generalisation' of results (Yin, 2003: 32–3), while the '*replication logic*' and '*explanation building*' involved help to ensure that the findings are externally and internally valid (ibid: 33–7).

Finally, I should also acknowledge that I had to make compromises in the selection of the case studies. Ideally, all cases should be completed interdisciplinary research projects so that the philosophical coherence of the project outputs can be examined. However, at the time of writing only the project in case study A was complete; the projects in case studies B and C were still in progress. Clearly, this situation made answering question 3 (about the conditions for achieving an integrated research outcome) slightly more difficult, although certain research outputs relating to case study B, in which there are clear philosophical tensions, were available for analysis. Furthermore, although the project team in case study C had yet to publish any findings, evidence obtained through interviews with team members helped to shed light on the social context of knowledge production, which, in any case, was the overriding rationale for choosing this case.

I am now in a position to discuss the final element of the research design: *methods of inquiry*. Here, I want to distinguish between methods of data construction and methods of data interpretation, which I discuss in turn. Now, given that the rationale for choosing three different interdisciplinary research projects is to ascertain how particular social and intellectual conditions affect researchers' decision making, it follows that in-depth interviewing of the researchers involved in these projects is an appropriate way of finding out about the operation of underlying structures and generative mechanisms. Pawson (1989: 287–322) and Pawson and Tilley (1997: 153–82) have set out a model of the interview that is consistent with the assumptions of critical realism and it is this model that guided the interview strategy in this investigation. Standard models of the interview, Pawson observes, effectively assume that the subject matter and subject of the interview are the same (an assumption rooted, unsurprisingly, in the epistemology of empiricism). In the structured approach, which positivists advocate, the researcher asks a series of predetermined 'neutral' questions that stimulate a response from the subject in the form of a 'true' answer. By contrast, in the unstructured approach, which interpretivists advocate, researcher and subject construct meaning together and certainly not in any predetermined way. The criticisms of the two approaches are of course well known. From a positivist perspective, the unstructured approach entails a lack of control over what data are generated, making comparison of responses across subjects impossible, and, from an interpretivist perspective, the structured approach runs the risk of imposing an invalid frame of reference on the subject. If the former criticism refers to the problem of *control* of meaning, the latter refers to the problem of *imposition* of meaning.

Pawson's model overcomes the polarization between the two standard models of the interview and thereby solves the problems of meaning control and imposition by drawing a clear distinction between the subject matter of the interview, which is the researcher's theory, and the subject of the interview, who is being interviewed because he or she is in the privileged position of being able to comment on a particular aspect of the researcher's theory. Hence, in making a clear distinction between theory and subject, we open up the possibility of a division of labour in the interview, based on a division of expertise, in which the researcher, who is in the privileged position of being able to develop scientific as opposed to commonsense explanations of social phenomena, 'teaches' the conceptual framework to the respondent, who 'learns' and 'applies' it to his or her own thinking.

Of course, the 'teacher–learner' aspect of the interview is very much an indirect affair. Thus, rather than simply offering a direct explication of the proposed theory, which would run the risk of the interview becoming a self-corroborating exercise, the researcher offers a series of theoretical cues or prompts, which the respondent takes to be the frame of reference for understanding the meaning of individual questions. For example, for this project all researchers interviewed were provided with a briefing note indicating which aspects of the practices they engaged in as researchers were of interest to the investigator, while opening statements to questions also indicated what sort of information was desired. Indeed, the individual questions asked typically focused on what were thought to be important decision-making points for the respondent. For example, the second section of the interview schedule addressed the issue of approach to social inquiry. Respondents were asked about typical problems and questions considered important in their field of inquiry, how they solved such problems, how they constructed an argument, how they fitted together theory and empirical evidence, and so on. These questions were designed to elicit responses, from which the investigator could then infer the existence of a particular philosophy of science implicit in the respondent's reasoning. When devising appropriate questions to ask, then, the researcher has to translate social scientific (or philosophical) discourse (in which the proposed theory is initially expressed) into the everyday discourse of the interview subject. If, for example, the interview subjects had been asked the sorts of questions that philosophers routinely ask about, say, the nature of social phenomena and the limits to knowledge of social phenomena, it is likely that the subject would have struggled to answer and would have asked the investigator what he or she meant (unless of course the subject had an adequate understanding of philosophy). Piloting of the interview schedule can therefore help the researcher to know when the translation has been successful; that is, to know when subjects understand what is being asked of them.

In addition to the 'teacher–learner' aspect of the interview, there is also the 'conceptual refinement' aspect. In other words, the subject of the interview not only learns and applies the researcher's conceptual framework but also comments on it (by virtue of the expertise the subject acquires as an occupant of a particular position in society) and thereby helps the researcher to refine the proposed theory. In revealing the structure of his or her thinking, the subject is in effect proposing his or her own 'theory', which the researcher, in turn, 'learns' and 'applies' by asking follow-up questions that paraphrase or summarize the subject's answer. In inviting comment on these paraphrases and summaries in the form of the subject's agreement or disagreement, the researcher is checking whether the reasoning process he or she has depicted is an accurate reflection of the subject's reasoning. Conceptual refinement, in short, enables the researcher to understand how the subject usually thinks in a particular sociocultural context; in understanding what courses of action are open to subjects and how subjects arrive at particular decisions, the researcher gains a bearing on how a particular sociocultural context influences human agency. For example, if an interview subject reveals that he or she has been offered the chance to take part in an interdisciplinary research project but has declined the offer for the reason that declining would be better for his or her career prospects, the researcher will be directed to the importance of the academic career structure in shaping researchers' decisions about what sort of research to pursue. The researcher could then ask further questions of the subject in order to understand the conditions for promotion through the academic career structure and why the subject thought that the pursuit of interdisciplinary research would be detrimental to career progression.

What I have just discussed is a model of the interview that overcomes the problems of meaning control and imposition. Now, it may be thought that in 'teaching' the conceptual framework to the subject, the researcher is imposing a particular framework of meaning on the subject. In fact, the researcher is simply orienting or channelling the subject towards some meanings and away from others, in recognition of the fact that the meaning of concepts is context specific. Moreover, in allowing the subject to comment on this conceptual framework (which, of course, the researcher has attempted to 'translate' into the everyday discourse of the subject) the researcher is in no way taking the proposed reasoning models to be a direct reflection of the way the subject usually thinks. By contrast, in the standard structured model of the interview the researcher lets the conceptual framework speak for itself and thereby assumes that the statements on which the subject is asked to offer an opinion (which the researcher typically ranks on a scale) do indeed reflect the subject's usual mode of reasoning. In practice, of course, the subject may struggle to offer a response for lack of context – a sign that the researcher has not addressed the imposition problem. Similarly, when the standard unstructured model is put into practice, the subject may also start looking for greater context from the interviewer if he or she is simply asked to define a situation from his or her own perspective – a sign that the researcher has not addressed the problem of control. Therefore, both problems – of meaning control and imposition – have to be negotiated if any conversation is to be mutually intelligible.

The mechanics of the interviews carried out for this research project can be summarized as follows. The interview schedule was designed in light of the theoretical framework elaborated in Chapter 3 and in light of the results of three exploratory interviews with researchers who had carried out interdisciplinary research projects in the past.[6] (These three informal interviews also served as pilot interviews, which meant that appropriate explanatory cues and prompts could be developed.) The questions were organized into four sections. The first section comprised a set of introductory questions concerned with the subject's disciplinary background, field of inquiry and general research interests. The second section focused more explicitly on the intellectual context of the subject's research activity. In this section, subjects were asked to describe how they usually approached a research task, be it a research problem or question, and to refer to specific examples so that the philosophical assumptions upon which they were (implicitly) drawing could be understood. The questions in the third section related explicitly to the social context of knowledge production and focused on how peer review and assessment mechanisms – in particular, the RAE – affected what sort of research the subjects chose to do and where to publish it. The fourth and final section focused on subjects' previous and current interdisciplinary research activity. Subjects were asked about their roles in any collaborative interdisciplinary research they had taken part in, how their role had related to the roles of their collaborators and what sorts of problems they had encountered in collaborating with researchers who came from different disciplinary backgrounds and adopted different methodological approaches.

The initial intention was to carry out interviews with all members of the three project teams (identified above as case studies A, B and C). However, practical constraints meant that only those who either had played or were playing a major role in the project – usually the principal investigators – could be interviewed.[7] The interviews themselves were recorded on tape with the permission of the interviewee and later transcribed in full. As with all conversations, interviews are subject to interviewee bias, poor recall and poor articulation. Indeed, these problems applied especially to the investigation of case study A, a project that was completed seven years ago. For example, the problem of poor recall was particularly evident in the interview with one team member, who had subsequently been appointed to a position in Her Majesty's Treasury and had therefore lost touch with the world of academic research, and another who had remained in academic research but whose approach to social inquiry had developed significantly since completion of the project. However, to a certain extent this problem was mitigated by the availability of individual team members' disciplinary research outputs published at the time of the interdisciplinary project, which could be examined for clues as to individuals' approach to social inquiry. Furthermore, team members' verbal reports about the nature of the interdisciplinary project could also be compared with the published outputs (such as books, reports, and journal articles) arising from the project. Hence, the use of multiple sources of evidence helped to increase the validity of data construction by establishing 'converging lines of inquiry' (Yin, 2003: 35–6, 97–101). However, it was much more difficult to rely on data triangulation procedures in the investigation of cases B and C because these two projects were still in progress and few research outputs arising specifically from the projects were available for examination. However, what the project team members lacked in research outputs they made up for in much clearer and more thorough recall of the problems involved in attempting to integrate knowledge.

Before I turn to the problem of the interpretation of the data constructed, I should mention how I have addressed the problem of reliability. Yin (2003: 37–9) recommends the creation of a 'case study protocol' (ibid: 67–77) and 'case study database' (ibid: 101–5) as ways of ensuring that a different investigator can either investigate the same case using the same procedures or re-examine extant data and thereby reach similar conclusions. From this investigation, therefore, I have compiled the following: an interview schedule and guide, transcripts of recorded interviews and notes of non-recorded interviews, documents describing the projects' aims and objectives that have been published on the internet, copies of any research outputs relating to the three projects, bibliographies of any published disciplinary research outputs relating to the individual researchers interviewed that were consulted during the course of the investigation and, finally, official policy documents produced by important actors in UK higher education. Now, in principle, all this material is available to anyone wishing to examine the findings of the investigation. However, because the interviewees wished to remain anonymous and because each project involved only a small number of researchers, I have decided to make access to the database subject to the agreement of the interviewees.

How, then, was the empirical evidence in the case study database interpreted? How was this evidence used to answer the three, key research questions about integrative, interdisciplinary research? We saw in the first section of Chapter 2 that the critical realist logic of explanation in science turns on the concept of retroduction from phenomena lying at one level of reality (the *explananda*) to phenomena lying at another, deeper level (the *explanans*). Now, in social science this mode of inference will typically involve the explication of the causal conditions for an observed event (or set of events) of interest (perhaps in the form of a contrastive, as we have seen). Thus, in this investigation the overriding concern was to identify the causal conditions for science, which, I hypothesized, are both social and intellectual in nature.

How, though, did I use the interview transcripts, official policy documents and published research outputs to justify the existence of underlying social and intellectual structures and generative mechanisms? In posing this question, I am in effect posing the question of what makes possible the production of scientific research. I used the interview evidence to help me to answer this question because the chains of reasoning that subjects revealed helped me to identify which social structures and which intellectual structures influenced their choices about what to research and how. It is because social structures modify human agency that I was able to use agents' reasoning as a means of identifying them; that is, by examining *how* agents made a decision I was able to make an inference about *what* was influencing them. Hence, social structures can be thought of as a way of channelling, or of giving specific content to, human agency. (This is why human agency is not possible without social structure.) Similarly, I used policymakers' documents to augment and corroborate what interviewees said and thereby increase my understanding of the way in which the relevant social structures operate. The identification of the socio-intellectual conditions of knowledge production, then, I take to be a basic task of the sociology of science.

However, I also used subjects' published research outputs to identify the intellectual frameworks – in this case, philosophies of science – on which they drew implicitly. Indeed, if interview subjects draw on a piece of work to exemplify how they understand the process of scientific inquiry, we can examine the philosophical presuppositions of that output and compare them with the philosophical presuppositions of subjects' reasoning as described in the interview. (We can do this because all scientific theories presuppose a set of philosophical assumptions about the nature of reality, how reality can be known and what are the most appropriate methods to use to acquire that knowledge – as should be clear from the argument of Chapter 2.) In short, we can also use published research outputs (as well as policymakers' documents) to augment and corroborate what interviewees say. The identification and elaboration of the presuppositions about knowledge and being, then, I take to be the basic task of 'ontographology' (Lawson, 2004: 2).[8] Given that its focus is the ideational aspect of social reality, ontographology can be considered to be distinct from, yet encompassed within, the sociology of science.[9]

Let me now consider these methods of interpretation in a little more depth. I mentioned above that the basic mode of inference involved in constructing a scientific explanation is backwards looking. In fact, this mode of inference takes on two slightly different forms according to the nature of the research being carried out. In the model of pure or theoretical explanation, devised by Bhaskar (and known as DREI for short), it is signified by the term 'retroduction':

> *description* of law-like behaviour; *retroduction*, exploiting analogies with already known phenomena, to possible explanations of the behaviour; *elaboration* and elimination of alternative explanations; issuing (ideally) in the empirically-controlled *identification* of the causal mechanism(s) at work.
>
> (Bhaskar, 1986: 68)

In the model of applied or practical explanation (known as RRRE for short) it is signified by the term 'retrodiction':

> *resolution* of a complex event (situation, etc.) into its components; *redescription* of these components in theoretically significant terms; *retrodiction*, via independently validated normic or tendency statements, to possible antecedents of the components; and *elimination* of alternative possible causes.
>
> (ibid: 68)

In theoretical research, then, the aim is to isolate[10] a structure or mechanism so as to understand its mode of operation when its causal powers and liabilities are exercised independently of the context in which it is located. (I say more about what this 'context' is below.) In applied research, by contrast, the aim is to apply knowledge of structures and mechanisms gained through pure research to explain a novel event of interest and thereby to understand how the context in which those structures and mechanisms operate modifies their operation. This investigation is primarily applied in orientation. However, as I noted above, in practice it may be difficult to separate applied research from theoretical research because, if the application of theory reveals its limitations in explaining events and states of affairs of interest, further theoretical work will be required to overcome these limitations. Indeed, much of the discussion in Chapter 3 is devoted to the development of theory; that is, the concern in Chapter 3 is to elaborate upon and thereby develop previously identified (but inadequately specified and related) conditions for scientific activity.

However, I want to focus here on applied explanation and to consider the specific form that each step in the RRRE model takes. Now, the argument of Chapter 1 suggests that the concrete episode in question may be *resolved* into three basic components:

- the fact that some scientists choose to pursue mainly specialized, monodisciplinary research, whereas others choose to carry out a much larger proportion of integrative, interdisciplinary research in addition to their usual monodisciplinary research activities;
- the fact that, whereas some of those who wish to integrate knowledge through interdisciplinary research manage to produce a coherent research output (according to the definition of 'coherence' discussed in Chapter 1), others have difficulty in achieving the same degree of coherence and integration in the research process;
- the fact that many of those claiming to be carrying out integrative, interdisciplinary research often seem confused about what this means.[11]

The arguments of Chapters 1 to 5 of this book also suggest that these three components may be *redescribed* in the following theoretically significant terms:

- the dominance of specialized forms of knowledge production, whether these be disciplinary or subdisciplinary;
- methodological conflict between scientists, presupposing hitherto unresolved philosophical differences;
- multiple conceptions of interdisciplinarity, entailing confusion about the meaning of integrating knowledge.

Now, it is a central contention of this book that *retrodiction* to social and intellectual structures and generative mechanisms is necessary to explain these components. Furthermore, it is the concept-dependence of social activity – the fact that social objects are already interpreted by lay agents – that makes such an explanation, whether pure or applied, possible; for the basic task in science is to transform lay conceptions of social reality, which are characteristically inadequate in some way or other, into scientific conceptions. (To return briefly to the earlier discussion of data construction, the implication of the distinction between lay and scientific thought is that the division of expertise in the interview is hierarchical in the sense that, although the lay agent may have 'expert' knowledge of the influence of a particular structure, it is the scientist ultimately who is in the position to understand the broader context in which that mechanism operates.)

Now, given the key ontological assumption of this investigation – that events and states of affairs are generated by conjunctions of different mechanisms – the scientist faces the difficult task of identifying which particular structures and mechanisms should be applied to the theoretically redescribed components in question. In other words, if there is a range of different mechanisms operating at different levels of reality, how can we divide these up in a way that is explanatorily fruitful for the research question of interest? In this respect Pawson (1989) and Pawson and Tilley (1997) offer assistance to social scientists. They have developed a model that specifies the 'logic' of realist explanation:

> The basic task of social inquiry is to explain interesting, puzzling, socially significant regularities (R). Explanation takes the form of positing some underlying mechanism (M) which generates the regularity and thus consists of propositions about how the interplay between structure and agency has constituted the regularity. Within realist investigation there is also investigation of how the workings of such mechanisms are contingent and conditional, and thus only fired in particular local, historical or institutional contexts (C).
>
> (Pawson and Tilley, 1997: 71)

Now this model, which Pawson and Tilley summarize as the basic formula '*outcome* = *mechanism* + *context*' (ibid: 57), has much to recommend it, not least its emphasis on the contingency of social causation. Yet, it is not entirely clear in this model what 'mechanism' and 'context' mean. Pawson and Tilley argue that a 'mechanism' is 'an account of the makeup, behaviour and interrelationships of those processes which are responsible for the regularity. A mechanism is thus a theory – a theory which spells out the potential of human resources and reasoning' (ibid: 68). However, a mechanism is not the same as a theory: it is a (philosophical) concept that describes something real – in this case the way of working, in general, of social structure. Thus, mass production is a specific kind of (social) mechanism that is set in motion when the causal powers of (capitalist) structures of production and exchange are triggered. The concept of mechanism, then, describes something that exists independently of our knowledge of it: as a concept it pertains to the transitive domain of reality, whereas the entity it refers to pertains to the intransitive domain.[12] Therefore, a mechanism is not the same as either a concept or a theory (which is an account of how a specific mechanism of interest tends to operate when its causal powers and liabilities are activated).

It is important to define the term 'mechanism' clearly because, if we accept the foregoing definition, we find that what Pawson and Tilley call 'context' also involves causal mechanisms. 'Context', they argue, comprises pre-existing social conditions into which, say, a programme of social change is introduced:

> By social context, we do not refer simply to the spatial or geographical or institutional location into which programs are embedded. So whilst indeed programs are initiated in prisons, hospitals, schools, neighbourhoods, and car parks, it is the prior set of social rules, norms, values and interrelationships gathered in these places which sets limits on the efficacy of program mechanisms.
>
> (Pawson and Tilley, 1997: 70)

But, if social context is essentially social structure, or the 'social rules, norms, values and interrelationships gathered in these places', it must also include social mechanisms, if we accept that by the term 'mechanism' we mean the way in which social structure is causally efficacious.

Implicit in Pawson and Tilley's model, then, is the idea that 'context' or 'C' pertains to a range of mechanisms *contingently related* to a set of mechanisms called 'mechanism' or 'M' that are the primary focus of the investigation. However, Bhaskar has argued that mechanisms may be related to each other not only contingently but also necessarily. When the relations between mechanisms are *contingent* we have what Bhaskar calls '"mechanical" complexes of externally related interacting structures' and when the relations are *necessary* we have '"organic" totalities of internally related intra-acting ones' (1986: 110). In other words, an internally complex system is one in which the structure of the system, as an emergent whole, and the individual elements of which it is composed, are ontologically interdependent; that is, the whole and its parts are irreducible to one another, yet mutually influential, being one another's conditions of existence. By contrast, in an externally complex system the elements are not ontologically interdependent so that no systemic causal properties emerge. However, the *interaction* between the elements of such a system may still be described as causal because the effect(s) of one mechanism may either override or reinforce the effect(s) of another mechanism, in virtue of the external relation between them (ibid: 109–10). Moreover,

> particular systems may contain both mechanical and organic connections, and pairs of structures may be related in both internal and external ways (as so indeed may their relations too). So that even where structures cohere as a totality, this does not mean that all causal interaction between them is internal, i.e. identity-affecting. Pervasive internality in a system is compatible with differentiated, and highly specific, causal roles within it; so that existential parity is quite concordant with ontological differentiation and depth.
> (Bhaskar, 1986: 110–11)

Therefore, the difficulty facing the applied social scientist when attempting to construct an intelligible and plausible explanation of concrete events lies in specifying as accurately as possible not only the nature of the connections between sociocultural objects but also the way in which the particular system they comprise is articulated – that is, the way in which sociocultural objects have differential causal force. In short, the crucial problem facing the applied social scientist when moving from the abstract to the concrete is how to capture the *complexity* of the interactions of different structures and mechanisms, their causal powers, and tendencies.[13] It is the notion of complexity, therefore, that is missing from Pawson and Tilley's model of explanatory inquiry.

How, then, does ontographology fit into the scheme of explanation? How exactly does it relate to the RRRE model? Now, I claimed above that ontographology is a method of interpretation in its own right so let me justify this claim. Ontographology is a distinct method because it is the sort of method that philosophers use; that is, it involves a special type of retroductive inference known as transcendental reasoning.[14] We have already encountered the transcendental mode of reasoning in the discussion of transcendental realism in Chapter 2, which Bhaskar (1975) derived from an inquiry into the possibility of successful scientific experimentation. Now, the premise of a transcendental argument does not have to be scientific experimentation; it can be any sort of human activity conceptualized in experience. However, in ontographology the premise is not so much a particular human activity *per se* as the *product* of that activity. Hence, the question ontographologists pose is not what must be the case for a particular scientific method to be employed successfully but what must be the case given the reality that a particular scientific theory describes. For example, Lawson has argued that orthodox general equilibrium theories in economics presuppose a deductivist methodology, a positivist epistemology, and a social atomistic ontology (1997).[15]

However, although ontographology is a distinctively philosophical method, the products of its analysis can still be used in the construction of a scientific explanation. That is why I claimed above that the sociology of science may be seen to encompass ontographology. For example, suppose we compare the philosophical presuppositions of a particular scientific theory with the philosophical assumptions that the author of that theory claims to hold. If we find agreement between the two, we will have corroborating evidence for what the author of the theory professes. But, if we find philosophical disagreement, we may want to explain this scientifically. For example, a social scientist may claim to hold assumptions consistent with a transcendental realist philosophy. Yet, examination of his or her work may reveal elements of a contradictory philosophy. Indeed, we may find – as we did in the works of the classical political economists discussed in the third section of Chapter 2 – unacknowledged philosophical contradictions not only between how scientists understand what they do and what their theories presuppose but also between different elements of the same theory – perhaps manifest in a confused understanding of causation. But, wherever we find such contradictions, their existence becomes a legitimate object of scientific explanation. Indeed, if we can show how false beliefs about knowledge and being are necessary in some way, we will be well on the way to understanding how particular philosophies of science serve as ideologies '*of*' and '*for*' science (Bhaskar, 1989: 23; 1998: 53).

In this appendix, I have set out and justified the specific research design that guided the social scientific investigation of the problem of integrative, interdisciplinary research. Although this particular research design does not involve the mixing of different scientific research methods – as is the traditional way of understanding mixed methods research – it does involve the mixing of one particular scientific research method – interviewing – with a particular philosophical method known as ontographology. I used the different types of data generated from the two methods – respectively, researchers' understandings of science and the philosophical presuppositions of scientific research – to construct a causal contrast explanation of the difficulties researchers have experienced in attempting to integrate knowledge through interdisciplinary research. This explanation forms the argument of Chapters 4 and 5 and reflects both the theoretical and applied nature of the inquiry. It is applied to the extent that the evidence generated is used to test existing theories about the underlying social and intellectual context of knowledge production and it is theoretical to the extent that the evidence generated is also used to help develop those theories. Hence, although I present the theoretical argument of the thesis in Chapter 3 before the discussion of the empirical evidence from the case studies of interdisciplinary research in Chapters 4 and 5, I do not want to suggest that the empirical evidence I generated had no influence over the development of the theoretical framework. I do not want to imply that I am simply testing theories of knowledge production other researchers have developed by applying them to the problem of interdisciplinarity because I used the evidence I generated to develop those theories as well as to test them. To clarify this point: if pre-existing theories of knowledge production did influence the construction of evidence, that evidence, in turn, influenced the process of critical theoretical development. In short, I see the relationship between theory and evidence as interdependent.

I have argued that an intensive empirical procedure was an appropriate type of research design for this investigation, given the nature of the questions posed and the underlying commitment to depth-realist forms of explanation. I have justified this choice of research design by showing how the research questions, research strategy, theory, sources, and methods fit together coherently. But, just as the relationship between scientific theory and empirical evidence is interdependent, so is the relationship between philosophical theory and scientific practice. Hence, the research design I have presented in this appendix should be regarded as, on the one hand, the pre-existing set of intellectual resources that guided my investigation and, on the other hand, as the reconstructed logic of my investigation as it actually occurred. But, to the extent that it is an explanation of how my investigation proceeded, it is a fallible and partial one because there may be certain aspects of my research practice that remain untheorized and so implicit to my inquiry.

# Notes

## 1 Introduction: the problem of integrating knowledge

1. For information about the programme and speakers see www.britac.ac.uk/events/2006/inter-disc/prog.html (accessed 3 April 2013). For a summary of the discussion see www.britac.ac.uk/news/release.asp?NewsID=199 (accessed 3 April 2013).
2. For full information about all the workshops in this series go to www.lancs.ac.uk/fass/projects/iass/workshops.html (accessed 3 April 2013).
3. See page 3 of the ICOSS brochure at www.shef.ac.uk/content/1/c6/03/27/91/Brochure.pdf (accessed 3 April 2013).
4. See www.dur.ac.uk/ias (accessed 3 April 2013).
5. See www.relu.ac.uk (accessed 3 April 2013) and also Lowe and Phillipson (2006).
6. They also define a third type of integration that is equivalent to 'a single overarching theoretical framework', although they thought that this was 'an idealized limit' and was 'unlikely to be attained soon' (Rossini and Porter, 1979: 72).
7. Tait *et al.* define 'mode 1' interdisciplinarity as research 'which has the aim of furthering the expertise and competence of academic disciplines themselves for example through developments in methodology which enable new issues to be addressed or new disciplines or sub-disciplines to be formed'. They define 'mode 2' interdisciplinarity as research 'which addresses issues of social, technical and/or policy relevance where the primary aim is problem-oriented and discipline-related outputs are less central to the project design' (2003a: 13).
8. See 'Rural Economy and Land Use Programme Specification for the Third Call for Proposals' at www.relu.ac.uk/funding/ThirdCallSpecification.pdf (accessed 3 April 2013).
9. However, the complexity of reality is not the only basis for justifying interdisciplinary research. Barry *et al.* identify three different motivations or 'logics' of interdisciplinary research: 'the logics of accountability, innovation and ontology' (2008: 22). The logic of complexity discussed in this section most closely resembles the 'logic of ontology', although if integrative, interdisciplinary research produces a cognitive advancement that can help policymakers to solve important problems of public interest, the logic of complexity will entail a 'logic of innovation' and 'logic of accountability' as well.
10. Repko also leaves the meaning of 'disciplinary insight' unclear. He tells us that 'An insight is a scholarly contribution to the clear understanding of a problem. Insights can be produced either by disciplinary experts or by interdisciplinarians' (2008: 12). However, at no point in his textbook does he explain what disciplinary insights are about – that is, what features of reality they refer to; and he fails to do this, as we have already seen, because his argument remains stuck at the level of methodology and epistemology.

11 See www.britac.ac.uk/news/release.asp?NewsID=199 (accessed 3 April 2013).
12 See www.lancs.ac.uk/fass/projects/iass/workshops.html (accessed 3 April 2013).
13 See Petts, J., Owens, S. and Bulkeley, H. 'Discussion Paper for Seminar 6', page 2 at www.planning-resnet.org.uk/seminars/19-10-04/esrc_position_paper.pdf (accessed 3 April 2013).
14 Ibid., page 5.
15 Ibid., page 6.
16 Available online at http://royalsociety.org/uploadedFiles/Royal_Society_Content/policy/publications/1996/10203.pdf (accessed 3 April 2013).
17 In fact, women's studies finds itself caught in a debate between those who reject an interdisciplinary approach and who want women's studies to become a discipline in its own right and those who fear that, in the absence of an explicitly interdisciplinary approach, women's studies will become dominated by a particular perspective and will thereby become part of the very problem of which it is critical. On this debate, see Bowles and Klein (1983).
18 Thus, when I say that the term 'critical realist sociology of knowledge' should be used to describe the nature of the assumptions guiding sociological inquiry, I am treating critical realism as an intellectual cause of the production of a sociological argument. Of course, critical realist philosophy does not determine the nature of that argument because scientific activity, like any other social activity, is subject to multiple causal determination; but, it does make the production of such an argument possible.
19 However, in Chapter 4, I do introduce the concept of the subconscious into my argument.

## 2 Critical realism and integrative interdisciplinary research

1 It must be remembered that, as a general movement in philosophy and social theory, critical realism is continually evolving in critique of itself. Accordingly, its categorical grammar is continually expanding. Indeed, its imminently critical character ensures that its development has been, and continues to be, a dialectical process, starting with *transcendental realism* and moving through *critical naturalism* and *explanatory critique* to *dialectical critical realism* and culminating in *transcendental dialectical critical realism*. (See the entry 'critical realism' in Hartwig [2007: 96–105] for a full exposition of the development of this philosophy of science.)
2 For an overview and selection of readings from this debate see Bryman (2006).
3 Lindesmith's (1968) work on opiate addiction is the most commonly cited example of analytic induction.
4 Turner (1981) provides a useful codification of this approach.
5 Hammersley and Atkinson also acknowledge the positivist presuppositions of the naturalist position in ethnography – that is, the idea that the social world should be studied in its natural state and in ways that are sensitive to that state. Indeed, they point to the 'tension within ethnography between the naturalism characteristic of ethnographers' methodological thinking and the constructivism and cultural relativism that shape their understanding of the perspectives and behaviour of the people they study' (1995: 10–11). In resolving this tension, they propose a third, alternative 'reconstructed logic of inquiry that shares much with positivism and naturalism but goes beyond them in important respects' (ibid: 21). This is also the position advocated here.
6 The following exposition of the assumptions of critical realism, which has had to be relatively concise given limitations of space, draws on a variety of sources: Bhaskar (1975, 1979, 1986, 1989, 1993, 1994), Archer *et al.* (1998), Sayer (1984, 2000b) and Danermark *et al.* (2002). Concise definitions of many of the terms critical realists use can be found in Hartwig (2007).
7 Of course, the fact that experimental event regularities can be produced at all

presupposes that the natural world must be open because it is only if something is open that part of it can then be closed off.

8 As Bhaskar points out, naturalism is manifest in two forms: '*reductionism*, which asserts that there is an actual identity of subject-matter as well, and *scientism*, which denies that there are any significant differences in the methods appropriate to studying social and natural objects, whether or not they are actually (as in reductionism) identified' (1998: 2). The form of naturalism with which I am principally concerned and refute at this point in the chapter, is scientism. However, as I show later in this chapter, where I introduce and defend the concept of emergence, I am also arguing against reductionist forms of naturalism, such as physicalism.

9 As I discuss in Chapter 4, sociologists of science working in the interpretivist tradition, such as Kuhn (1962), have extended the position of methodological difference into a thorough-going methodological relativism (thereby implying historicism), the upshot of which is that there is nothing essential about the method of scientific inquiry (Feyerabend, 1975).

10 Lawson (1997: 199–204) in fact argues that the inability to achieve experimental closures in the social realm does not constitute a limit to a naturalistic social science because not all natural sciences can achieve experimental closure. Indeed, this argument suggests that the standard distinction between open and closed systems that critical realists have tended to rely on requires further clarification in acknowledgement of the possibility of systems being open and closed to different degrees or 'partly open' and 'partly closed' (Karlsson, 2011: 161).

11 Danermark *et al.* prefer to use the term 'critical methodological pluralism' (2002: 150–70).

12 For a definition of the concept of duality see Bhaskar (1993: 397) and the entry 'duality and dualism' in Hartwig (2007: 149–50).

13 More precisely, we can say that theory and practice and being and thought constitute types of *constellational unity or duality*. So, for example, a scientific practice presupposes and so depends on a theory of science, while scientific theorizing presupposes and so depends on practical engagement with the world (such as experimentation). But, note that we also have a *constellational identity* here in the sense that scientific theorizing is but one type of, and so is contained within, practice, just as thought is but one feature of, and so is contained within, being. See the definition of constellation in Bhaskar (1993: 395–6) and also the entry for this concept in Hartwig (2007: 78–9).

14 Referential detachment is 'The detachment of the act of reference from that to which it refers. This establishes at once its existential intransitivity and the possibility of another reference to it, a condition of any intelligible discourse at all' (Bhaskar, 1993: 402–3).

15 No wonder, then, that Carp (2001), Bailis (2001) and Klein (2001) are all resistant to what they see as Newell's attempt to impose a particular meaning of interdisciplinarity across the scholarly community (an attitude that Klein sums up in the comment that Newell's unification agenda is just another 'modernist agenda in the midst of postmodern skepticism' [Klein, 2001: 44]).

16 This happens by virtue of what critical realists call the *reality principle*. It is synonymous with the concept of *alethic truth*, defined as 'The truth of, or real reason(s) for, or dialectical ground of, *things*, as distinct from *propositions*, possible in virtue of the ontological stratification of the world and attainable in virtue of the dynamic character of science' (Bhaskar, 1993: 394). The concept of alethic truth is in turn synonymous with the concept of (epistemologically mediated) *axiological necessity*. See the entry 'reality principle' in Hartwig (2007: 401–2) and 'alethia' (ibid: 24–30).

17 For a comprehensive discussion of 'irrealism' see Hartwig (2007: 268–71).

18 Note that certain realists are also highly sceptical about the possibility of scientific integration. Dupré (1993), for example, follows postmodernists in criticizing what he

sees as the three related sins of the Western intellectual tradition – determinism, reductionism and essentialism – and claims to discern a prevailing 'disorder' in the world. (Dupré describes his ontological position as a 'metaphysics of radical ontological pluralism, what I have referred to as "promiscuous realism"' [ibid: 18].) Given the prevailing disorder in the world, Dupré argues, the sciences cannot be unified via reductionism because science is a 'mixed bag' of theories and methods that reflects a diversity of objects of inquiry (ibid: 242). But, the question facing radical pluralists such as Dupré remains: if there is nothing essential to science, how can we demarcate science from non-science?

19 We can also use the dialectical critical realist concept of *mediation* to describe the relationship between emergent levels of reality (Bhaskar, 1993: 112–34). For example, human agency is determinative of social structure, in the sense that it could not exist without human agency, but mediating of its effect, in the sense that the causal impact of social structure must always work through human agency. Likewise, social structure is determinative of human agency, in the sense of setting the conditions for its exercise, but mediating of the effect of the exercise of human agency because human agency is always operative through social structure. See also Norrie (2010: 98–9) and the entry 'mediate' in Hartwig (2007: 294–5).

20 Bhaskar also uses the concept of interaction in this way – for example, when defining '"mechanical" complexes of externally related interacting structures' (1986: 110). However, when describing the relationship between internally related structures, as in a totality, he refers to 'intra-acting' rather than interdependent structures (ibid.). I am not sure too much hangs on this difference in terminology. However, in this work, I use the concept of interdependence, rather than intra-action, because I wish to clarify the precise mode of connection between causal objects lying at different levels of reality and where the higher-level object is emergent from the lower-level objects. Perhaps the concept of intra-action is more appropriate when thinking about the totality of the causal processes pertaining to an entity – that is, when thinking about the entity as an emergent whole – because the prefix 'intra' means 'within' (so that causal intra-action means the causal processes going on within an entity to make it what it is). For a definition of intra-action from the perspective of dialectical critical realism see Bhaskar (1993: 123). See also the entry 'relationality' in Hartwig (2007: 410–11).

21 Bhaskar's theory of integrative pluralism has close affinities with integral theory, an intellectual movement centred in the United States that focuses on the integration of knowledge (Marshall, 2012). However, the neo-Kantian ontological commitments of integral theory call into question its ability to help us to understand the real conditions of possibility of integrating knowledge from different sciences – on which, see Rutzou (2012).

22 For reasons that I make clear later, my representation of the stratification of being differs from Collier's because, whereas Collier places the psychological and semiological sciences at the top of the ladder, with the social sciences beneath them, I prefer to place the social, semiological and psychological sciences all on one level and at the top of the ladder.

23 Existential constitution is a type of internal relationality, where 'one element or aspect (moment, determination, relation, etc.), $e_2$, is essential and intrinsic to… another, $e_1$' (Bhaskar, 1993: 123). This means that $e_2$ 'is not necessarily a physical part of' $e_1$ (ibid.). Note also that it does not imply a causal relation: that is implied by the third type of internal relationality, 'intra-*connection*', where 'one element, $e_2$, is causally efficacious on an element internally related to it, $e_1$' (ibid.). The significance of all this is that, whereas the differentiation of social structure by aspect implies only the first type of internal relationality (existential constitution), the differentiation of social structure by its parts – for example, the identification of an internal relationship between landlord and tenant – implies both the first and third types because landlord

and tenant are essential to one another and causally efficacious one another. See also the entry 'relationality' in Hartwig (2007: 410–11).

24 On the nature and different types of totality, see the entry 'totality' in Hartwig (2007: 470–3).

25 For a definition of 'conjuncture' see Hartwig (2007: 76).

26 On multiple control as a species of multiple determination see the entry 'determination, determinism' in Hartwig (2007: 122–3) and also 'infra-/intra-/super-structure' (ibid: 257–8).

27 In the phase of development of original critical realism, Bhaskar identifies 'mechanical complexes' and 'organic totalities' as distinct types of 'system'. He writes:

> Where thoroughgoing internal relationality prevails it is natural to think of the structures 'interpenetrating' and as comprising a '*totality*'. But causal structures may interact in a normic or a systematic way, without being internally related... Accordingly systems can be bifurcated into two polar types: 'mechanical' complexes of externally related interacting structures; and 'organic' totalities of internally related intra-acting ones.
>
> (Bhaskar, 1986: 109–10)

However, in the phase of dialectical critical realism, Bhaskar appears to have dropped the concept of mechanical complex and developed the concept of totality. I continue to use the concept of mechanical complex but in recognition that this is not a type of system because a system is an emergent entity (Mingers, 2011). Therefore, we may regard a totality, but not a mechanical complex, as a type of system because a mechanical complex does not involve internal relationality – only external relationality.

28 On the concept of 'partial totality', see Bhaskar (1993: 126–7, 133–4) and (1994: 76).

29 See also Bhaskar (1994: 84). Among systems theorists, the concept of recursive embeddedness is known as *nesting*. For example, Mingers, in his astute comparison of the concepts of (dialectical) critical realism and systems theory, identifies a similarity of meaning between a 'hierarchy or nesting of systems' and 'recursive embeddings' (2011: 315). However, Mingers also appears to have doubts about using the concept of hierarchy, claiming that it 'can be misleading' and that emergence 'is better described as a nesting of systems within systems much like Russian dolls' (ibid: 307). Now, although the concept of nesting does capture the emergent relationship between parts and whole (where the parts are nested within the whole), it would be misleading to claim that emergence is analogous to the situation with Russian dolls because this analogy fails to capture the essential feature of emergence, which is that it is the relations between the parts that give rise to a new entity possessing distinctive properties. With Russian dolls we see only how one doll fits inside another, larger doll.

Mingers also describes the relationship between component parts and emergent whole as one of 'local-to-global causation' (ibid: 322). Now, using the terms 'local' and 'global' suggests that causal objects can be differentiated according to the *scale* at which they are effective. I prefer not to use these terms when identifying entities emergent at different levels of reality because, in my view, the terms 'local' and 'global' are concerned with the differentiation of space (and are therefore commonly used by geographers). To equate causation at the level of structure and system/totality with 'local' and 'global' causation, respectively, is to miss the point that both structures and systems/totalities can operate at both 'local' and 'global' scales. Think, for example, of the possibility of categorizing goods and labour markets in the UK according to the distance between potential buyers and sellers. From a Marxian perspective, such markets constitute parts of the capitalist system of production and exchange, which, if it possesses properties that are unique to the UK, may be considered to be 'local' in scale – at least in relation to the capitalist systems of other countries; yet, the markets on which the system depends may be 'global' in scale.

Perhaps a more appropriate term to use to distinguish between the different levels of reality within an emergent entity such as a totality is *scope*, which signals the different view we may take of an object's constitution. This term, rather than scale, is indicative of the sense in which emergent entities are 'compounds' (Bhaskar, 1986: 107). Thus, we may refer to the 'macroscopic' level when considering the object as an emergent whole and the 'microscopic' level when considering its constitutive parts.

30 See the entry 'social form' in Hartwig (2007: 421–2).

31 Central to the practice of dialectic is what Bhaskar refers to as 'the art of thinking the *coincidence of distinctions and connections*' (1993: 180).

32 I consider political economy, as a particular example of integrative social science, in the next section of this chapter.

33 Bhaskar makes further distinctions in this respect. For example, he also identifies 'concrete' sciences, such as history, which 'study the ensemble of epistemically significant truths about a given thing, especially as these are formed in the context of what it does and what happens to it' (1986: 112). If that definition is accepted, concrete sciences such as history must be considered to be implicitly integrative forms of knowledge because in focusing on the development through time of a phenomenon of interest a concrete science such as history takes for granted an understanding of the modes of connection of the different aspects of a phenomenon. However, in focusing on the historical dimension of phenomena in abstraction from their spatial dimension a concrete science such as history is not a completely integrative form of knowledge because it misses out a full understanding of 'process' or 'the mode of spatio-temporalising structural effects', one of the four moments of the 'concrete singular' (Bhaskar, 1993: 129). Moreover, this abstraction would be 'illicit' if it rested on an (implicit) understanding that the historical and spatial exist in separation – a problem of 'deprocessualization' (ibid: 130). Indeed, to the extent that the study of history betrays the influence of empiricism, rooted in the epistemic fallacy, and to the extent that this has led to an (untenable) split between questions about agency and questions about social structure, it may also be considered to be afflicted by problems of 'destratification', 'demediation' and 'desingularization', corresponding to the three other moments of the concrete singular (ibid.). What is perhaps most distinctive about Marxian social science is its (implicit) aim of capturing all four moments of the concrete singular in its theorisation of 'the *pan-concrete* totality (of totalities)' (ibid: 128). On the study of history see the entry 'historiography' in Hartwig (2007: 236–7); on the nature of the concrete see the entries 'concrete/abstract' (ibid: 71–3) and 'concrete universal↔singular' (ibid: 73–4).

34 Consideration of the embeddedness of human agency takes us to the concept of 'four-planar social being', a dialectical enrichment of the transformational model of social activity (Bhaskar, 1993: 160–1).

35 Dow, for example, argues that one of the distinguishing features of the work of the early Scottish political economists was their 'preference for drawing on several disciplines in an integrated manner' (1987: 342). Similarly, Jessop and Sum state that:

> classical political economy was pioneered by polymaths who believed that political economy should comprise the integrated study of economic organization and wealth creation, good government and good governance, and moral economy (including language, culture, and ethical issues).
>
> (Jessop and Sum, 2003: 996)

And Milonakis and Fine argue:

> All classical writers wrote at a time when political economy was the only identifiable social science, with the fragmentation of the latter lying far ahead in the future. As such, most of them were able to range freely across the economic and the non-economic, to incorporate the social and the psychological into their

> analyses, and to move from historical narrative to theoretical discourse without apology. Indeed, for most classical writers, especially Smith, Mill and Marx, political economy was seen as a unified social science, rather than simply as the science of the economy.
>
> (Milonakis and Fine, 2009: 1–2)

36 To the extent that Smith also refers to 'a certain propensity in human nature ... the propensity to truck, barter, and exchange one thing for another' and to 'self-love' (ibid: 25–7), Smith's *Inquiry* maintains a psychological aspect as well.

37 More accurately, we should say that Smith's political economy presupposes a critical realist philosophy of science because Smith is investigating social objects in a way that is in accordance with the principles of both transcendental realism and critical naturalism.

38 Just as the social system that Smith sets out in his *Inquiry* embraces both social scientific specialization and integration, so does Smith's scientific work as a whole. Indeed, the advertisement in the sixth edition of *The Theory of Moral Sentiments* suggests that Smith explicitly recognized a connection between the focus of the *Inquiry* and the focus of a planned but never executed work on jurisprudence:

> In the last paragraph of the first Edition of the present work, I said, that I should in another discourse endeavour to give an account of the general principles of law and government, and of the different revolutions which they had undergone in the different ages and periods of society; not only in what concerns justice, but in what concerns police, revenue, and arms, and whatever else is the object of law. In the *Enquiry concerning the Nature and Causes of the Wealth of Nations*, I have partly executed this promise; at least so far as concerns police, revenue, and arms. What remains, the theory of jurisprudence, which I have long projected, I have hitherto been hindered from executing, by the same occupations which had till now prevented me from revising the present work.
>
> (cited in Skinner, 1979: 12)

The connection between the *Inquiry* and the planned work on jurisprudence would have appeared as an overlap of subject matter in the sense that the production of legal rules, which would have been the focus of the theory of jurisprudence, would have entered into the argument of the *Inquiry* as the causal effect of government regulations. But, it is apparent that the subject matter of *The Theory of Moral Sentiments* also fits into this wider scheme of thought at least to the extent that the principle of 'self-love' enters into the argument of both works. The wider scheme of thought is of course the field of moral philosophy, on which Smith gave lectures at the University of Glasgow, and the specific areas of which were natural theology, ethics, justice and expediency (Stewart, [1795] 1980: 274–5).

39 However, man can use knowledge of natural laws to his advantage.

40 See Marx (1969: 173–216, 373–425).

41 Mill is quite clear that the 'method *à priori*' is the essential mode of reasoning in social science. In fact, he claims that it is the 'only' one that is applicable: 'But we go farther than to affirm that the method *à priori* is a legitimate mode of philosophical investigation in the moral sciences: we contend that it is the only mode' ([1844] 1967: 327).

42 O'Brien (1975: 70–3) notices the methodological differences within the works of Senior and Cairnes, and also the 'hybrid' character of J. S. Mill's methodological position, but fails to explain them as the result of a philosophical contradiction between an implicit empirical realism and an implicit transcendental realism.

43 The dual, reinforcing influences of empiricism and rationalism constitute 'primal squeeze' (Bhaskar, 1993: 402), the third member of the 'unholy trinity', whose other two members are the 'epistemic fallacy' and 'ontological monovalence' (ibid: 406).

### 3 Towards a theory of knowledge production

1 In Merton's functional account, the 'ethos of science' consists of a series of institutional norms – 'universalism', 'communism', 'disinterestedness' and 'organized skepticism' – and technical norms – 'empirical evidence' and 'logical consistency' – which serve a particular end, that is, 'the extension of certified knowledge' (1973: 270). It is clear from Merton's choice of technical norms that he implicitly accepts the positivist account of scientific development. For a critique of Merton's account, see Barnes and Dolby (1970) and also Whitley (1972).

2 The assumptions that ontological questions can be reduced to epistemological questions and that epistemological questions can be reduced to sociological questions implicitly inform two key neo-Kuhnian offshoots in the sociology of science. The first is the microsociological study of scientific laboratory work, associated with the work of Latour and Woolgar (1979) and Knorr-Cetina (1981). The problem driving this line of work is the social construction of knowledge (Knorr-Cetina and Mulkay, 1983). The second is the closely related 'strong programme' in the sociology of knowledge (Bloor, 1981; Barnes and Bloor, 1982), which takes as problematic the relationship between material interests and scientific ideas (Bloor, 1976; Barnes, 1974, 1977; Barnes *et al.*, 1996). For a critique of the strong programme by a philosopher, see Laudan (1981); for a critique by a sociologist, see Whitley (1983).

3 See also the entry 'intransitive, transitive and metacritical dimensions' in Hartwig (2007: 263–5), where it is made clear that the transitive dimension is constellationally contained within the intransitive dimension because knowledge is part of reality and as such may be treated as an intransitive object of inquiry through referential detachment.

4 In the 'Postscript – 1969' to the second edition of *The Structure of Scientific Revolutions* (1970c: 174–210), in 'Reflections on my Critics' (1970b), and in 'Second Thoughts on Paradigms' (1974), Kuhn does attempt to clarify the meaning of the term 'paradigm'. Indeed, he introduces a new concept, 'disciplinary matrix', to describe all the various 'elements' that he had previously brought together under the term 'paradigm' and reserves the latter term for a particular subset of the former – 'exemplars' – which he describes as 'concrete problem solutions, accepted by the group as, in a quite usual sense, paradigmatic'. The remaining elements of the disciplinary matrix are 'symbolic generalizations' – that is, formal 'expressions' of scientific laws – and 'models', which are both 'heuristic' devices and 'the objects of metaphysical commitment' (Kuhn, 1977: 297–8). But, what this clarification of the intellectual context of knowledge production still lacks is a clear differentiation between *scientific* and *philosophical* commitments.

5 Each of the three collaborative interdisciplinary research projects discussed in Chapters 4 and 5 exemplifies a particular organization of research.

6 Indeed, such is the array of internal relations pertaining to education that we should perhaps designate education a system rather than a structure.

7 Of course, I acknowledge that there may be other social structures and other connections out there that I have not considered. However, the literature suggests that the structures set out in Figure 3.1 are of particular importance.

8 Although the term 'research methods' is typically used rather confusingly to refer to both the construction and interpretation of data, Whitley avoids this confusion by distinguishing clearly between technical and interpretative norms.

9 Social scientific ontology has to be more specific because it is by virtue of the empirical assessments that social scientists make that they can make claims about the nature of specific social objects. Philosophers cannot make such claims because the knowledge they develop is *à priori* – that is, immanent to and conditional upon, science. Hence, social philosophical ontology has to be more general than social scientific ontology. For an explanation of the difference between philosophical and scientific reasoning see Bhaskar (1998: 50–1).

10 Note that this possibility is also implicit in Leftwich's distinctions between 'arena' and 'process' conceptions of the political and the further distinctions between 'extensive' and 'limited' versions of the two. Although those advocating a 'process' conception do so implicitly from a non-positivist standpoint, it is clearly an option for those whose philosophical position is non-positivist to investigate the formal arenas of politics from a non-positivist position because the process conception is more encompassing than the arena conception and one could identify unobservable political processes within, say, the formal institutions of government. However, the reverse does not hold: if one were a positivist, one would not accept the reality of a domain of unobservable objects, so that one would not accept the process conception of the political – at least as this is defined by Leftwich (2004a: 13–16).

11 For example, in this book, I am arguing that scientific research should be explained as the outcome of the interaction of a particular set of social and intellectual structures. But, it is open to other social scientists to propose alternative explanatory accounts that invoke the operation of a different set of social and intellectual structures.

12 However, note that at least two of the approaches Marsh and Stoker (2002a, 2010) identify – institutionalism and feminism – reflect the investigation of a distinctive *social* category rather than a distinctive philosophical position, while Marxism is an approach based on a particular theory of history and society. But, we can still identify distinctive philosophical positions within these approaches, particularly institutionalism and feminism, as a reading of the chapters on these approaches shows.

13 There has been considerable debate as to whether contemporary mainstream economics can indeed be described as positivist. Some have pointed to the practices of orthodox 'pure' theorists, whereby mathematical models are formulated but not tested empirically, as evidence that at least some parts of mainstream economics are not positivist (Wade Hands, 1999; Walters and Young, 2001), while others have noted that, even when orthodox economists do test their models in the spirit of positivism, the repeated predictive failures have not led them to reject this mode of reasoning as the positivist principle of falsification requires (Canterbery and Burkhardt, 1983; Eichner, 1983). However, Fleetwood (2005) has argued that, whether or not one regards 'pure' theorizing as consistent with the assumptions of positivism – however these are defined – both orthodox theoretical and applied economics presuppose the same empirical realist ontology, which is the key presupposition of positivism.

14 However, I recognize that the linkages between social science and society may be more subtle and diffuse than this. We cannot discount the possibility that scientists will be attracted to the assumptions of positivism because these fit with their pre-existing worldview and because scientists have grounds for thinking that positivist science is intellectually valuable – even if they are completely unaware of the ideological effect of positivism.

15 The University of Sheffield, for example, recently introduced a series of nine 'grade profiles' that describe the typical responsibilities and requirements for all non-clinical jobs up to the position of senior lecturer equivalent. Grades 8 and 9 describe the roles of academic staff involved in both teaching and research, with the exception of readers and professors. See http://hr.dept.shef.ac.uk/reward/usgs_grade_profiles.pdf (accessed 3 April 2013).

16 There are differences in the literature as to what constitutes the essence of 'mainstream' and 'non-mainstream' economics. For example, Harley and Lee locate the essence at a scientific level:

> Economics can be divided into a mainstream, called neoclassical economics, and a non-mainstream, which broadly consists of Marxian, Post Keynesian, Institutional, and Sraffian economics. The distinction between neoclassical and non-mainstream economics can be broadly conceived in terms of theoretical and

> methodological concepts such as relative scarcity, rationality, atomistic individualism, equilibrium, and ergodicity which are central to the former but are not to the latter. This difference is succinctly expressed in their definition of economics. Neoclassical economists define economics broadly as the study of how people and societies deal with scarcity; whereas the non-mainstream economists support various combinations of the following definitions – economics is the investigation of the nature and causes of the wealth of nations, of the laws of motion of capitalism, and/or the behaviour, institutions, and culture which underlie evolving capitalist economies.
>
> (Harley and Lee, 1998: 26)

Lawson, by contrast, prefers to locate the essential difference between the mainstream and non-mainstream at a methodological rather than theoretical level not least because this sort of definition can allow for the fact that, although mainstream economists' assumptions and solution concepts may change, their commitment to deductivism remains. Lawson argues this point explicitly from the philosophical perspective of critical realism:

> One primary object of critical realism in economics has been to identify the basic nature or character of mainstream economics. Most critics of the mainstream project have, in attempting to characterise it, isolated particular substantive claims, such as theories of rationality, or of equilibrium. It has been the contention of critical realism, in contrast, that it is at the level of method that its essence lies. In fact the insight that it is not substantive theory that defines the project is clear enough once we recognize that, despite the mainstream project being widely regarded as persisting, specific substantive theories come and go, often with some rapidity. Even the cherished conceptions of rationality and equilibrium have been dispensed with in recent contributions regarded as central to the mainstream.
>
> (Lawson, 1999: 3–4)

For a defence of this argument, see also Lawson (2006).

17 There have been various attempts to construct formal lists and rankings of economics journals, either using citation index data (Liebowitz and Palmer, 1984; Diamond, 1989; Laband and Piette, 1994; Burton and Phimister, 1995; Liner, 2002) or using respondent evaluation data (Hawkins *et al.*, 1973). By far the best known – and most notorious – of these is the so-called Diamond list of 'core journals' (Diamond, 1989).

18 All this is not to say that it will be impossible for non-mainstream economics to survive in UK universities, as Harley and Lee (1998) rather pessimistically conclude; as I discuss later in this section, it may be that student dissatisfaction with the nature of economics will lead to falling enrolments at undergraduate level – in which case, the economics elite may be forced to reconsider the nature of the economics curriculum. Therefore, it is to say that if the Research Assessment Exercise (now the Research Excellence Framework) continues in its present form, the possibility of pursuing non-mainstream work in UK universities will tend to be severely constrained.

19 Lawson (1997: 3–4) gives some examples of criticism internal and external to economics, including a UK *Observer Magazine* article and an article from the *New Scientist*. However, in the past few years, following the onset of the economic crisis in the UK and other industrialized countries, the economics profession has come under public scrutiny to a much greater extent than before – thanks largely to Her Majesty Queen Elizabeth II, who, during a visit to the London School of Economics and Political Science in November 2008, asked Professor Luis Garicano why nobody had foreseen the economic crisis. Her question, which was widely reported in the British media, led the British Academy to organize a Forum on 17 June 2009, 'The

Global Financial Crisis – Why Didn't Anybody Notice?', at which selected academic social scientists, economics journalists and civil servants discussed her question. See www.britac.ac.uk/events/archive/forum-economy.cfm (accessed 3 April 2013), subsequently published in the *British Academy Review* (November 2009, issue 14, pages 8–10). The result of the Forum was a joint letter sent to Her Majesty in July 2009 (see www.britac.ac.uk/news/newsrelease-economy.cfm, accessed 13 February 2013).

What is interesting about the letter sent to the Queen is that it makes no reference to the key economic ideas informing economic policymaking in the years leading up to the crisis. Indeed, the letter appears to hold on to a positivist conception of science for, despite acknowledging that 'the exact form' of the crisis 'and the timing of its onset and ferocity were foreseen by nobody', it states that 'What matters in such circumstances is not just to predict the nature of the problem but also its timing'. Yet, from a critical realist perspective, it is not surprising that no one should have predicted the exact realization and timing of the crisis precisely because the capitalist system is an open rather than a closed system and is thus susceptible to continual change, making prediction an impossibility. At best, one can speak of the way the system tends to work and, despite claiming honours for their predictive success, many heterodox economists did indeed do so in the years leading up to the crisis (Keen, 2011: ch. 1). Yet, the letter makes no reference to heterodox thinking, except to say that 'Many people did foresee the crisis'. Moreover, the letter concludes that:

> The failure to foresee the timing, extent and severity of the crisis and to head it off, while it had many causes, was principally a failure of the collective imagination of many bright people, both in this country and internationally, to understand the risks to the system as a whole.

This conclusion seems to suggest that the forecasting failure was somehow a failure of human agency – of the scientific and policymaking elite's power of reasoning. Yet, if, as appears to be the case, academics and policymakers were not lacking in the capacity to be imaginative (otherwise they could not be described as 'bright people'), surely we need to examine the ideas that were (in part) the conditions for the intentionality of scientists and policymakers – not least the idea that markets are self-equilibrating. Of course, this is exactly what heterodox critics of orthodox economists have been doing for years. But, certain economics journalists now appear to be taking their lead – see the following articles by Aditya Chakrabortty in *The Guardian* newspaper:

- 'Economics has failed us: but where are the fresh voices?', *The Guardian*, 16 April 2012, available online at www.guardian.co.uk/commentisfree/2012/apr/16/economics-has-failed-us-alternative-voices (accessed 3 April 2013);
- 'Angry academics can't answer my criticism that there's too little analysis of our current crisis', *The Guardian*, 7 May 2012, available online at www.guardian.co.uk/commentisfree/2012/may/07/academics-cant-answer-criticism-analysis (accessed 3 April 2013);
- 'Big business has corrupted economics', 26 November 2012, available online at www.guardian.co.uk/commentisfree/2012/nov/26/big-business-corrupted-economics (accessed 3 April 2013).

The first article, on the present condition of the social sciences in the UK, prompted a sharp riposte from Professor Andrew Gamble of the University of Cambridge – 'Have the social sciences failed us?' (www.britac.ac.uk/policyperspectives/Have-the-social-sciences-failed-us.cfm, accessed 3 April 2013). The second article refers to the 'intellectual cleansing' of economics departments in UK universities, which is the implication of my own argument about the practice of economics in the UK; while the third article points to the important relationship between academic economics and society – again, one of the themes of my argument in this chapter.

20 There has been a relatively limited amount of press coverage of the development of the post-autistic economics movement. See, for example, the following articles:

- Jacobsen, K. 'Unreal, man', *The Guardian*, 3 April 2001, available online at www.guardian.co.uk/education/2001/apr/03/highereducation.socialsciences (accessed 3 April 2013);
- Jacobsen, K. and MacLeod, D. 'Fired up for battle' in *The Guardian*, 9 September 2003, available online at www.guardian.co.uk/education/2003/sep/09/highereducation.economics (accessed 3 April 2013);
- Boyle, D. 'The storming of the accountants' in *The New Statesman*, 21 January 2002, available online at www.newstatesman.com/node/142029 (accessed 3 April 2013).

21 Machin and Oswald do not provide data on this but Tables 1 and 2 in the longer version of their paper suggest that applications in sociology and psychology have remained stable or even increased slightly during the 1990s (1999: 21).

22 Machin and Oswald even give examples of such 'non-economist jobs' and the typical salaries attached to each (2000: F341).

23 Freeman's suggestion was, of course, ignored by the editors of the symposium of papers on the state of British academic economics (in which Freeman's paper was included). One of the two editors of the symposium was the then President of the Royal Economic Society. See Propper and Dasgupta (2000).

24 In October 2006, the ESRC introduced a 'disciplinary enhanced stipend' of £3,000 for the economics postgraduates it supported. This policy caused some disquiet amongst other social scientists, not least political scientists, whose ESRC postgraduate studentship quota allocation was reduced. See the 'Letter sent from Professor Ian Diamond, Chief Executive, ESRC to Professor Jon Tonge, Chair, Political Studies Association on 4th May regarding ESRC Quota Awards in Politics' available online at www.psa.ac.uk/PSAnews/PSANews0607.pdf (accessed 20 February 2013).

25 We have already seen that politics is divided into various schools of thought that presuppose incompatible philosophical assumptions (Marsh and Stoker, 2002a, 2010). Law, too, is characterized by what Toma has called 'alternative inquiry paradigms' (1997), while the intellectual cleavages within sociology have reached such an extent that that discipline is now said to be suffering from a crisis of identity (Turner, 1990; Crane and Small, 1992).

**4 The intellectual context of knowledge production**

1 See 'A Stratified Model of the Self' in Bhaskar (1993: 148–9) and 'The Stratification of the Subject' in Bhaskar (1994: 98–9).

2 Explaining this difference will be a task for further research. One possible explanation may be that the nature of intellectual development within the professional persona depends on the strength of the dominant philosophy embodied within the lay persona. Thus, it may be the case that the dominance of transcendental realism within the lay persona of the research officer in case study A explains the nature of the intellectual changes within the research officer's professional persona.

3 Note that philosophical contradiction may characterize the lay as well as the professional persona, a possibility I have already hinted at in distinguishing between the 'everyday empiricism of common sense' and 'everyday depth–realism'.

4 The logic of scientific discovery, which Bhaskar sets out in *A Realist Theory of Science* (1975: Chapter 3) and which I discuss in the second section of Chapter 2, lies at the core of what Bhaskar later refers to as the 'epistemological dialectic' in *Dialectic* (1993: 33–5). See also the entry 'epistemological dialectic' in Hartwig (2007: 175–7).

## 5 The social context of knowledge production

1 We encountered the distinction between scientific ontology and philosophical ontology in Chapter 4. The former is concerned with the nature of the specific entities that scientists investigate and thus has implications for the boundaries between disciplines and fields, which lay claim to the investigation of particular objects, whereas the latter is concerned with developing a more fundamental set of categories that draws out the commonalities of all the specific entities scientists investigate and from which follow theories of the nature of knowledge and how best to acquire it.

2 However, we must remember that content analyses of journals, such as Riba's study (1996), can give us only a rough-and-ready indication of the relative dominance of philosophical approaches to inquiry. Even if an article contains, say, the 'empirical–inductive' variety of mathematics, this does not necessarily mean that the overall argument of the article will reflect a positivist approach to scientific inquiry. The use of a regression model, for example, could be consistent with a transcendental realist philosophy of science if the results were interpreted as empirical patterns to be explained at a deeper level of reality. The use of statistical analysis *per se*, then, does not necessarily imply that a political scientist is drawing only on a positivist approach to scientific inquiry. Given the possibility of internal philosophical contradictions that I discussed in the previous chapter, it may be that the argument of a particular journal article presupposes more than one type of philosophical approach.

3 Unfortunately, we cannot compare the data for *Political Studies* across the two periods because Marsh and Savigny make a mistake when constructing Table 3. The percentages they quote for *Political Studies* for the period 1975–1979 are exactly the same as those they quote for the *American Journal of Political Science*, yet their commentary indicates that the figures for *Political Studies* are very different (2004: 162–4). In fact, this mistake and others lead them astray, for they go on to claim that 'positivism has a very strong hold in these UK journals outside the area of normative political theory' (ibid: 164). However, the percentages they cite in Tables 3 and 4 suggest that this claim can apply only to the *British Journal of Political Science* and not to *Political Studies*. If the latter journal is not and has not been dominated by positivism, this may explain Marsh and Savigny's rather puzzling conclusion in which they note that, despite a positivist 'bias' in leading UK politics journals, 'this does not reflect the interests and concerns of the UK profession' (ibid: 166). Indeed, they go on to cite Hayward's (1999) overview of UK political science, which supports my claim that the UK politics profession is more tolerant of different approaches to scientific inquiry than its US counterpart and not biased in a certain philosophical direction.

4 On *resonance*, see the entry 'reflection' in Hartwig (2007: 408–9).

5 McLean *et al.*'s (2009) survey of UK, US and Canadian political scientists' evaluations of political science journals gives similar results. Among British political scientists quite a few specialist journals such as *Political Analysis*, *History of Political Thought*, *Political Theory* and *Philosophy and Public Affairs* ranked at least as high as, if not higher than, generalist journals such as *Political Studies* when it came to quality. However, the journals that had the most 'impact' were all generalist journals such as *British Journal of Political Science*, *American Political Science Review*, *Political Studies*, *International Organization* and *American Journal of Political Science* – to name the top five. By contrast, the American political scientists ranked the generalist journals consistently at the top according to both quality and impact.

6 I have not explored the operation of education and training structures to the same extent as I have explored the (combined) operation of peer review, the scientific division of labour and the academic career hierarchy. But, it is clear, I think, that education and training are important mechanisms through which disciplinary norms are defined and reproduced because entrance to the academic profession depends (amongst other things) on the acquisition of the requisite set of qualifications. Of

course, in acquiring the relevant qualifications the student acquires a disciplinary mindset. Why some students choose to challenge this mindset by developing an interest in integrative, interdisciplinary research and why others do not are questions for further research.

7 Bhaskar defines '*Tina formations*' as:

> internally contradictory, more or less systemic, efficacious, syntonic... ensembles, only demonstrable as such... insofar as they have been transcendentally or otherwise refuted, displaying duplicity, equivocation, extreme plasticity and pliability and rational indeterminacy (facilitating their ideological and manipulative use).
>
> (Bhaskar, 1993: 117)

The Tina formation is composed of three elements: a 'Tina compromise', a 'Tina connection' and a 'Tina defence mechanism' (ibid: 116–17). In the case of economics, the Tina *connection* is between an explicit, positivist understanding of economic inquiry and an implicit, conventionalist understanding of the economic. The latter is grafted on to the former in an attempt to deal with the lack of a conception of ontological depth within positivism – an absence that undermines the identification of the economic as a distinct yet interdependent aspect of social reality. This connection is the condition for the *compromise* with a differentiated and interconnected reality, and the axiological necessity to understand it as such, and takes the form of 'orthodox interdisciplinarity or 'economics imperialism', which I discussed at the end of Chapter 2. The Tina *defence mechanism* is the injunction not to study methodology because this is superfluous to the successful pursuit of economics. Of course, as Lawson (1997: 11–14) points out, in practice, orthodox economists have violated this injunction – a violation that points to the inherent instability of Tina formations – in virtue of their contradictory nature – and the consequential necessity to introduce further compromises, connections and defence mechanisms. Indeed, the contradictory nature of the Tina formation allows us to identify sub-totalities as an important feature of the social context of knowledge production – in addition to the presence of partial totalities.

In politics the elements of the Tina formation have a different content. In this case, the relevant *connection* is between positivist and interpretivist approaches to political inquiry on the one hand and a transcendental realist understanding of the political as a distinct yet interdependent aspect of social reality on the other. The positivist and interpretivist influences, to the extent that they rest on the epistemic–ontic fallacy, undercut the transcendental-realist-inspired recognition of the stratification of social reality, resulting in a *compromise* which takes the form of ontological independence or, translated into the language of scientific practice, of *interdisciplinary-research-as-multidisciplinary-research*. In this way, the integration of multiple, disciplinary perspectives is subverted. The *defence mechanism* – even if this is only unintentional – is the injunction to respect or 'celebrate' the diversity of approaches to political inquiry. As Stoker and Marsh put it:

> There is a pluralism of method and approach out there that should not be denied; however it should not be 'isolative', but rather interactive. It should be eclectic and synergistic. That is what is meant by our claim to celebrate diversity.
>
> (Stoker and Marsh, 2010: 12)

8 See, for example, the 'School Research Vision' of the School of Sociology, Politics and International Studies at the University of Bristol, at www.bristol.ac.uk/spais/research/ researchvision (accessed 3 April 2013). This School, we are told,

> is an interdisciplinary scholarly environment producing leading research which is international in its focus and relevant to the changing circumstances of our

> increasingly interconnected world. We are committed to rigorous conceptual and empirical research that is politically and socially relevant and problem oriented. We aim to advance theory, knowledge and methods at the interface between the disciplines of sociology, politics and international relations. The questions addressed recognize that political structures are related in complex ways to the social conditions that underlie them, and equally, that social conditions are affected in complex ways by political structures.

Under 'Research Themes' we are told:

> Our research activity is guided by a focus on key themes: International Relations, Global Development and Security; Ethnicity and Migration; Europe and Europeanization; and Culture, Politics, and Society. All researchers across the School identify with one or more of the themes. This enables collective identification over themes within the School and aims to further collaboration and interdisciplinarity in our research activities.

See the relevant web page at www.bristol.ac.uk/spais/research/researchthemes (accessed 3 April 2013).

Similarly, the University of Manchester has published a 'Research Strategy' of which interdisciplinarity is a significant feature. On page 7 of the Strategy, under 'Focus and Interdisciplinarity', it states:

> We will exploit our wide range of capabilities to form new and ground-breaking interdisciplinary combinations across the full range of subjects. Our institutes will play an important role in taking forward this agenda but no internal structure, process or system should be a barrier to interdisciplinary working.

On page 8, it states under 'Actions': 'Form cross-faculty groupings around emergent research themes and in particular target cross-faculty opportunities with task forces to develop an integrated strategy'. See 'University of Manchester Research Strategy' at http://documents.manchester.ac.uk/display.aspx?DocID=9823 (accessed 3 April 2013).

## 6 Conclusion

1 It is important to consider the relationship between postmodernism and interdisciplinarity, not least because postmodernism appears to be increasingly influential – if not, hegemonic – within other fields of social scientific inquiry – especially sociology. Understanding the precise structuring of the field of sociology must be a topic for further research.

2 For a definition of subject–object identity theory see the entry 'identity theory' in Bhaskar (1993: 399). See also the entry 'identity theory' in Hartwig (2007: 250–1).

3 On the reification, including hypostatization, of scientific ideas in irrealist forms of thought, see the entry 'rationalism' in Hartwig (2007: 395–7). Note also Bhaskar's identification of:

> the *tacit* duplicity of dialectical antagonists, such as subjective empiricism and objective idealism... or of empirical realism and conceptual realism. For, epistemologically, what are the ideas of conceptual realism but brute facts, established results, while, ontologically, what are facts but hypostatized ideas?
>
> (Bhaskar, 1993: 313)

4 See Higher Education Funding Council for England, 'Research Excellence Framework. Second consultation on the assessment and funding of research', HEFCE, September 2009/38, p. 24, available online at www.hefce.ac.uk/media/hefce1/pubs/hefce/2009/0938/09_38.pdf (accessed 3 April 2013).

5 Ibid., p. 5.

6 See Higher Education Funding Council for England, 'Research Excellence Framework: Second consultation on the assessment and funding of research. Summary of responses', HEFCE, March 2010, pp. 15–16, available online at www.hefce.ac.uk/media/hefce/content/pubs/consultationoutcomes/2009/200938outcomes-secondconsultationontheref/REF2_0310.pdf (accessed 3 April 2013).

7 The authors of the consultation document asked respondents to set out 'further measures' that they should consider in order to ensure that interdisciplinary research 'is assessed on an equal footing with other types of research'. See 'Consultation question 9' in 'Research Excellence Framework' (note 4), p. 24.

8 See 'Panel Criteria and Working Methods', HEFCE, January 2012, p. 59 available online at www.ref.ac.uk/pubs/2012-01/ (accessed 3 April 2013).

9 See 'Joint AHRC ESRC Statement on Subject Coverage: Interfaces between the arts and humanities and the social sciences' available online at www.esrcsocietytoday.ac.uk/ESRCInfoCentre/opportunities/ahrc_esrc (accessed 3 April 2013).

10 Two of the objectives of the RELU Programme, for example, are 'to deliver integrative, interdisciplinary research of high quality' and 'to enhance capabilities for interdisciplinary research' (Lowe, 2006: 4).

**Appendix: research design**

1 I should explain that the contrast in question 2 is an observation I have made from a reading of the literature on interdisciplinarity. Certainly, implicit in much of the discussion in this literature is the observation that interdisciplinary research is a minority pursuit. Moreover, the long-standing concerns expressed by policymakers about the need for more interdisciplinary research and the ongoing attempts to promote this form of inquiry through the establishment of specialized research centres attest to a general absence of integrative forms of knowledge and a general desire to rectify this deficiency. However, the extent to which monodisciplinary research dominates interdisciplinary research is a question that can only be answered accurately through a survey of the research community, of the sort that the Centre for Educational Research and Innovation (CERI, 1972) carried out. For practical reasons, and because I believe that the more urgent need is to explain the difficulties researchers have experienced in integrating knowledge, I decided not to pursue this line of inquiry.

2 See Chapter 2, 'Introducing critical realism: the philosophy of social research' for a discussion of an intensive empirical procedure.

3 In using the term 'retroductive' to describe a particular research strategy, I do not want to suggest that I accept completely Blaikie's view about research strategies and paradigms. Blaikie argues that the researcher can combine different methods, whether quantitative or qualitative, in two different ways: either the researcher uses different methods in combination in the service of the same research strategy and philosophical approach or the researcher uses different methods in sequence in the service of different research strategies and philosophical approaches. As he puts it:

> While methods for collecting and analysing data can be used in the service of different research strategies, they can only be combined when they are used within the same ontological assumptions. Alternatively, if a variety of methods are used with different ontological assumptions they can be used in sequence, with careful attention being given to the shifts in ontological assumptions that are involved.
>
> (Blaikie, 2000: 261)

Now, the implication of methodological 'sequencing' of this sort, which is also advocated by Creswell (1994) and Padgett (1998), is that the researcher flips from one set of philosophical assumptions to another during the course of the same inquiry. Yet, in light of the argument that I developed in the third section of Chapter 2, 'Social scientific integration in practice', such an approach is liable to generate weaknesses or difficulties at a scientific level. This is also the fundamental problem with the pragmatist approach to the mixing of research methods, an approach that Blaikie seems to favour when he states that the four different research strategies (inductivist, deductivist, retroductivist and abductivist) cannot be synthesized because this is 'methodologically impossible' (2000: 261). Yet, as I argued in the first section of Chapter 2, critical realists have found a way of synthesizing these research strategies so as to accommodate elements of all four within a new philosophy of science. Blaikie seems not to have realized this, despite claiming familiarity with the work of prominent critical realists such as Bhaskar. Therefore, I use the term 'retroductive' to describe what I regard as the fundamental movement in all science. But, this does not mean that I regard inductive, deductive and abductive modes of inference as irrelevant to science – far from it. For example, if we have engineered a closed system in a laboratory, we can apply deductive and inductive logics but the fact remains that our overriding logic, the one that motivated the closure, was retroductive.

4 Lawson defines a *contrast space* as 'a domain over which it is meaningful, given our current understandings... to draw comparisons. It is a space over which any observed systematic contrasts can be regarded as *prima facie* significant or of interest' (2003: 89).
5 Note that, although the goal of scientific integration was the chief criterion for project selection, it was not necessarily the case that members of each project team understood scientific integration in the same way. What mattered was that they all *claimed* to be practising integrative, interdisciplinary research and recognized the need to incorporate different disciplinary perspectives in the inquiry; whether or not they actually achieved a coherent scientific synthesis is a separate question.
6 Again, the exploratory interviews were carried out with researchers who understood interdisciplinarity in different ways.
7 However, one of the key researchers involved in case study A – the project in comparative political economy – had died. This researcher was the sole representative of law, which was one of the controlling disciplines in the project (alongside political science).
8 'Ontographology' means, literally, the study of the representation of being. Lawson uses the term 'opology' to describe the same practice, 'where the op stands in for **o**ntological **p**resuppositions (incorporating **o**ntological **p**remises and **o**ntological **p**osits)' (2004: 2). The term ontographology is preferred here because its etymology is more obvious, although it is still a slightly misleading term to use because it seems to imply that it is only ontological presuppositions that are being identified, when, in fact, those presuppositions have to be logically derived from methodological and epistemological presuppositions in the first and second instances.
9 The implication of this is that sociologists of science ought to be philosophers as well as social scientists, if they are to understand more clearly the relationship between the nature or content of science and its mode of production.
10 Of course, isolation in many of the natural sciences is performed with the help of laboratory experimentation. In the social sciences, by contrast, the conditions for local closure do not apply so that isolation or abstraction from the concrete has to take place entirely in thought.
11 Clearly, these three components are related because whether or not coherent integration occurs presupposes that there was a choice as to whether or not to conduct integrative, interdisciplinary research and that the understanding of interdisciplinary research was sufficient to the task.
12 Hence, the use of the term 'mechanism' to describe the ways of working of social structure is open to revision.
13 Indeed, a similar problem arises when moving from the concrete to the abstract

because complexity is a characteristic not only of the domain of the 'real' – as we have just seen – but also of the domain of the 'empirical', in the sense that concrete events may be multifaceted. Hence, just as structures and causal mechanisms may be internally related, thereby forming an organic totality, so the different facets of a concrete event may be internally related, thereby forming a 'nexus' (Bhaskar, 1986: 109). It may be more appropriate, therefore, to speak, not of a concrete event but of a 'concrete episode', the character of which influences the different facets that comprise it and that, in turn, influence the character of the episode as a whole (ibid: 111). The possibility arises, therefore, that a nexus of aspects of a historical episode is generated by an organic totality of causal mechanisms and structures.

14 Transcendental reasoning is a special type of retroductive inference because in philosophy the concern is to establish *à priori*, that is, necessary, conditions for the premise of an argument, whereas in science the concern is to establish both *à priori* and *à posteriori*, that is, both necessary and sufficient conditions – hence the crucial role that empirical validation plays in both the DREI and RRRE models of explanation. Moreover, the implication of the difference in objectives is that the conclusions of a transcendental argument in philosophy will be formal, syncategorematic and concerned with only one domain of reality (the domain of generative objects *in general*), whereas in science the conclusions of a retroductive argument will be historical (since they may be revised), will refer directly to *specific* objects thought to be the conditions for the premise of the argument, and thus will be concerned with two domains of reality – the domain of generative objects and the domain of their empirical effects (Bhaskar, 1998: 50–1). In other words, in science the construction of an explanation involves a movement back and forth between the concrete situation of interest (the *explanandum*) and abstract descriptions of those structures and mechanisms thought to be responsible for generating the situation of interest (the *explanans*). In philosophy, by contrast, it is necessary to move only backwards to reveal what must in general be the case for something to be possible.

15 Of course, identifying such presuppositions does not mean that we have to accept that reality is as described. As Lawson puts it, 'there is an extra conceptual step required to move from 1) *identifying* or *recognizing* the presuppositions of such theories and 2) *accepting the plausibility* of those theories and so their ontological presuppositions' (2004: 2). For example, if it is found that policy changes issuing from a particular theory turn out to be unsuccessful, the philosophical presuppositions of the unsuccessful theory can be contrasted with those of a more successful theory and an appropriate conclusion drawn as to the relative plausibility and intelligibility of the two theories. Lawson (1997, 2003) has done exactly this in his critique of contemporary economics.

# References

Archer, M. S. (1995) *Realist Social Theory. The Morphogenetic Approach*. Cambridge: Cambridge University Press.

Archer, M. S. and Tritter, J. Q. (eds) (2000) *Rational Choice Theory. Resisting Colonization*. London: Routledge.

Archer, M. S., Bhaskar, R., Collier, A., Lawson, T. and Norrie, A. (eds) (1998) *Critical Realism. Essential Readings*. London: Routledge.

Ashworth, J. and Evans, J. L. (2001) 'Modeling Student Subject Choice at Secondary and Tertiary Level: A Cross-Section Study', *Journal of Economic Education*, 32(4): 311–20.

Ayer, A. J. (ed.) (1959) *Logical Positivism*. Glencoe, IL: Free Press.

Bachrach, P. and Baratz, M. S. (1962) 'Two Faces of Power', *American Political Science Review*, 56(4): 947–52.

Bachrach, P. and Baratz, M. S. (1963) 'Decisions and Non-Decisions: An Analytical Framework', *American Political Science Review*, 57(3): 632–42.

Bachrach, P. and Baratz, M. S. (1970) *Power and Poverty: Theory and Practice*. Oxford: Oxford University Press.

Bailis, S. (2001) 'Contending with Complexity: A Response to William H. Newell's "A Theory of Interdisciplinary Studies"', *Issues in Integrative Studies*, 19: 27–42.

Ball, S. J. (1984) 'Beachside Reconsidered: Reflections on a Methodological Apprenticeship', in R. G. Burgess (ed.) *The Research Process in Educational Settings: Ten Case Studies*, Lewes: Falmer Press, pp. 69–96.

Barber, W. J. (1991) *A History of Economic Thought*. London: Penguin. (Originally published by Pelican in 1967.)

Barnes, B. (1974) *Scientific Knowledge and Sociological Theory*. London: Routledge and Kegan Paul.

Barnes, B. (1977) *Interests and the Growth of Knowledge*. London: Routledge and Kegan Paul.

Barnes, B. and Bloor, D. (1982) 'Relativism, Rationalism, and the Sociology of Knowledge', in M. Hollis and S. Lukes (eds) *Rationality and Relativism*, Oxford: Blackwell, pp. 21–47.

Barnes, S. B. and Dolby, R. G. A. (1970) 'The Scientific Ethos: A Deviant Viewpoint', *Archives Européennes de Sociologie*, XI: 3–25.

Barnes, B., Bloor, D. and Henry, J. (1996) *Scientific Knowledge: A Sociological Analysis*. Chicago: University of Chicago Press.

Barry, A., Born, G. and Weszkalnys, G. (2008) 'Logics of Interdisciplinarity', *Economy and Society*, 37(1): 20–49.

Beam, D. (1982) 'Fragmentation of Knowledge: An Obstacle to its Full Utilization', in K. E. Boulding and L. Senesh (eds) *The Optimum Utilization of Knowledge: Making Knowledge Serve Human Betterment*, Boulder, CO: Westview Press, pp. 160–74.

Bell, D. and Kristol, I. (eds) (1981) *The Crisis in Economic Theory*. New York: Basic Books.

Bell, S., Marzano, M. and Carss, D. N. (2005) *Calming Troubled Waters: Making Interdisciplinarity Work*. Final Report to RELU (Project No. ESRC: RES-224-25-0110). Obtained from authors.

Bennett, A., Barth, A. and Rutherford, K. R. (2003) 'Do We Preach What We Practice? A Survey of Methods in Political Science Journals and Curricula', *PS: Political Science and Politics*, 36(3): 373–78.

Benson, T. C. (1982) 'Five Arguments Against Interdisciplinary Studies', *Issues in Integrative Studies*, 1: 38–48.

Bhaskar, R. (1975) *A Realist Theory of Science*. Leeds: Leeds Books.

Bhaskar, R. (1978) *A Realist Theory of Science*, 2nd edn. Brighton: Harvester Press.

Bhaskar, R. (1979) *The Possibility of Naturalism. A Philosophical Critique of the Contemporary Human Sciences*. Brighton: Harvester Press (2nd edn, Harvester Wheatsheaf, 1989).

Bhaskar, R. (1986) *Scientific Realism and Human Emancipation*. London: Verso.

Bhaskar, R. (1989) *Reclaiming Reality. A Critical Introduction to Contemporary Philosophy.* London: Verso.

Bhaskar, R. (1993) *Dialectic. The Pulse of Freedom*. London: Verso.

Bhaskar, R. (1994) *Plato Etc. The Problems of Philosophy and their Resolution*. London: Verso.

Bhaskar, R. (1998) *The Possibility of Naturalism. A Philosophical Critique of the Contemporary Human Sciences*, 3rd edn. London: Routledge.

Bhaskar, R., Frank, C., Høyer, K. G., Næss, P. and Parker, J. (eds) (2010) *Interdisciplinarity and Climate Change: Transforming Knowledge and Practice for our Global Future.* London: Routledge.

Birnbaum, P. (1978) 'Academic Contexts of Interdisciplinary Research', *Educational Administration Quarterly*, 14(2): 80–97.

Birnbaum, P. (1979) 'A Theory of Academic Interdisciplinary Research Performance: A Contingency and Path Analysis Approach', *Management Science*, 25(3): 231–42.

Birnbaum, P. (1981) 'Integration and Specialization in Academic Research', *Academy of Management Journal*, 24(3): 487–503.

*BJPIR* (1999) 'Editorial: Studying British Politics', *British Journal of Politics and International Relations*, 1(1): 1–11.

Blackburn, S. (2004) 'Social Science: In Retrospect and Prospect', *Graduate Journal of Social Science*, 1(1): 167–88.

Blaikie, N. (2000) *Designing Social Research*. Cambridge: Polity.

Bloor, D. (1976) *Knowledge and Social Imagery*. London: Routledge and Kegan Paul.

Bloor, D. (1981) 'The Strengths of the Strong Programme', *Philosophy of Social Science*, 11: 199–213.

Blume, S. S. (1977) 'Introduction. Sociology of Sciences and Sociologies of Science', in S. S. Blume (ed.) *Perspectives in the Sociology of Science*, Chichester: Wiley, pp. 1–20.

Boisot, M. (1972) 'Discipline and Interdisciplinarity', in CERI, *Interdisciplinarity: Problems of Teaching and Research in Universities*, Paris: Organisation for Economic Cooperation and Development, pp. 89–97.

Boulding, K. E. (1981) *A Preface to Grants Economics. The Economy of Love and Fear*. New York: Praeger.

Bowles, G. and Klein, R. D. (eds) (1983) *Theories of Women's Studies*. London: Routledge and Kegan Paul.

Brannen, J. (1992) *Mixing Methods*. Aldershot: Avebury.

Bruce, A., Lyall, C., Tait, J. and Williams, R. (2004) 'Interdisciplinary Integration in Europe: The Case of the Fifth Framework Programme', *Futures*, 36(4): 457–70.

Bryman, A. (1984) 'The Debate About Quantitative and Qualitative Research: A Question of Method or Epistemology?', *British Journal of Sociology*, 35(1): 75–92.

Bryman, A. (1988) *Quantity and Quality in Social Research*. London: Unwin Hyman.

Bryman, A. (ed.) (2006) *Mixed Methods*. London: Sage.

Buchanan, D. R. (1992) 'An Uneasy Alliance: Combining Qualitative and Quantitative Research Methods', *Health Education Quarterly*, 19(1): 117–35.

Bulmer, M. (1979) 'Concepts in the Analysis of Qualitative Data', *Sociological Review*, 27(4): 651–77.

Bunge, M. (1973) *Method, Model and Matter*. Dordrecht: Reidel.

Burton, M. P. and Phimister, E. (1995) 'Core Journals: A Reappraisal of the Diamond List', *Economic Journal*, 105(429): 361–73.

Cairncross, A. (1986) *Economics and Economic Policy*. Oxford: Blackwell.

Cairnes, J. E. (1875) *The Character and Logical Method of Political Economy*, 2nd edn. London: Macmillan and Co. (1st edn, Longman, Brown, Green, Longmans and Roberts, 1857).

Canterbery, E. R. and Burkhardt, R. J. (1983) 'What Do we Mean by Asking Whether Economics is a Science?', in A. S. Eichner (ed.) *Why Economics is not yet a Science*, London: Macmillan, pp. 15–40.

Carp, R. M. (2001) 'Integrative Praxes: Learning from Multiple Knowledge Formations', *Issues in Integrative Studies*, 19: 71–121.

CERI (1972) *Interdisciplinarity: Problems of Teaching and Research in Universities*. Centre for Educational Research and Innovation, Paris: Organisation for Economic Cooperation and Development.

Chubin, D. E., Rossini, F. A., Porter, A. L. and Mitroff, I. I. (1979) 'Experimental Technology Assessment: Explorations in Processes of Interdisciplinary Team Research', *Technological Forecasting and Social Change*, 15(2): 87–94.

Coats, A. W. (1967) 'Sociological Aspects of British Economic Thought (ca. 1880–1930)', *Journal of Political Economy*, 75(5): 706–29.

Coats, A. W. (1968) 'The Origins and Early Development of The Royal Economic Society', *Economic Journal*, 78(310): 349–71.

Coats, A. W. (1975) 'The Development of the Economics Profession in England: A Preliminary Review', in L. Hournanidis (ed.) *International Congress of Economic History and History of Economic Theories, Proceedings*, Piraeus, Greece: Piraeus Graduate School of Industrial Studies, pp. 277–90.

Collier, A. (1989) *Scientific Realism and Socialist Thought*. Hemel Hempstead: Harvester Wheatsheaf.

Collier, A. (1994) *Critical Realism. An Introduction to Roy Bhaskar's Philosophy*. London: Verso.

Colvin, P. (1985) *The Economic Ideal in British Government*. Manchester: Manchester University Press.

Committee on Facilitating Interdisciplinary Research, National Academy of Sciences, National Academy of Engineering, Institute of Medicine (2004) *Facilitating Interdisciplinary Research*. Washington, DC: National Academies Press. Available online at www.nap.edu/catalog.php?record_id=11153 (accessed 1 April 2013).

Crane, D. (1967) 'The Gatekeepers of Science', *American Sociologist*, 2: 195–201.

Crane, D. and Small, H. (1992) 'American Sociology since the Seventies: The Emerging Identity Crisis in the Discipline', in T. C. Halliday and M. Janowitz (eds) *Sociology and its Publics: The Forms and Fates of Disciplinary Organization*, Chicago: University of Chicago Press, pp. 197–234.

Creswell, J. (1994) *Research Design: Qualitative and Quantitative Approaches*. London: Sage.

Crewe, I. and Norris, P. (1991) 'British and American Journal Evaluation: Divergence or Convergence?', *PS: Political Science and Politics*, 24(3): 524–31.

Crick, B. (1959) *The American Science of Politics: Its Origins and Conditions*. London: Routledge and Kegan Paul.

Dahl, R. (1957) 'The Concept of Power', *Behavioral Science*, 2(3): 201–15.

Daily, G. C. and Ehrlich, P. R. (1999) 'Managing Earth's Ecosystems: An Interdisciplinary Challenge', *Ecosystems*, 2(4): 277–80.

Danermark, B. (2002) 'Interdisciplinary Research and Critical Realism. The Example of Disability Research', *Journal of Critical Realism*, 5(1): 56–64.

Danermark, B., Ekström, M., Jakobsen, L. and Karlsson, J. C. (2002) *Explaining Society. Critical Realism in the Social Sciences*. London: Routledge.

Denzin, N. (1970) *The Research Act in Sociology. A Theoretical Introduction to Sociological Methods*. London: Butterworths.

Devine, F. and Heath, S. (1999) *Sociological Research Methods in Context*. London: Macmillan.

Diamond, A. M. (1989) 'The Core Journals in Economics', *Current Contents*, 21(1): 2–9.

Dogan, M. and Pahre, R. (1990) *Creative Marginality. Innovation at the Intersections of Social Sciences*. Boulder, CO: Westview Press.

Dow, S. (1987) 'The Scottish Political Economy Tradition', *Scottish Journal of Political Economy*, 34(4): 335–48.

Dunleavy, P., Kelly, P. J. and Moran, M. (2000) 'Characterizing the Development of British Political Science', in P. Dunleavy, P. J. Kelly and M. Moran (eds) *British Political Science. Fifty Years of Political Studies*, Oxford: Blackwell, pp. 3–9.

Dupré, J. (1993) *The Disorder of Things. Metaphysical Foundations of the Disunity of Science*. Cambridge, MA: Harvard University Press.

Eichner, A. S. (1983) 'Why Economics is not yet a Science', in A. S. Eichner (ed.) *Why Economics is not yet a Science*, London: Macmillan, pp. 205–41.

Elder-Vass, D. (2005) 'Emergence and the Realist Account of Cause', *Journal of Critical Realism*, 4(2): 315–38.

Elias, N., Martins, H. and Whitley, R. D. (eds) (1982) *Scientific Establishments and Hierarchies*. Sociology of the Sciences, Volume VI. Dordrecht: Reidel.

Evaluation Associates (1999) *Interdisciplinary Research and the Research Assessment Exercise*. A Report by Evaluation Associates Ltd, March 1999, for the UK Higher Education Funding Bodies.

Evans, M. and Macnaughton, J. (2004) 'Should Medical Humanities be a Multidisciplinary or an Interdisciplinary Study?', *Medical Humanities*, 30(1): 1–4.

Feyerabend, P. K. (1975) *Against Method. Outline of an Anarchistic Theory of Knowledge*. London: New Left Books (revised edn, Verso, 1988; 3rd edn, Verso, 1993).

Fine, B. (2003) 'A Brief History of Economics Imperialism', presented to the Cambridge Realist Workshop, 3 November.

Fine, B. and Milonakis, D. (2009) *From Economics Imperialism to Freakonomics. The Shifting Boundaries Between Economics and Other Social Sciences*. London: Routledge.

Firestone, W. A. (1990) 'Accommodation. Toward a Paradigm–Praxis Dialectic', in E. G. Guba (ed.) *The Paradigm Dialog*, Newbury Park: Sage, pp. 105–24.
Fleetwood, S. (2005) 'A Critical Realist Reply to Walters and Young', *Review of Political Economy*, 17(4): 587–600.
Fleetwood, S. (2006) 'Rethinking Labour Markets: A Critical-realist-socioeconomic Perspective', *Capital and Class*, 89: 59–89.
Freeman, R. B. (2000) 'The Changing State of Economics in the United Kingdom and United States', *Economic Journal*, 110(464), F355–57.
Fullbrook, E. (2003) *The Crisis in Economics*. London: Routledge.
Fullbrook, E. (ed.) (2004) *A Guide to What's Wrong with Economics*. London: Anthem Press.
Fullbrook, E. (ed.) (2007) *Real World Economics: A Post-Autistic Economics Reader*. London: Anthem Press.
Furner, M. O. (1975) *Advocacy and Objectivity. A Crisis in the Professionalization of American Social Science, 1865–1905*. Lexington: The University Press of Kentucky.
Gamble, A. M. (1995) 'New Political Economy', *Political Studies*, 43(3): 516–30.
Geertz, C. (1993) 'Thick Description: Toward an Interpretive Theory of Culture', in C. Geertz, *The Interpretation of Cultures: Selected Essays*, New York: Basic Books, pp. 3–30.
Goodin, R. E. and Klingemann, H.-D. (eds) (1996) *A New Handbook of Political Science*. Oxford: Oxford University Press.
Goodlad, S. (1979) 'What is an Academic Discipline?', in R. Cox (ed.) *Cooperation and Choice in Higher Education*, London: University of London Teaching Methods Unit, pp. 10–20.
Gould, F. (1975) 'Interdisciplinary Studies at the Polytechnic of Central London', in *Case Studies in Interdisciplinarity. Group 3: Integrated Social Science*. Group for Research and Innovation in Higher Education, London: The Nuffield Foundation.
Grace, N. M. (1996) 'An Exploration of the Interdisciplinary Character of Women's Studies', *Issues in Integrative Studies*, 14: 69–86.
Greenleaf, W. H. (1993) *The British Political Tradition. Volume One. The Rise of Collectivism*. London: Methuen.
Guba, E. and Lincoln, Y. (1982) 'Epistemological and Methodological Bases of Naturalistic Inquiry', *Educational Communication and Technology Journal*, 30(4): 233–62.
Gunnell, J. (2006) 'The Founding of the American Political Science Association: Discipline, Profession, Political Theory and Politics', *American Political Science Review*, 100(4): 479–86.
Hagstrom, W. O. (1965) *The Scientific Community*. New York: Basic Books.
Hammersley, M. and Atkinson, P. (1995) *Ethnography: Principles in Practice*, 2nd edn. London: Routledge (1st edn, Tavistock, 1983).
Hammersley, M., Scarth, J. and Webb, S. (1985) 'Developing and Testing Theory: The Case of Research on Pupil Learning and Examinations', in R. G. Burgess (ed.) *Issues in Educational Research: Qualitative Methods*, Lewes: Falmer Press, pp. 48–66.
Harley, S. and Lee, F. S. (1997) 'Research Selectivity, Managerialism, and the Academic Labor Process: The Future of Nonmainstream Economics in U.K. Universities', *Human Relations*, 50(11): 1427–60.
Harley, S. and Lee, F. S. (1998) 'Peer Review, the Research Assessment Exercise and the Demise of Non-Mainstream Economics', *Capital and Class*, 66: 23–51.
Hartwig, M. (ed.) (2007) *Dictionary of Critical Realism*. London: Routledge.

Haskell, T. S. (1977) *The Emergence of Professional Social Science*. Urbana, IL: University of Illinois Press.

Hawkins, R. G., Ritter, L. S. and Walter, I. (1973) 'What Economists Think of Their Journals', *Journal of Political Economy*, 81(4): 1017–32.

Hay, C. (2002) *Political Analysis. A Critical Introduction*. Basingstoke: Palgrave.

Hayward, J. (1999) 'British Approaches to Politics. The Dawn of a Self-Deprecating Discipline', in J. Hayward, B. Barry and A. Brown (eds) *The British Study of Politics in the Twentieth Century*, Oxford: Oxford University Press, pp. 1–35.

Heckhausen, H. (1972) 'Discipline and Interdisciplinarity', in CERI, *Interdisciplinarity: Problems of Teaching and Research in Universities*, Paris: Organisation for Economic Cooperation and Development, pp. 83–9.

Heilbroner, R. (2000) *The Worldly Philosophers. The Lives, Times, and Ideas of the Great Economic Thinkers*, rev. 7th edn. London: Penguin (1st edn, Viking, 1969).

Hempel, C. G. (1966) *Philosophy of Natural Science*. Englewood Cliffs, NJ: Prentice-Hall.

Hickman, R. J. S. (1980) 'Interdisciplinarity: A Cutting Edge for Higher Education', *Pivot*, 7(3): 49–52.

Hix, S. (2004) 'A Global Ranking of Political Science Departments', *Political Studies Review*, 2(3): 293–313.

Howe, K. R. (1988) 'Against the Quantitative–Qualitative Incompatibility Thesis or Dogmas Die Hard', *Educational Researcher*, 17(8): 10–16.

Hunt, E. K. (2002) *History of Economic Thought. A Critical Perspective*. New York: M. E. Sharpe.

Ichimura, S. (1975) 'Interdisciplinary Research and Area Studies', *Journal of Southeast Asian Studies*, 6 (2): 112–20.

Ikenberry, S. I. and Friedman, R. C. (1972) *Beyond Academic Departments: The Story of Institutes and Centres*. San Francisco: Josey Bass.

Jessop, B. and Sum, Ngai-Ling (2003) 'Pre- and Post-Disciplinarity Perspectives in (Cultural) Political Economy', *Économies et Sociétés*, 39(6): 993–1015.

Johnson, R. B. and Onwuegbuzie, A. J. (2004) 'Mixed Methods Research: A Research Paradigm Whose Time Has Come', *Educational Researcher*, 33(7): 14–26.

Karlqvist, A. (1999) 'Going Beyond Disciplines. The Meanings of Interdisciplinarity', *Policy Sciences*, 32(4): 379–83.

Karlsson, J. C. (2011) 'People Can Not Only Open Closed Systems, They Can Also Close Open Systems', *Journal of Critical Realism*, 10(2): 145–62.

Keen, S. (2011) *Debunking Economics–Revised and Expanded Edition: The Naked Emperor Dethroned?* London: Zed Books (1st edn, Zed Books, 2001).

Kenny, M. (2004) 'The Case for Disciplinary History: Political Studies in the 1950s and 1960s', *British Journal of Politics and International Relations*, 6(4): 565–83.

King, M. D. (1971) 'Reason, Tradition, and the Progressiveness of Science', *History and Theory*, 10(1): 3–32.

Kinzig, A. (2001) 'Bridging Disciplinary Divides to Address Environmental and Intellectual Challenges', *Ecosystems*, 4(8): 709–15.

Klein, J. T. (1985) 'The Evolution of a Body of Knowledge', *Knowledge: Creation, Diffusion, Utilization*, 7(2): 117–42.

Klein, J. T. (1990) *Interdisciplinarity: History, Theory, and Practice*. Detroit: Wayne State University Press.

Klein, J. T. (1996) *Crossing Boundaries: Knowledge, Disciplinarities, and Interdisciplinarities*. Charlottesville: University Press of Virginia.

Klein, J. T. (2001) 'Interdisciplinarity and the Prospect of Complexity. The Tests of Theory', *Issues in Integrative Studies*, 19: 43–57.

Knorr, K. D., Strasser, H. and Zilian, H. G. (eds) (1975) *Determinants and Controls of Scientific Development*. Dordrecht: Reidel.

Knorr, K. D., Krohn, R. and Whitley, R. D. (eds) (1980) *The Social Process of Scientific Investigation*. Sociology of the Sciences, Volume IV. Dordrecht : Reidel.

Knorr-Cetina, K. D. (1981) *The Manufacture of Knowledge: An Essay on the Constructivist and Contextual Nature of Science*. Oxford: Pergamon Press.

Knorr-Cetina, K. D. and Mulkay, M. (1983) 'Introduction: Emerging Principles in Social Studies of Science', in K. D. Knorr-Cetina and M. Mulkay (eds) *Science Observed: Perspectives on the Social Study of Science*, London: Sage, pp. 1–17.

Kuhn, T. (1962) *The Structure of Scientific Revolutions*. Chicago: University of Chicago Press.

Kuhn, T. (1970a) 'Logic of Discovery or Psychology of Research?', in I. Lakatos and A. E. Musgrave (eds) *Criticism and the Growth of Knowledge*, London: Cambridge University Press, pp. 1–23.

Kuhn, T. (1970b) 'Reflections on my Critics', in I. Lakatos and A. E. Musgrave (eds) *Criticism and the Growth of Knowledge*, London: Cambridge University Press, pp. 231–78.

Kuhn, T. (1970c) *The Structure of Scientific Revolutions*, 2nd edn, enlarged. Chicago: University of Chicago Press.

Kuhn, T. (1974) 'Second Thoughts on Paradigms', in F. Suppe (ed.) *The Structure of Scientific Theories*, Urbana, IL: University of Illinois Press, pp. 459–82.

Kuhn, T. (1977) 'Second Thoughts on Paradigms', in T. Kuhn, *The Essential Tension*, Chicago: University of Chicago Press, pp. 293–319.

Kuhn, T. (1996) *The Structure of Scientific Revolutions*, 3rd edn. Chicago: University of Chicago Press.

Laband, D. N. and Piette, M. J. (1994) 'The Relative Impacts of Economics Journals: 1970–1990', *Journal of Economic Literature*, 32(2): 640–66.

Lakatos, I. (1970) 'Falsification and the Methodology of Scientific Research Programmes', in I. Lakatos and A. E. Musgrave (eds) *Criticism and the Growth of Knowledge*, London: Cambridge University Press, pp. 91–196.

Lakatos, I. and Musgrave, A. E. (eds) (1970) *Criticism and the Growth of Knowledge*. London: Cambridge University Press.

Latour, B. and Woolgar, S. (1979) *Laboratory Life. The Social Construction of Scientific Facts*. London: Sage.

Lattuca, L. R. (2001) *Creating Interdisciplinarity. Interdisciplinary Research and Teaching among College and University Faculty*. Nashville: Vanderbilt University Press.

Laudan, L. (1981) 'The Pseudo-Science of Science?', *Philosophy of the Social Sciences*, 11: 173–98.

Lawson, T. (1997) *Economics and Reality*. London: Routledge.

Lawson, T. (1999) 'Developments in Economics as Realist Social Theory', in S. Fleetwood (ed.) *Critical Realism in Economics: Development and Debate*, London: Routledge, pp. 3–20.

Lawson, T. (2003) *Reorienting Economics*. London: Routledge.

Lawson, T. (2004) 'A Conception of Ontology'. Available online at www.csog.group.cam.ac.uk/A_Conception_Of_Ontology.pdf (accessed 3 April 2013).

Lawson, T. (2006) 'The Nature of Heterodox Economics', *Cambridge Journal of Economics*, 30(4): 483–505.

LeCompte, M. and Goetz, J. (1982) 'Problems of Reliability and Validity in Ethnographic Research', *Review of Educational Research*, 52(1): 31–60.
Leftwich, A. (ed.) (2004) *What is Politics? The Activity and its Study*, 2nd edn. Cambridge: Polity (1st edn, Blackwell, 1984).
Leftwich, A. (2004a) 'Thinking Politically: On the Politics of Politics', in A. Leftwich (ed.) *What is Politics? The Activity and its Study*, 2nd edn, Cambridge: Polity, pp. 1–22.
Lewis, P. (2000) 'Realism, Causality and the Problem of Social Structure', *Journal for the Theory of Social Behaviour*, 30(3): 249–68.
Liebowitz, S. J. and Palmer, J. P. (1984) 'Assessing the Relative Impacts of Economics Journals', *Journal of Economic Literature*, 22(1): 77–88.
Lindesmith, A.R. (1968) *Additives and Opiates*. Chicago: Aldine.
Liner, G.H. (2002) 'Core Journals in Economics', *Economic Inquiry*, 40(1): 138–45.
Lowe, P. (2006) *Programme Director's Annual Report 2006*. Swindon: ESRC. Available online at www.relu.ac.uk/news/Annual%20%20Report%202006%20web%20version.pdf (accessed 3 April 2013).
Lowe, P. and Phillipson, J. (2006) 'Reflexive Interdisciplinary Research: The Making of a Research Programme on the Rural Economy and Land Use', *Journal of Agricultural Economics*, 57(2): 165–84.
Lukes, S. (1974) *Power: A Radical View*. London: Macmillan (2nd edn, Palgrave Macmillan, 2005).
Machin, S. and Oswald, A. (1999) *Signs of Disintegration: A Report on UK Economics PhDs and ESRC Studentship Demand*. Available online at www2.warwick.ac.uk/fac/soc/economics/staff/faculty/oswald/esrcrep.pdf (accessed 3 April 2013).
Machin, S. and Oswald, A. (2000) 'UK Economics and the Future Supply of Academic Economists', *Economic Journal*, 110(464): F334–49.
McKay, D. (1991) 'Is European Political Science Inferior to or Different from American Political Science?', *European Journal of Political Research*, 20(3–4): 459–66.
Mackey, J. L. (2001) 'Another Approach to Interdisciplinary Studies', *Issues in Integrative Studies*, 19: 59–70.
McLean, I., Blais, A., Garand, J. C. and Giles, M. (2009) 'Comparative Journal Ratings: A Survey Report', *Political Studies Review*, 7(1): 18–38.
Malthus, T. R. ([1823] 1986) 'The Measure of Value Stated and Illustrated, with an Application of it to the Alterations in the Value of the English Currency Since 1790', in *Essays on Political Economy*, published as Volume Seven of *The Works of Thomas Robert Malthus, eds E. A. Wrigley and D. Souden*, London: Pickering, pp. 175–253.
Malthus, T. R. ([1836] 1986) *Principles of Political Economy Considered with a View to their Practical Application*, published as Volume Five of *The Works of Thomas Robert Malthus, eds E. A. Wrigley and D. Souden,* London: Pickering.
Mar, B. W., Newell, W. T. and Saxberg, B. O. (1981) 'Interdisciplinary Research – A Dilemma for University Central Administration', *Journal of the Society of Research Administrators*, 13(2): 25–43.
Marsh, D. and Savigny, H. (2004) 'Political Science as a Broad Church: The Search for a Pluralist Discipline', *Politics*, 24(3): 155–68.
Marsh, D. and Stoker, G. (eds) (2002a) *Theory and Methods in Political Science*, 2nd edn. Basingstoke: Palgrave Macmillan (1st edn, Macmillan, 1995).
Marsh, D. and Stoker, G. (2002b) 'Introduction', in D. Marsh and G. Stoker (eds) *Theory and Methods in Political Science*, 2nd edn, Basingstoke: Palgrave Macmillan, pp. 1–16.
Marsh, D. and Stoker, G. (2002c) 'Conclusion', in D. Marsh and G. Stoker (eds) *Theory*

*and Methods in Political Science*, Basingstoke: Palgrave Macmillan, 2nd edn, pp. 311–17.

Marsh, D. and Stoker, G. (eds) (2010) *Theory and Methods in Political Science*. Basingstoke: Palgrave Macmillan, 3rd edn.

Marshall, P. (2012) 'The Meeting of Two Integrative Metatheories', *Journal of Critical Realism*, 11(2): 188–214.

Martin, R. (1999) 'The New "Geographical Turn" in Economics: Some Critical Reflections', *Cambridge Journal of Economics*, 23(1): 65–91.

Martins, H. (1972) 'The Kuhnian "Revolution" and its Implications for Sociology', in T. S. Nossiter, A. H. Hanson and S. Rokkan (eds) *Imagination and Precision in the Social Sciences*, London: Faber and Faber, pp. 13–58.

Marx, K. (1969) *Theories of Surplus Value. Part II*. London: Lawrence & Wishart.

Masterman, M. (1970) 'The Nature of a Paradigm', in I. Lakatos and A.E. Musgrave (eds) *Criticism and the Growth of Knowledge*, London: Cambridge University Press, pp. 59–89.

Mendelsohn, E., Weingart, P. and Whitley, R. D. (eds) (1977) *The Social Production of Scientific Knowledge*. Sociology of the Sciences, Volume I. Dordrecht: Reidel.

Merton, R. (1973) *The Sociology of Science*. Chicago: University of Chicago Press.

Miles, M. B. and Huberman, A. M. (1984) 'Drawing Valid Meaning from Qualitative Data: Toward a Shared Craft', *Educational Researcher*, 13(5): 20–30.

Mill, J. S. ([1844] 1967) 'On the Definition of Political Economy; And on the Method of Investigation Proper to It', in J. M. Robson (ed.) *Essays on Economics and Society*, published as Volume IV of *Collected Works of John Stuart Mill*, Toronto: University of Toronto Press, London: Routledge and Kegan Paul, pp. 309–39.

Miller, R. C. (1982) 'Varieties of Interdisciplinary Approaches in the Social Sciences', *Issues in Integrative Studies*, 1: 1–37.

Mills, C. W. (1959) *The Sociological Imagination*. Oxford: Oxford University Press.

Milonakis, D. and Fine, B. (2009) *From Political Economy to Economics. Method, the Social and the Historical in the Evolution of Economic Theory*. London: Routledge.

Mingers, J. (2011) 'The Contribution of Systemic Thought to Critical Realism', *Journal of Critical Realism*, 10(3): 303–30.

Molteberg, E., Bergstrøm, C. and Haug, R. (2000) 'Interdisciplinarity in Development Studies: Myths and Realities', *Forum for Development Studies*, 27(2): 317–30.

Monroe, K. R. (ed.) (2005) *Perestroika! The Raucous Rebellion in Political Science*. New Haven: Yale University Press.

Moran, J. (2002) *Interdisciplinarity*. London: Routledge.

Newby, H. (1977) 'In the Field: Reflections on the Study of Suffolk Farm Workers', in C. Bell and H. Newby (eds) *Doing Sociological Research*, London: Allen and Unwin, pp. 108–29.

Newell, W. H. (1983) 'The Case for Interdisciplinary Studies: Response to Professor Benson's Five Arguments', *Issues in Integrative Studies*, 2: 1–19.

Newell, W. H. (2001) 'A Theory of Interdisciplinary Studies', *Issues in Integrative Studies*, 19: 1–25.

Newell, W. H. and Green, W. (1982) 'Defining and Teaching Interdisciplinary Studies', *Improving College and University Teaching*, 30(1): 23–30.

Norrie, A. (2010) *Dialectic and Difference. Dialectical Critical Realism and the Grounds of Justice*. London: Routledge.

O'Brien, D. P. (1975) *The Classical Economists*. Oxford: Clarendon Press.

Ormerod, P. (1994) *The Death of Economics*. London: Faber and Faber.

Padgett, D. (1998) *Qualitative Methods in Social Work Research*. London: Sage.

Pawson, R. (1989) *A Measure for Measures. A Manifesto for Empirical Sociology*. London: Routledge.

Pawson, R. and Tilley, N. (1997) *Realistic Evaluation*. London: Sage.

Petts, J., Owens, S. and Bulkeley, H. 2004. Discussion Paper for Seminar 6. ESRC Transdisciplinary Seminar Series: 'Knowledge and Power: Exploring the Science/Society Interface in the Urban Environment Context', University of Birmingham and University of Cambridge, 2004. Available online at www.planning-resnet.org.uk/seminars/19-10-04/esrc_position_paper.pdf (accessed 3 April 2013).

Popper, K. (1959) *The Logic of Scientific Discovery*. London: Hutchinson (2nd revised edn, 1968).

Popper, K. (1963) *Conjectures and Refutations: The Growth of Scientific Knowledge*. London: Routledge and Kegan Paul (2nd edn [revised], 1965; 3rd edn [revised], 1969; 4th edn [revised], 1972; 5th edn, 1974; 5th edn [revised], 1989).

Popper, K. (1970) 'Normal Science and its Dangers', in I. Lakatos and A. E. Musgrave (eds) *Criticism and the Growth of Knowledge*, London: Cambridge University Press, pp. 51–8.

Propper, C. and Dasgupta, P. (2000) 'The State of British Academic Economics: Editorial Introduction', *Economic Journal*, 110(464): F291–92.

*PS* (2006) 'Editorial', *Political Studies*, 54(1): 1–2.

Pye, L. W. (ed.) (1975) *Political Science and Area Studies: Rivals or Partners?* Bloomington: Indiana University Press.

Qin, J., Lancaster, F. W. and Allen, B. (1997) 'Types and Levels of Collaboration in Interdisciplinary Research in the Sciences', *Journal of the American Society for Information Science*, 48(10): 893–916.

Ray, L. and Sayer, A. (eds) (1999) *Culture and Economy after the Cultural Turn*. London: Sage.

Read, M. and Marsh, D. (2002) 'Combining Quantitative and Qualitative Methods', in D. Marsh and G. Stoker (eds) *Theory and Methods in Political Science*, 2nd edn, Basingstoke: Palgrave Macmillan, pp. 231–48.

Redman, D. A. (1997) *The Rise of Political Economy as a Science. Methodology and the Classical Economists*. Cambridge, MA: The MIT Press.

Reichardt, C. S. and Cook, T. D. (1979) 'Beyond Qualitative versus Quantitative Methods', in T. D. Cook and C. S. Reichardt (eds) *Qualitative and Quantitative Methods in Evaluation Research*, Beverly Hills: Sage, pp. 7–32.

Repko, A. F. (2008) *Interdisciplinary Research. Process and Theory*. Los Angeles: Sage.

Rhoten, D. (2003) *A Multi-method Analysis of the Social and Technical Conditions for Interdisciplinary Collaboration*. Final Report for the Hybrid Vigor Institute, San Francisco CA. Available online at www.ncar.ucar.edu/Director/survey/Rhoten_NSF-BCS.FINAL.pdf (accessed 3 April 2013).

Riba, C. (1996) 'The Use of Mathematics in Political Science: A Survey of European and American Journals', *European Journal of Political Research*, 29(4): 477–508.

Ricardo, D. (1951[1821]) *On the Principles of Political Economy and Taxation*, published as Volume I of *The Works and Correspondence of David Ricardo, eds P. Sraffa and M. H. Dobb*, London: Cambridge University Press.

Ricardo, D. ([1820] 1952) 'Ricardo To Malthus', in *Letters 1819–June 1821*, published as Volume VIII of *The Works and Correspondence of David Ricardo, eds P. Sraffa and M. H. Dobb*, London: Cambridge University Press, pp. 183–86.

Ricardo, D. ([1821] 1952) 'Ricardo To Mill', in *Letters 1819–June 1821*, published as

Volume VIII of *The Works and Correspondence of David Ricardo, eds P. Sraffa and M. H. Dobb*, London: Cambridge University Press, pp. 329–31.

Rist, R. (1977) 'On the Relations among Educational Research Paradigms: From Disdain to Détente', *Anthropology and Education Quarterly*, 8(2): 42–9.

Roberts, G. (2003) *Review of Research Assessment. Report by Sir Gareth Roberts to the UK Funding Bodies.* Available online at www.ra-review.ac.uk/reports/Roberts.asp (accessed 20 February 2013).

Robertson, I. T. (1981) 'Some Factors Associated with Successful Interdisciplinary Research', *Journal of the Society for Research Administrators*, 13(2): 44–50.

Rossini, F. A. and Porter, A. L. (1979) 'Frameworks for Integrating Interdisciplinary Research', *Research Policy*, 8(1): 70–9.

Rossini, F. A. and Porter, A. L. (1981) 'Interdisciplinary Research: Performance and Policy Issues', *Journal of the Society of Research Administrators*, 13(2): 8–24.

Rossini, F. A., Porter, A. L., Kelly, P. and Chubin, D. E. (1981) 'Interdisciplinary Integration within Technology Assessments', *Knowledge: Creation, Diffusion, Utilization*, 2(4): 503–28.

Rutzou, T. (2012) 'Integral Theory: A Poisoned Chalice?', *Journal of Critical Realism*, 11(2): 215–24.

Sale, J. E. M., Lichfield, L. H. and Brazil, K. (2002) "Revisiting the Quantitative–Qualitative Debate. Implications for Mixed-Methods Research', *Quality and Quantity*, 36(1): 43–53.

Sayer, A. (1984) *Method in Social Science. A Realist Approach.* London: Routledge (2nd edn, Routledge, 1992).

Sayer, A. (2000a) 'For Postdisciplinary Studies: Sociology and the Curse of Disciplinary Parochialism/Imperialism', in J. Eldridge, J. MacInnes, S. Scott, C. Warhurst and A. Witz (eds) *For Sociology. Legacies and Prospects*, Durham: Sociologypress/British Sociological Association, pp. 83–91.

Sayer, A. (2000b) *Realism and Social Science.* London: Sage.

Shapere, D. (1964) 'The Structure of Scientific Revolutions', *Philosophical Review*, 73(3): 382–94.

Shapiro, I. (2005) *The Flight from Reality in the Human Sciences.* Princeton: Princeton University Press.

Siegelman, L. (2002) 'Notes from the (New) Editor', *American Political Science Review*, 96(1): viii–xvi.

Skinner, A. S. (1979) *A System of Social Science. Papers Relating to Adam Smith.* Oxford: Clarendon Press.

Smith, A. ([1776] 1976) *An Inquiry into the Nature and Causes of the Wealth of Nations,* published as Volume II of *The Glasgow Edition of the Works and Correspondence of Adam Smith, eds R. H. Campbell and A. S. Skinner*, Oxford: Clarendon Press.

Smith, J. K. and Heshusius, L. (1986) 'Closing Down the Conversation: The End of the Quantitative–Qualitative Debate among Educational Inquirers', *Educational Researcher*, 15(1): 4–12.

Squires, G., Simons, H., Parlett, M. and Becher, T. (1975) *Interdisciplinarity.* Group for Research and Innovation in Higher Education, London: Nuffield Foundation.

Steinmetz, G. and Chae, O.-B. (2002) 'Sociology in an Era of Fragmentation: From the Sociology of Knowledge to the Philosophy of Science, and Back Again', *The Sociological Quarterly*, 43(1): 111–37.

Stewart, D. (1980[1795]) 'Account of the Life and Writings of Adam Smith, LL.D.', in *Essays on Philosophical Subjects*, published as Volume III of *The Glasgow Edition of the Works and Correspondence of Adam Smith, eds W. P. D. Wightman, J. C. Bryce and I. C. Ross*, Oxford: Clarendon Press, pp. 269–351.

Stilwell, F. (2006) *Political Economy. The Contest of Economic Ideas*, 2nd edn. Oxford: Oxford University Press (1st edn, 2002).

Stoker, G. and Marsh, D. (2010) 'Introduction', in D. Marsh and G. Stoker (eds) *Theory and Methods in Political Science*, 3rd edn, Basingstoke: Palgrave Macmillan, pp. 1–12.

Storer, N. (1966) *The Social System of Science*. New York: Holt, Rinehart and Winston.

SURPC (1997) *Interdisciplinary Research: Process, Structures and Evaluation*. Edinburgh: Scottish Universities Research Policy Consortium.

Swedberg, R. (1990) *Economics and Sociology. Redefining their Boundaries. Conversations with Economists and Sociologists*. Princeton: Princeton University Press.

Szostak, R. (2007) 'How and Why to Teach Interdisciplinary Research Practice', *Journal of Research Practice*, 3(2): 1–20. Article M17, available online at http://jrp.icaap.org/index.php/jrp/article/viewArticle/92/89 (accessed 3 April 2013).

Tait, J., Williams, R., Bruce, A., Lyall, C., Grávalos, E., Rodriquez, P., Jolivet, E., Jorgensen, U. and Læssøe, J. (2003a) *Interdisciplinary Integration in the Fifth Framework Programme* (II-FP5). Final Report. EC Accompanying Measure. Contract No: SEAC-1999-00034. University of Edinburgh: Scottish Universities Policy Research and Advice Network. Available online at www.supra.ed.ac.uk/Publications/FINAL%20REPORT.pdf (accessed 3 April 2013).

Tait, J., Williams, R., Bruce, A., Lyall, C., Grávalos, E., Rodriquez, P., Jolivet, E., Jorgensen, U. and Læssøe, J. (2003b) *Interdisciplinary Integration in the Fifth Framework Programme* (II-FP5). Annexes to Final Report. EC Accompanying Measure. Contract No: SEAC-1999-00034. University of Edinburgh: Scottish Universities Policy Research and Advice Network. Available online at www.supra.ed.ac.uk/Publications/FINAL_REPORT_ANNEXES.pdf (accessed 18 April 2008).

Toma, J. D. (1997) 'Alternative Inquiry Paradigms, Faculty Cultures and the Definition of Academic Lives', *Journal of Higher Education*, 68(6): 679–705.

Turner, B. A. (1981) 'Some Practical Aspects of Qualitative Data Analysis: One Way of Organising the Cognitive Processes Associated with the Generation of Grounded Theory', *Quantity and Quality*, 15(3): 225–47.

Turner, R. H. (1990) 'The Many Faces of American Sociology. A Discipline in Search of Identity', *American Behavioral Scientist*, 33(6): 662–84.

Von Mises, R. (1951) *Positivism*. Cambridge, MA: Harvard University Press.

Wade Hands, D. (1999) 'Empirical Realism as Meta-method: Tony Lawson on Neoclassical Economics', in S. Fleetwood (ed.) *Critical Realism in Economics. Development and Debate*, London: Routledge, pp. 169–85.

Walters, B. and Young, D. (2001) 'Critical Realism as a Basis for Economic Methodology: A Critique', *Review of Political Economy*, 13(4): 483–501.

Watson, M. (2005) *Foundations of International Political Economy*. Basingstoke: Palgrave Macmillan.

Wear, D. N. (1999) 'Challenges to Interdisciplinary Discourse', *Ecosystems*, 2(4): 299–301.

Weber, M. (1904) 'The "Objectivity" of Knowledge in Social Science and Social Policy', in S. Whimster (ed.) (2004) *The Essential Weber*, London: Routledge, pp. 359–404.

Weingart, P. and Stehr, N. (eds) (2000) *Practising Interdisciplinarity*. Toronto: University of Toronto Press.

Whitley, R. D. (1972) 'Black Boxism and the Sociology of Science: Discussion of the Major Developments in the Field', in P. Halmos (ed.) *The Sociology of Science*, Sociological Review Monograph No. 18, Keele: Keele University Press, pp. 61–92.

Whitley, R. D. (ed.) (1974a) *Social Processes of Scientific Development*. London: Routledge and Kegan Paul.

Whitley, R. D. (1974b) 'Cognitive and Social Institutionalization of Scientific Specialties and Research Areas', in R. D. Whitley (ed.) *Social Processes of Scientific Development*, London: Routledge and Kegan Paul, pp. 69–95.

Whitley, R. D. (1977a) 'The Sociology of Scientific Work and the History of Scientific Development', in S. S. Blume (ed.) *Perspectives in the Sociology of Science*, Chichester: Wiley, pp. 21–50.

Whitley, R. D. (1977b) 'Changes in the Social and Intellectual Organisation of the Sciences', in E. Mendelsohn, P. Weingart and R.D. Whitley (eds) *The Social Production of Scientific Knowledge*, Sociology of the Sciences, Volume I, Dordrecht: Reidel, pp. 143–69.

Whitley, R. D. (1980) 'The Context of Scientific Investigation', in K. D. Knorr, R. Crohn and R. D. Whitley (eds) *The Social Process of Scientific Investigation*, Sociology of the Sciences, Volume IV, Dordrecht: Reidel, pp. 297–321.

Whitley, R. D. (1982) 'The Establishment and Structure of the Sciences as Reputational Organizations', in N. Elias, H. Martins and R.D. Whitley (eds) *Scientific Establishments and Hierarchies*, Sociology of the Sciences, Volume VI. Dordrecht: Reidel, pp. 313–57.

Whitley, R. D. (1983) 'From the Sociology of Scientific Communities to the Study of Scientists' Negotiations and Beyond', *Social Science Information*, 22(4/5): 681–720.

Whitley, R. D. (1984) *The Intellectual and Social Organisation of the Sciences*. Oxford: Clarendon Press (2nd edn, Oxford University Press, 2000).

Whitley, R. D. (1986) 'The Structure and Context of Economics as a Scientific Field', *Research in the History of Economic Thought and Methodology*, 4: 179–209.

Whitley, R. D. (1991) 'The Organisation and Role of Journals in Economics and Other Scientific Fields', *Economic Notes by Monte dei Paschi di Siena*, 20(1): 6–32.

Wiles, P. and Routh, E. (1984) *Economics in Disarray*. Oxford: Blackwell.

Willis, P. (1980) 'Notes on Method', in S. Hall, D. Hobson, A. Lowe and P. Willis (eds) *Culture, Media, Language*, London: Hutchinson, in association with the Centre for Contemporary Cultural Studies, University of Birmingham, pp. 88–95.

Woods, P. (1985) 'Ethnography and Theory Construction in Educational Research', in R. G. Burgess (ed.) *Field Methods in the Study of Education*, Lewes: Falmer, pp. 51–78.

Yin, R. K. (2003) *Case Study Research. Design and* Methods, 3rd edn. Thousand Oaks, CA: Sage (1st edn, 1984; 1st edn [revised], 1989; 2nd edn, 1994).

# Index

Printed in Great Britain
by Amazon